Communal Solitude

The Carthusian Lay Brethren in Great Britain and Ireland, 1178-1569

Francesca Breeden

BAR BRITISH SERIES 675 | 2022

Published in 2022 by
BAR Publishing, Oxford, UK

BAR British Series 675

Communal Solitude

ISBN 978 1 4073 5975 5 paperback
ISBN 978 1 4073 5976 2 e-format

DOI https://doi.org/10.30861/9781407359755

A catalogue record for this book is available from the British Library

© Francesca Breeden 2022

COVER IMAGE *Friary reconstruction, illustration courtesy of Roger Barnes*

The Author's moral rights under the 1988 UK Copyright,
Designs and Patents Act, are hereby expressly asserted.

All rights reserved. No part of this work may be copied, reproduced, stored, sold, distributed, scanned, saved in any form of digital format or transmitted in any form digitally, without the written permission of the Publisher.

Links to third party websites are provided by BAR Publishing in good faith and for information only. BAR Publishing disclaims any responsibility for the materials contained in any third party website referenced in this work.

BAR titles are available from:

BAR Publishing
122 Banbury Rd, Oxford, OX2 7BP, UK
info@barpublishing.com
www.barpublishing.com

Of Related Interest

Excavations at Minster House, Bristol, 1992
From abbey cellarium and prior's lodging to cathedral prebendal house
John Bryant

BAR British Series **669** | 2021

The 'Obese Medieval Monk'
A multidisciplinary study of a stereotype
Pip Patrick

BAR British Series **590** | 2014

Dalla villa al monastero: Nuovi dati archeologici da S. Maria di Grottaferrata
Francesca Zagari

BAR International Series **2632** | 2014

Stanley Abbey and its Estates 1151-c1640
A Cistercian monastery and its impact on the landscape
Graham Brown

BAR British Series **566** | 2012

The Affinities and Antecedents of Medieval Settlement
Topographical perspectives from three of the Somerset hundreds
Nick Corcos

BAR British Series **337** | 2002

Shaping Community: The Art and Archaeology of Monasticism
Papers from a symposium held at the Frederick R. Weisman Museum University of Minnesota March 10-12, 2000
Edited by Sheila McNally

BAR International Series **941** | 2001

Advances in Monastic Archaeology
Edited by Roberta Gilchrist and Harold Mytum with contributions by C J Bond, L A S Butler, T P O'Connor, P H Cullum, S Moorhouse, D M Palliser, J Schofield, D Stocker, J Stopford and S H Ward

BAR British Series **227** | 1993

San Vincenzo al Volturno
The Archaeology, Art and Territory of an Early Medieval Monastery
Edited by Richard Hodges, John Mitchell

BAR International Series **252** | 1985

Acknowledgements

As with any publication, there are many people I need to thank. Tansy at BAR Publishing, thank you for being patient with me and helping me navigate the publishing process. Penny and Richard, thank you for letting me survey your home, and for providing me with opportunities to share my research with the local community. Glyn, you always have an extra bit of information up your sleeve when it comes to the Carthusians. Thank you for all your very useful comments while this was going through the review process, and for getting me in touch with various interesting people. Thank you also to the peer reviewers who gave some very helpful pointers and helped me to transform my thesis into a book.

Hugh, thank you for badgering me to publish my work. It probably wouldn't have happened otherwise. You read this as a thesis multiple times and I'm grateful that you stuck with me through the particularly awful writing.

My family have supported me from day one, with their unconditional love and encouragement. Thank you for always being willing to procrastinate with me, for gifting me a lifelong tea habit, and reminding me of how proud you are.

Bre, you are the family I picked, and I am thankful every day that I did. I'm not sure I would have got to this point without your brutal honesty, unwavering love, and unending encouragement. Thank you for always fighting my corner.

Contents

List of Figures ix
List of Tables xi
List of Abbreviations xii
Abstract xiii

1. Introduction 1
1.1 Data Set and Chronology 1
1.2 A Brief History of the Carthusian Order 1
1.3 Primary Written Sources 3
1.4 Previous Archaeological Research 4

2. The Carthusians in Great Britain 7
2.1 Hugh of Lincoln and the first English foundation: 1178–1221 7
2.2 Expansion and Royal Benefaction: 1222–1500 7
2.3 The Carthusians during the Reformation: 1518–1569 9
2.4 The Aftermath of the Dissolution and the Re-use of Carthusian Buildings 11
2.5 Conclusions 12

3. Church, Cloister, and Cell: The Inner Charterhouse Complex 13
3.1 Overview of the Charterhouse Complex 13
3.2 Previous Excavations and Resistivity Surveys 18
    3.2.1 Witham Charterhouse 18
    3.2.2 Hinton Priory and Friary 21
3.3 The Carthusian Church: Use, Expansion and Decoration 22
3.4 The Cloister 23
3.5 The Cell 24
3.6 Conclusions 25

4. Daily Life in the Charterhouse 27
4.1 The Daily Schedule 27
4.2 Prayer and Spiritual Exercises 27
4.3 Manual Works 29
4.4 Meals 30
4.5 Silence 32
4.6 Death and Memory 33
4.7 Conclusions 38

5. The Wider Landscape of the Carthusian Precinct 41
5.1 Siting of the Charterhouse 41
5.2 Water Management 42
5.3 Topographic Analysis: Using LiDAR to assess landscape changes 43
5.4 The Influence of the Carthusians on the Local Landscape 49
5.5 Carthusian Estates 51
5.6 Conclusions 51

6. Material Culture of the Charterhouse 55
6.1 A Comparative Study of Monastic Material Culture recovered from English Charterhouses 55
    6.1.1 Ceramic Cooking and Dining Vessels 55
    6.1.2 Writing and Book Manufacture Implements 60
    6.1.3 Dress Accessories 64
    6.1.4 Summary 66
6.2 Material Culture of the Lay Brethren 66
    6.2.1 Mount Grace Priory 66

    6.2.2 The London Charterhouse 67
    6.2.3 Coventry Charterhouse 67
    6.2.4 Documentary Evidence 67
    6.2.5 Summary 68
  6.3 Conclusions 68

7. The Lower House: An Archaeological Investigation at the sites of Hinton and Witham Friary 69
  7.1 A Divided House 69
  7.2 Case Study 1 – Witham Friary 70
  7.3 Case Study 2 – Hinton Friary 70
  7.4 Geophysical Survey 71
    7.4.1 Witham Friary Earth Resistance Survey 71
    7.4.2 Hinton Friary Earth Resistance Survey 73
    7.4.3 Hinton Friary Magnetometer Survey 73
  7.5 Synthesis of Data 76
  7.6 Conclusions 76

8. Conclusions 79
  8.1 Can the Lay Brother be identified as archaeologically distinct? 79
  8.2 Layouts and Landscapes: Arrangement and Organisation 79
  8.3 Interactions with the Secular World 80
  8.4 The Role of the Lay Brother 80
  8.5 Scope and Recommendations for Further Research 81

Bibliography 83

List of Figures

Figure 1.1. Map of all the charterhouses included in the present study.. 2

Figure 3.1. Zoning plan of Mount Grace Priory, based on the methodology of Del Espino Hidalgo and
García Fernández (2015)... 14

Figure 3.2. Diagram illustrating areas of access in the charterhouse.. 16

Figure 3.3. The layout of Mount Grace Priory, indicating drainage routes and numbered cells........................ 17

Figure 3.4. Space Syntax Analysis access plan for Mount Grace Priory, a rural charterhouse 18

Figure 3.5. The layout of Cell 13 at Mount Grace Priory, an example of the monks' cells. This illustration
shows the bricks found *in situ* during excavations at the site and indicates the division of space within the cell 19

Figure 3.6. Space Syntax Analysis access plan of a Carthusian cell, based on cell 13 at Mount Grace Priory 19

Figure 3.7. Layout of the London Charterhouse (after Barber and Thomas 2002, 38-39)................................. 20

Figure 3.8. Space Syntax Analysis access plan of the London Charterhouse, an urban Carthusian monastery................ 21

Figure 3.9. The nesting holes still visible in the Witham Friary dovecote (now used as an architect's office).................. 25

Figure 3.10. Painted letter above a cell door at La Musée de la Grande Chartreuse 25

Figure 4.1. Graph illustrating the increase in the number of bequests to charterhouses between 1200 and 1539 34

Figure 4.2. The de la Pole family tree, fourteenth-fifteenth centuries 36

Figure 4.3. The Mowbray-Holland family tree, fourteenth-fifteenth centuries 36

Figure 4.4. The Longspée family tree, twelfth-fourteenth centuries 37

Figure 4.5. The La Zouche-Cantilupe family tree, twelfth-fifteenth centuries... 37

Figure 4.6. Graph illustrating the number of burial requests made to charterhouses from 1200 to 1539 38

Figure 4.7. Graph illustrating male and female bequests to charterhouses from 1200 to 1539.......................... 39

Figure 5.1. The London Charterhouse in the context of other religious houses in London 44

Figure 5.2. Swiss and Cluster hillshaded LiDAR at Witham Charterhouse.. *44*

Figure 5.3. LiDAR at Witham Charterhouse with resistivity survey data added (after Gaffney 1994) *46*

Figure 5.4. LiDAR at Witham Charterhouse with location of post-Dissolution buildings added...................... 46

Figure 5.5. Cluster hillshade LiDAR at Hinton Priory with resistivity survey data added (after Gaffney 1995b) 47

Figure 5.6. Cluster hillshade LiDAR at Hinton Friary, with additional interpretation.. *47*

Figure 5.7. Cluster hillshade LiDAR at Sheen Charterhouse 48

Figure 5.8. Swiss hillshade LiDAR at Axholme Charterhouse 48

Figure 5.9. Cluster and Swiss hillshade LiDAR at Mount Grace Priory 49

Figure 5.10. Map of estates owned by Sheen Charterhouse.. 52

Figure 5.11. Map of estates owned by London Charterhouse 52

Figure 6.1. Chart showing the percentage of domestic and imported ceramics excavated at Mount Grace Priory 56

Figure 6.2. Proportions of domestic fabric types excavated at Mount Grace Priory.. 58

Figure 6.3. Chart comparing the proportions of domestic and imported ceramics recovered from excavations
at Mount Grace Priory, London Charterhouse, and St Anne's, Coventry 59

Figure 6.4. Example of margin pricking to guide ruled lines from BL Lansdowne MS 1201, f. 9r................... 61

Communal Solitude

Figure 6.5. Example of missing illumination from TNA E 328/310, letters patent granting the Charterhouse at Hinton 50 marks annually 61

Figure 6.6. Folio 15v from BL Harley MS 2373, where a reader has added notes to the margins of the manuscript 62

Figure 6.7. Example of correction of a manuscript in red ink from BL Add. MS 61823, f. 19r 62

Figure 6.8. Another example from BL Lansdowne MS 1201, f. 35r, where space has been left for another scribe to add the correct sentence 62

Figure 6.9. Lead-drawn illustration of Queen Elizabeth I, filling the 'O' of 'omnibus', never fully illuminated, from a document detailing the sale of granges owned by Hinton Priory (TNA CRES 38/514/6/1) 62

Figure 7.1. Location of Witham Friary and Witham Hall Farm in relation to each other 71

Figure 7.2. Interior or the lay brothers' church at Witham Friary, showing the vaulted ceiling added by the Carthusians during renovations 71

Figure 7.3. Exterior of the lay brothers' church at Witham Friary, showing the buttresses added in 1875 72

Figure 7.4. The site of Hinton Priory and the village of Friary in relation to one another 72

Figure 7.5. Interpretation of resistivity survey conducted at Witham Friary 74

Figure 7.6. Resistivity survey results for Friary 74

Figure 7.7. Interpretation of resistivity survey data at Friary 75

Figure 7.8. Magnetometry survey results for Friary 75

Figure 7.9. Interpretation of magnetometry survey results at Friary 77

Figure 7.10. Combined interpretation of Friary resistivity and magnetometry interpretations with LiDAR interpretation 77

Figure 7.11. Photograph of Woodman's Cottage in Friary from 1909 facing south east, with upstanding remains in foreground, possibly site of lay brothers' church 78

Figure 7.12. Potential layout of the lay brothers' complex at Friary based on survey data and 1909 photo 78

List of Tables

Table 1.1. Charterhouses founded in Great Britain and Ireland, with their foundation and dissolution dates and founders 3

Table 3.1. Nagel's (2015) phasing of medieval to early modern charterhouse constructions, with the addition of how British and Irish charterhouses fit into the categories 15

Table 4.1. The daily schedule for both Carthusian monks and lay brothers. After Thompson 1930 and 'Un Chartreux' 1984, 46 28

Table 6.1. Types of pottery excavated at Mount Grace Priory according to categories 56

Table 6.2. Dress accessories excavated from different areas at Mount Grace Priory 64

List of Abbreviations

B.L.	British Library, London
Bodl.Lib.	Bodleian Library, University of Oxford
Bristol	Notes or Abstracts of the Wills contained in the volume entitled The Great Orphan Book and Book of Wills in the Council House at Bristol
C.C.	Coutumes de Chartreuse
C.M.	Charterhouse Muniments, Sutton's Hospital
C.Pap.Reg.	Calendar of entries in the Papal Registers relating to Great Britain and Ireland
C.P.R.	Calendar of the Patent Rolls preserved in the Public Record Office
C.U.L.	Cambridge University Library
Derbyshire	Derbyshire Wills proved in the Prerogative Court of Canterbury, 1393-1574
Eng.Epis.Acta	English Episcopal Acta 37: Salisbury 1263-1297
GSB	Geophysical Surveys of Bradford
G.U.L.	Glasgow University Library
Hustings	Calendar of Wills proved and enrolled at the Court of Husting, London, AD1258-AD1688. Part II, AD1358-AD1688
Itineraries	William Worcestre, *Itineraries*
L&P Hen. VIII	Letters and Papers, Foreign and Domestic, of the Reign of Henry VIII
Liturgy Office	Universal Norms on the Liturgical Year and the General Roman Calendar
Lon. Consist.	London Consistory Court Wills, 1492-1547
LPL	Lambeth Palace Library, London
Magna Vita	Magna Vita S. Hugonis Episcopi Lincolniensis
Maisons	Maisons de l'ordre des Chartreux : vues et notices
North Country	North Country Wills, 1383-1558
OED	Oxford English Dictionary
Pat.Lat.	Patrologia Latina
PCC	Prerogative Court of Canterbury
RCHME	Royal Commission on the Historical Monuments of England
Reg. Bekynton	The Register of Thomas Bekynton, Bishop of Bath and Wells, 1443-1465
Somerset	Somerset Medieval Wills, 1383-1500
Somerset II	Somerset Medieval Wills, 1501-1530
Somerset III	Somerset Medieval Wills, 1531-1558
Southwell	Wills proved before the Chapter of Southwell, D.D. 1470-1541
SRO	Somerset Record Office, Taunton
Statutes	Tertio compilation of the Carthusian Statutes (1510)
Test.Ebor.	Testamenta Eboracensia
Test.Vet.	Testamenta Vetusta
TNA	The National Archives, Kew
UB	Universitatsbibliothek Basel

Abstract

This study examines the Carthusians in Great Britain and Ireland from an archaeological standpoint and highlights the role of the lay brother in the everyday life of the charterhouse.

Using the case studies of Witham Charterhouse and Hinton Priory, the layouts of the lay brothers' complexes are explored through geophysical survey and comparison with Carthusian material culture assemblages from other British charterhouses. This method of investigation provides a singular view of the lay brother in medieval society and for the first time proposes a layout of an English Carthusian lower house.

The investigation begins with an introduction to the topic and gives an overview history of the Carthusians in Great Britain, before discussing in more detail areas of the charterhouse complex – the cell, church and cloister. Following this is a discussion of everyday life for the monks and lay brothers, exploring various facets including death and memory. The study then moves on to investigate the wider landscape of the monastery complex, and how the local area was exploited and utilised by the Carthusians. The monks' and lay brothers' interactions with secular society are considered through excavated assemblages from a number of charterhouses, which also demonstrates specific occupations for each of the inhabitants. The final chapter presents the results of resistivity and magnetometer surveys at the two Somerset charterhouses and provides an interpretation of these results. It is concluded that it is not currently possible to identify the Carthusian lay brother as archaeologically distinct as there are not sufficient assemblages to provide an accurate understanding of the differences in monastic and lay objects. More research is therefore required before the lay brother can be properly understood.

1

Introduction

Only those who have experienced the solitude and silence of the wilderness can know what benefit and divine joy they bring to those who love them...There, for their labour in the contest, God gives his athletes the reward they desire: a peace that the world does not know and joy in the Holy Spirit.

St Bruno to Raoul le Verd[1].

The need for solitude fuelled the unique lifestyle of the Carthusian Order. This ideal was incorporated into the founding institution at La Grande Chartreuse, as seen by the above letter, and promulgated throughout the Carthusian Order, which, out of all the monastic orders, carried the need for isolation to the extreme. However, their existence would have been impossible without a select group of men known as the lay brothers, to enable this life of silence and solitude. Despite the lay brothers' invaluable contribution to the Order, they have been overlooked in both historical and archaeological studies: an imbalance this study seeks to redress.

This study aims to examine the role of the lay brother in Carthusian communities by examining the monastic houses of the Order in Great Britain and Ireland and combining a wide range of information to give context for the archaeological evidence that follows. A historically contextualised study of the Carthusian lay community will be provided through two research questions:

1. Is it possible to identify the lay brethren as an archaeologically distinct element of the community?
2. How was the lay brothers' precinct arranged and organised?

This research will examine the material remains, the surviving documentary sources, previous excavations, and available cartographic data to understand how the lay brothers shaped their landscapes and environments. These research questions will be answered using previously excavated material assemblages and new geophysical surveys at the two correries of Witham and Hinton Charterhouses.

1.1 Data Set and Chronology

The sites included in this study are all those from Great Britain and Ireland[2] (fig. 1.1) and were selected based on regionality, rather than the provinces they were assigned to by the Carthusian Order. The reason for the dates chosen is that it encompasses the foundation of the first charterhouse at Witham in 1178 (table 1.1), up until the formal suppression of the Perth Charterhouse in 1569. These dates do not in all cases account for post-Dissolution activity at the sites, although this is addressed where necessary. The two key research sites are Witham Friary[3] and Hinton Friary, both in Somerset, and the first two English charterhouses. These were chosen for further archaeological research as they are the only two Carthusian 'lower houses' known to have existed in Britain, and therefore give a singular opportunity to examine the lay brethren.

1.2 A Brief History of the Carthusian Order

The beginnings of the Carthusian Order lie within a broader phenomenon of twelfth-century religious revival. Their reversion to the early Christian hermitic lifestyle was not unique, being contemporary with the Camaldolese (f. c.1012) and the Vallombrese (f. c.1036), all three of which addressed an increasing disenchantment with the current monastic lifestyle and challenged the existing Benedictine monasticism. These three orders were part of the 'New Hermits', along with the Grandmontines (f. 1076), the Cistercians (f. 1098), the Tironensians (f. 1109), the Savignacs (f. 1112), and the Premonstratensians (f. 1121) (Leyser 1984, 113-118). In contrast to traditional hermits, the New Hermits saw solitude as excluding secular society, not fellow religious, and thus sought to create communities of hermits (Monti 2003, 245). In this sense, the Carthusians, Camaldolese, and Vallombrese most similarly mirror each other, living in individual cells and coming together for worship, while the day-to-day running of the house was left to the lay brothers (Monti 2003, 246-247). The over-arching aim of the New Hermits was to relive the *vita apostolica* (life of the apostles) and the *vita primitiva* (the early Church) (Leyser 1984, 26). In this way, they hoped to counter the lax lifestyle that had come to be associated with monasticism.

The Carthusian Order was founded in 1084 by St Bruno, who decided to take up the solitary life permanently after spending some months in a remote hermitage. With six companions, he travelled to the wilderness of the Chartreuse mountains, near Grenoble, arriving in June 1084. The site chosen for the new hermitage was in the

---

[1] *Lettres des premiers chartreux* I, 71
[2] As concerns the location of the houses within the Carthusian provinces, all the English charterhouses were included in the *Provincia Anglie*, but the house at Perth was first attached to the *Provincia Picardie*, then from 1456-1460 became part of the English Province. Since this move was somewhat unpopular, the house then moved to the *Provincia Gebennensis*, where it remained until the Reformation (Fawcett and Hall 2005, 49).

[3] 'Friary' here does not refer to the religious houses of Friars, but is an anglicisation of 'frèrie', meaning a house of brothers. This will be explained in further detail on page 64.

Communal Solitude

Figure 1.1. Map of all the charterhouses included in the present study.

Table 1.1. Charterhouses founded in Great Britain and Ireland, with their foundation and dissolution dates and founders.

	Foundation Date	Founder	Dissolution Date
Witham	1178	Henry II	15 March 1539
Hinton	1222	William Longespée	31 March 1539
Kilnalahanin	1249	Richard de Burgo	1321
Beauvale	1343	Nicholas de Cantilupe	18 July 1539
London	1370	Sir Walter Manny	10 June 1537 (formally suppressed 15 November 1538)
Hull	1377	Michael de la Pole	9 November 1539
Coventry	1381	William la Zouche / Richard II	16 January 1539
Axholme	1397	Thomas Mowbray	18 June 1538
Mount Grace	1398	Thomas Holland	18 December 1539
Sheen	1414	Henry V	20 August 1539
Perth	1429	James I (of Scotland)	9 August 1569

centre of a valley, and surrounded by high cliffs, making it particularly inaccessible to outsiders and thus ensuring the monks' solitude (Jotischky 1995, 42). The monastic precinct was called the 'desert,' drawing directly upon the experiences and teachings of the first Christian hermits (Brantley 2007, 33; Gilbert 2014, 378).

The monks' cells were situated slightly higher up the mountain than the lay-brothers' quarters, hence earning the names 'upper house' and 'lower house'. The lay brethren enabled the monks' way of life, providing food and fuel and working the land around the monastery. The lower house also functioned as a gatehouse, so any visitors to the charterhouse had to be received there first (Bligny 1986, 8). This further increased the monks' inaccessibility and ensured that unwelcome or unexpected visitors would not disturb their silence. From the beginning, the Carthusian monks relied on lay brothers and hired servants to provide for the community through growing food, tending livestock, and maintaining the smooth running of the house; indeed, two of the first companions, Andrew and Guarin, are noted as being lay brethren (Thompson 1930, 7).

The distinctive Carthusian layout, a central cloister surrounded by individual cells, began to emerge in around 1104, as extensions were made to the first two charterhouses, and the way of life was consolidated (Aston 1993, 141). Guibert de Nogent, who visited La Grande Chartreuse in 1112, described thirteen monks living around a central cloister, each with their own cell, where they worked, slept and ate (Bruce 2007, 158).

Until 1115, only three charterhouses existed: La Grande Chartreuse in France, and La Torre and St-Stephen-in-the-Wood in Italy[4], which Bruno founded while acting as an advisor to Pope Urban II (Rowntree 1981, 3). Between 1115 and 1116, six new charterhouses were founded: Portes (1115), Saint-Sulpice en Bugey (1115), Meyriat (1116), Les Écouges (1116), Durbon (1116) and La Sylve-Bénite (1116) (Coppack and Aston 2002, 17). These new houses stimulated the expansion of the Carthusian Order in Europe, and by 1200, 37 houses had been established in France, Italy, England, Slovenia, Spain and Denmark (Braunfels 1972, 117). By 1521, at the Order's peak, there were 195 Carthusian houses across Europe, having expanded into countries including Germany, Sweden, Hungary, Belgium and Switzerland. Each of the houses belonged to one of eighteen provinces from which visitors were chosen to report on the condition of the relevant houses to the General Chapter and ensure that capitular decrees were enacted (Knowles 1955, 135).

1.3 Primary Written Sources

The Carthusian Statutes or *Consuetudines Cartusiae*[5] (hereafter C.C.) were based on St Bruno's ideals of desert solitude but were enhanced with Guigo I's[6] own experiences of living as a hermit in the Carthusian Order, and his thoughts on solitude (Hogg 2014, 35; Ritchey 2014, 171). The Statutes were initially written as a set of guidelines for the six new houses established in 1115-1116 so they could continue Bruno's vision. The further editions gave additional information, reflecting current issues within the Order[7].

---

[4] These two foundations were at some point amalgamated into one community under the name of *Serra San Bruno* (Rowntree 1981, 3).

[5] All references to the Carthusian Statutes come from the 1984 Cerf edition. This edition has transcribed the 1121-1128 Carthusian Statutes. References from the later Statutes (1510 edition printed in Basel) are stated.

[6] Guigo I was the fifth prior of La Grande Chartreuse, from 1109 to 1137.

[7] The first edition of the Statutes was that written by Guigo I, the Carthusian Statutes, completed in 1127. Following this, three further revisions were compiled, the *Antiqua Statuta* in 1259-1271, the *Nova Statuta* in 1368, and the *Tertio Compilatio* in 1509. This last revision is considered the most complete, and the edition published in Basle in 1510 (Universitätsbibliothek Basel AK VI 21) is used as the basis for today's Statutes (Introduction to *Coutumes de Chartreuse* 2001, 125).

The Statutes covered a range of topics, designed to answer any queries members of the Carthusian community may have about how to conduct themselves, and also instructing them on how the divine office should be carried out. It is in the Statutes that specific instructions regarding the community began to coalesce, such as the number of occupants, limited by Guigo to thirteen monks and sixteen lay brothers; the maximum number which could be supported without asking for alms (C.C. 7:1-2). As a historical reference, the Statutes provide a vital source of information as to how the charterhouse was intended to be run. This set of rules influenced the construction and design of the charterhouses, ensuring solitude for the inhabitants, which has an important bearing on research into the architecture of Carthusian buildings.

The *Chartae* of the General Chapter, on the other hand, records the proceeds of the annual meeting at La Grande Chartreuse of the Carthusian Order. As a documentary source, it is invaluable. It lists the obits for every monk or lay brother who died that year, as well as the visitors to each province, and short reports from each charterhouse. To supplement the Statutes, it also gives ordinations which lay out explicitly how the rule is to be applied, often in answer to queries from different houses, or where the statutes do not address specific issues. The *Chartae* make it possible to track the most important issues for the Carthusian Order from 1217 into the eighteenth century and understand how they dealt with crises such as epidemic diseases and famines.

1.4 Previous Archaeological Research

Sir William Henry St John Hope (1854-1919) was one of the most important influences in monastic archaeology in England. He undertook excavations and academic research at many monasteries, including Mount Grace Priory (1905), and the London Charterhouse (published posthumously in 1925). The excavation at Mount Grace Priory allowed Hope to complete a plan of the building phases of the charterhouse, which consequently shaped the study of the earliest phase of research on the Carthusian houses in England. His work, however, is wholly surpassed by Coppack and Keen's 2019 monograph *Mount Grace Priory: Excavations of 1957-1992*, which provides much more detail from the excavations and long-running research they carried out. Likewise, some of Hope's work on the London Charterhouse has been superseded, first by Knowles and Grimes' (1954) post-war excavation, and later by Barber and Thomas' 2002 monograph on excavations at the site, although Hope's publication still stands as a beneficial source of documentary evidence relating to the charterhouse, as it gives transcriptions of the Charterhouse Register, documenting the early history of the monastery.

At the same time as Hope's studies, Beauvale Charterhouse was excavated by Du Boulay Hill and Gill (1908). The study revealed four cells, the church, little cloister and some other conventual buildings. The reconstruction was based upon Hope's 1905 study of Mount Grace, providing a detailed plan of one cell and illustrating the partitions within the cell (Du Boulay Hill and Gill 1908, 75). Their detailed large-scale plan, also inspired by Hope's Mount Grace publication, illustrated the excavated areas as well as conjectural structures.

The only Irish charterhouse, Kilnalahanin, was similarly the subject of a number of scholarly articles at the beginning of the twentieth century, but little has been written concerning the charterhouse since, and it is still relatively obscure. W. H. Grattan Flood (1907, 304) described the situation of the house's foundation and its location in the diocese of Clonfert, and was the first to publicise the site as one of particular historical significance. The paper was rather short and gave the most basic facts concerning the monastery, and in 1909, J. P. Dalton attempted to build upon Grattan Flood's work. Dalton (1909, 13) investigated the archaeology of the site much more thoroughly, indicating that due to later usage of the monastery as a Franciscan house, and more recently as a cemetery, the ground plan cannot be traced.

During the post-War period, Hinton Priory, in Somerset, was owned by Major Philip Fletcher, who was able to conduct his own excavations in the walled garden and the area around it, completing the first full excavation of the cloister and cells of any British or Irish charterhouse. The first report (Fletcher 1951) describes in detail the excavations from 1950 up to the point of this interim publication and makes some comparisons with the London Charterhouse and Parkminster, particularly the carved letters above each cell door (Fletcher 1951, 163). The additional report published in 1958 discussed the general layout of the house, as a complete plan could now be established (Fletcher 1958).

The late 1960s to late 1970s saw somewhat of a resurgence in Carthusian interest, with two substantial excavations carried out as well as an extensive academic study. Excavations at Witham Priory were conducted from 1965-9 by P. Barlow and R. Reid. The subsequent report, published in the *Proceedings of the Somerset Archaeological and Natural History Society* in 1990, describes the excavations, as well as illustrating the artefacts found on the site (Burrow and Burrow 1990).

The charterhouse at Coventry was studied at a similar time, from 1968-1987 by Iain Soden. This excavation was slightly less ambitious than that at Witham but achieved excellent results, and the subsequent plans are very useful for understanding the architecture, as Soden (1995) ensured that each of the stones and the bricks in walls were drawn in the plan and included in the report. Compared with the report from Witham or some of the early excavations, this gives a much better idea of the ground plan as excavated.

Although unexcavated, the charterhouse at Sheen, in Richmond, was thoroughly studied by John Cloake (1977). Working backwards through estate maps, documentary sources, and historical descriptions, Cloake was able to illustrate how the monastic complex at Sheen evolved from a fifteenth-century Carthusian house to being part of the Royal Gardens of Richmond in 1771 (Cloake 1977, 158-160, 182). With a full survey of the area, it would be possible to match up Cloake's conjectural plan with geophysical results, which may reveal new features. The Bradford geophysical survey (Gaffney 1997) covered only the area near the King's Observatory, to the north of the precinct, but unfortunately, given the area's current usage as a golf course, it is unlikely that a full geophysical survey will be completed in the near future.

In the early 1990s, the Royal Commission on the Historical Monuments of England (RCHME) undertook surveys of eight of the British and Irish charterhouses, examining all but London, Hull and Kilnalahanin. The importance of these surveys is that they combine not only archaeological information but also geographical, topographical, historical and cartographic sources. In combination with the geophysical surveys carried out by Geophysical Surveys Bradford (GSB) under the same project, each site is provided with a well-rounded base from which to attempt further research[8].

The geophysical surveys have not yet been re-evaluated in light of new survey techniques and equipment, but the original results still provide an excellent view of the sites and have revealed much that was missed in earlier excavations. GSB enhanced the data in a number of ways, to reveal as many of the features of the site as possible, using detailed relief plots, grey-scale plots and colour plots. Their interpretations are also a useful addition to the data, as it provides context for the results and their consequent plots.

The most recent publication on the subject, Glyn Coppack and Mick Aston's 2002 book *Christ's Poor Men* was the first study that successfully amalgamated the known archaeological information about the English charterhouses. However, it only discussed the English houses, despite Aston's original goal to also investigate Kilnalahanin and Perth (Aston 1993; 1997). An important point to note is that the publication also looks solely at the monks' environment and there is little discussion of the lay brethren and their place in the order.

Evidently, then, the Carthusians have been subject to some archaeological examination. However, these investigations have been somewhat sporadic, and there has been no attempt to amalgamate the data to gain better insight into the Carthusian Order as a community, rather than as distinct monasteries. Previous studies at the two main research sites of Hinton and Witham will be discussed in further detail in chapter 5, which will provide context to the rest of the content of that section.

---

[8] See Chapter 3 for further discussion of the surveys at Witham and Hinton

2
The Carthusians in Great Britain

The Carthusian Order's isolated nature lent itself to the small communities it nurtured, ensuring that silence and solitude could be maintained. Their presence in Great Britain and Ireland continued this tradition; only nine houses were established in England, and one each in Scotland and Ireland, compared with 87 in France and 43 in Italy during the medieval period (*Maisons* 1913-1919). This chapter will provide a brief history of each charterhouse, giving background for later discussion of archaeological and material remains at the sites.

2.1 Hugh of Lincoln and the first English foundation: 1178–1221

Witham was the last of three penitential monasteries, founded in 1178 by Henry II to expiate his role in the murder of Thomas Becket; it was also the sole Carthusian foundation. A site was chosen in the Royal Forest of Selwood, in Somerset, and was established by a monk and two lay brothers from La Grande Chartreuse. It is reported that Henry did little to aid the foundation of the Charterhouse at Witham[1] (Hallam 1977, 114). Although he gave the monks his own land, the current inhabitants were not removed, and no provision of shelter was given to the monks. This caused tension between both parties, which would not have been helped by the language barrier. The first prior was unable to manage the difficulties he faced, and so returned to the mother house (Appleby 1962, 212). The second prior sent to establish the house died only a few months after he arrived[2], and so the first charterhouse in England remained unestablished, its monks living in mud huts, and without a church (*Magna Vita* II, v; Appleby 1962, 212).

It was thus not until 1179 that the charterhouse could be adequately founded, when the procurator[3] of La Grande Chartreuse, Hugh, was sent for (Leyser 1987, 5). Hugh arrived at the priory in 1180 and began removing the tenants of the land (*Magna Vita* II, v; Coppack and Aston 2002, 28). With the king's authority, he offered the tenants emancipation of their servitude to Henry II or alternative accommodation similar to that which they had lost (Farmer 1989, 10). Hugh also persuaded the king to provide further funds to aid the construction of the site, as the Pipe Rolls from 1179 to around 1186 show payments for clothing of the brethren, sowing land, and for the building of the church and other structures (*Pipe Roll Society* vol. 30: 4, 11, 96; vol. 31: 109, 115; vol. 32: 27, 112, 141; vol. 33: 74, 122; vol. 34: 173; vol. 36: 135; vol. 37: 187). Unlike other English houses, such as Hinton, under Hugh's strict guidance the monastery never expanded but maintained an apostolic number of monks, twelve plus a prior, and around sixteen lay brethren to take care of the day-to-day running of the house (Coppack and Aston 2002, 30).

2.2 Expansion and Royal Benefaction: 1222–1500

Following the foundation of Witham in 1178, expansion throughout Great Britain and Ireland was slow. In 1222, the second English house was founded by William Longespée, the illegitimate son of Henry II and half-brother of Richard I and John (Strickland 2010, para. 1). A site in Hatherop, Gloucestershire was initially given to the community but, finding the location unsuitable, the monks petitioned to be moved, and Longespée's widow, Ela, Countess of Salisbury, offered them her manors of Hinton and Norton St Philip in exchange for the original site (Coppack and Aston 2002, 31).

Isolated in Somerset, Hinton and Witham remained the only charterhouses in England for over 100 years. However, in Ireland Richard de Burgo established a Carthusian house in 1249 named *Domus Dei* (House of God), or Kilnalahanin, near Loughrea, in Co. Galway (Grattan Flood 1907, 307). The house never flourished – in 1307, a tax survey valued the house at only £6 13s. 4d. – and this remained the only charterhouse in Ireland (Gray 1959, 45). Eventually, the house was suppressed by the Carthusian General Chapter in 1321[4], and by 1340 it had been abandoned completely (Gratton Flood 1907, 306-3-9; Dalton 1909, 25). The Franciscans took up the abandoned buildings, adapting and renovating the existing fabric, and so the ruins that remain on the site are Franciscan, not Carthusian (Gray 1959, 38).

Edward III granted the licence for a charterhouse in Exeter (Coppack and Aston 2002, 33), but nothing ever came of this proposal, and so it was not until 1343 that the third English house, Beauvale was founded. Situated near Greasley in Nottinghamshire, the priory sat on the edge of what is now called Abbey Wood, with plentiful supplies of fresh water from a nearby spring. Nicholas de Cantilupe

---

[1] The reported role of Henry II and Hugh of Lincoln in the establishment of Witham Charterhouse is discussed in further detail in Chapter 4 (see 4.1).
[2] The exact date of his death is unknown, though it must have been between 1178 and 1180. Much of what is understood about the early days of Witham Charterhouse is taken from the *Magna Vita*, which is undated.
[3] The procurator was the monk in charge of the lower house, who led the lay brothers' worship.
[4] On the suppression of Kilnalahanin the English priors were ordered to extract whatever rents and money they could from the house, as it was useless to the Order. 'De domo Hiberniae extrahant quidquid poterunt in redditibus et pecunia Priores Angliae, cum sit inutilis Ordini' (MS. GC 1, 82).

was responsible for this foundation of twelve monks and a prior, also endowing them with a significant amount of land and the right to quarry stone for the buildings (Du Boulay Hill and Gill 1908, 68-69).

The early charterhouses were typically characterised by having separate upper and lower houses, as at La Grande Chartreuse. The correrie (lower house) at Hinton was located a few miles to the east, at a site which is now merely called 'Friary,' a corruption of *frèreie*, or where the lay brethren resided (Coppack and Aston 2002, 15). Similarly, at Witham, the local village of Witham Friary is so named because the parish church was formerly the chapel of the lay brethren (McGarvie 1989, 11).

After the Black Death in the mid-fourteenth century, there was an upsurge in the number of Carthusian houses established. This is reflected by a phase of urban constructions, a relatively obscure concept at the beginning of the Order, as in general, the Carthusians sought isolation and austerity, away from the distractions of ordinary society. These urban houses also combined the upper and lower houses, manipulating and adapting the traditional layout of the monks' house to accommodate the lay brethren into the general charterhouse. At the London Charterhouse, each cell was sponsored by a different benefactor or benefactress, as the founder, Sir Walter Manny, died before the buildings could be completed (Knowles and Grimes 1954, 24-25; Wines 2008, 63-70). Sponsoring a cell performed a similar function to sponsoring a chantry chapel; the inhabitant of the cell was bound to pray for the souls of the benefactor and his or her family in perpetuity, ensuring their smooth passage to heaven. The impact of lay benefaction will be discussed in greater detail in chapter 3 (see 3.6).

After the establishment of the London Charterhouse in 1370, two other urban foundations quickly followed; Hull in 1377, and Coventry in 1381. Less is known about the Hull Charterhouse than other English Carthusian foundations, both archaeologically and historically. It was situated on the northern side of the city, outside the walls, and founded by Michael de la Pole, who dedicated it to St Michael (Hull City Council 2010, 4). De la Pole's father, William, had intended to found a house for the nuns of St Clare, but following his death, his son Michael altered the bequest to endow the Carthusians instead. As at the London Charterhouse, a number of the cells were endowed by wealthy local nobles. For example, John Colthorpe, mayor of Hull from 1389-90, sponsored a cell before his death in 1394, ensuring prayer in perpetuity for the souls of himself and his family (Lister 1924, 113; Page 1974, 191). The house was dissolved in 1539, and some of the buildings were destroyed, but the most considerable destruction came in 1642 when the remaining buildings were demolished before the second siege of Hull in the English Civil War (Hull City Council 2010, 4). Sir John Hotham blew up the remains of the charterhouse to remove any potential cover for the attacking Royalists (Evans 2018, 129). Consequently, there are no upstanding remains, and the precinct has long since been built over.

The Coventry Charterhouse, situated on the banks of the River Sherbourne to the south of the city, was founded by William, Lord Zouche of Harringworth, but when he died in 1382, the foundation stone of the church was laid by Richard II in 1385 (Soden 1995, 5). As the buildings were left incomplete, local notables contributed not only to the building of cells but also to the church, cloister, supplying the library and enabling the construction of fishponds, which will be further discussed in chapter 3 (Soden 1995, 6-7; see section 3.6). Benefaction at the Coventry Charterhouse continued throughout its existence, but at the time of the *Valor Ecclesiasticus* (vol. 3, 53-54), the house was still valued below the £200 threshold required to stay in operation, and it only managed to avoid suppression through a favourable review of being 'in virtue, contemplation and religion excellent' (Edwards 1946, 116). The house was, however, later dissolved in 1539 with the other charterhouses (TNA E 322/63).

By the end of the fourteenth century, charterhouses were once again being built in the countryside, and Axholme and Mount Grace Priory were established within a year of each other (1397 and 1398 respectively). Axholme was situated on the Isle of Axholme in northern Lincolnshire, on the site of a chapel to the Virgin Mary and was endowed for twelve monks and a prior, with some lay brothers to assist (TNA E 135/2/24, ff. 2, 8). The prior of the house at the time of the Dissolution was Augustine Webster, notably one of the three Carthusian monks who was executed when he failed to acknowledge Henry VIII as the Supreme Head of the Church of England and refused to denounce the Pope (TNA SP 1/92, ff. 26-35; BL Cotton Cleop. E/VI, f. 231).

Mount Grace Priory, near Northallerton in North Yorkshire, was founded by Thomas Holland, Duke of Surrey, in 1398, and was initially designed for a prior and twelve monks, although it was later expanded to accommodate a further six monks (Coppack and Keen 2019). A number of the monks were imprisoned for failing to swear the oath of supremacy in 1534 and in 1539 the house was surrendered, having been valued at £323 2*s*. 10½*d*. in the *Valor Ecclesiasticus* (Vol. 5, 84-85). Today, the priory is the best-preserved site of all the charterhouses in Great Britain and Ireland.

The last charterhouses to be established before the Reformation were also among the richest. Sheen Priory, in Richmond, was founded by Henry V in 1414, with the intention to house 40 monks, exceeding the standard apostolic number (Cloake 1977, 150). It would seem that, through its foundation, Henry V was attempting to expiate his father's sins for the role he played in the murder of Archbishop Scrope and the alleged murder of Richard II (Bernard 2012, 200). The Sheen Charterhouse was built for just 30 monks, reducing the original design, but this did not impact the wealth of the house. (Malden 1967, 89). Despite only being established the previous century, at the Dissolution the house was valued at £800 5s. 4½d. in the *Valor Ecclesiasticus* (Vol. 2, 51-54) and the prior was awarded a pension of £133 6s. 8d., more than some monasteries were worth (TNA E 315/234, f. 3b). The implications of royal patronage for the monastery cannot be understated. Beckett (1992, 11) suggested that the foundation at Sheen was 'designed to place the monarchy at the spiritual centre of English life', and the endowment made by Henry V would appear to agree with this. In total, over a series of three separate charters, around £900 was given to the new charterhouse, as well as an annual allowance of 2 tuns of wine, fishing rights on the Thames, and exemption from taxation (Hogg 2016, 50; Beckett 1992, 59). As Hogg suggests (2016, 50), the fishing rights would have been particularly important, as fish was one of the costliest outgoings for the Carthusian communities[5].

The Sheen Charterhouse was also closely linked with nearby Syon Abbey, a male and female Bridgettine house across the Thames, and there are many records of books and treatises written by the Carthusians for the nuns at Syon. These include the first English translation of *Imitatio Christi* (GUL Hunter MS 136), which was written in the early sixteenth century by William Darker for Elizabeth Gibb, the abbess of Syon (Herbert McAvoy 2004, 227; Patterson 2011, 137). The Sheen Charterhouse was the only Carthusian monastery to be re-founded by Queen Mary I (Haigh 1993, 226).

The only Carthusian house to be founded in Scotland, the Perth Charterhouse, was another royal foundation, in this case, that of James I of Scotland, who established the house in 1429. The house was designed for twelve monks and a prior and was first endowed with 200 marks (Ferguson 1910-11, 183; Beckett 1988, 2). The charterhouse was also intended to function as the king's mausoleum, and this is where he was buried in 1437, following his assassination, and his wife, Queen Joan was buried next to him in 1445. Sister to Henry VIII and wife of James IV, Margaret Tudor was also buried at the charterhouse after her death in 1541 (Fawcett and Hall 2005, 48).

2.3 The Carthusians during the Reformation: 1518–1569

From the late fifteenth century, there had been concern throughout the country as to the condition of the monasteries, and in 1518 Cardinals Wolsey and Campeggio began pressing for a reformation of the religious houses, using visitations to highlight where changes could be made (Bernard 2011, 394). The opposition from a minority of religious orders to Henry's divorce from Catherine of Aragon solidified the need for reformation, as they were seen as challenging the King's authority. Two monks of the London Charterhouse, the prior John Houghton, and the procurator Humphrey Middlemore, were jailed in the Tower of London in 1534 with Sir Thomas More and Bishop John Fisher[6] (TNA SP 3/4 f. 141; TNA SP 3/7 f. 17), for failing to acknowledge the succession. Houghton opined that it was not his place to discuss the affairs of the king, although he was unable to understand how a marriage that had been lawful for so many years and had been sanctified by the church could now be annulled (Chauncy 1550, sig. M3v; Whatmore 1983, 27; Gray 2013, 1). Both later agreed to the act 'as far as it might be lawful' and were released from the Tower by the end of May that year (Bernard 2005, 161).

Bernard (2011, 396) describes the compilation of the *Valor Ecclesiasticus* between 1535 and 1536 as aiming to 'provide a body of information on which taxation could be based and to assert royal authority'. Thomas Cromwell, the chief minister to Henry VIII from 1532 to 1540 appointed a number of commissioners by letters patent to survey ecclesiastical buildings and land, under the premise of calculating tax liability under the First Fruits and Tenths statute[7], but in reality, the survey served many different purposes (Hoyle 1995, 294; Solt 1990, 32; Heal 2003, 143; Bernard 2011, 396). The commissioners were charged with examining each monastery for morality and quality, indicating where reforms might be considered, and required the monks to acknowledge the royal supremacy over the pope (Hoyle 1995, 294). In April 1535, the priors of the London, Beauvale and Axholme Charterhouses, John Houghton, Robert Lawrence, and Augustine Webster presented themselves to Thomas Cromwell to plead for exemption from the Oath of Supremacy, with the hope that they could swear an oath more acceptable to the ideals of the Order (Whatmore 1983, 39-40; Bernard 2005, 162). They were immediately arrested and taken to the Tower of London. Under interrogation, the priors stated that they could not accept Henry as the Supreme Head of the Church of England, asserting that there was only one Church, which was that led by the pope, and so they were arrested (TNA SP 1/92, ff. 26-35; Bernard 2005, 162). On 4 May 1535 at Tyburn, the three priors were hung and 'while they were still alive the hangman cut out their hearts and bowels and burned them. Then they were beheaded and quartered, and the parts placed in public places on long spears' (L&P Hen. VIII, viii, 661).

The *Compendium Compertorum* for the Northern Visitation recorded the visitations of Doctors Richard

---

[5] The procurator's accounts for the London Charterhouse for 1492 list fish as the most expensive outgoing, totalling £104 17s. 8½d. of the annual total for the house of £588 12s. 10d. (Hogg 2016, 50).

[6] More and Fisher were arrested in 1534 for their objection to both the Act of Succession, illegitimising Katherine's daughter Mary, and the Oath of Succession, which required renunciation of foreign authorities (the pope), and annulled Henry and Katherine's marriage following its reinstatement by Pope Clement in 1534. Both men were beheaded in 1535.
[7] The First Fruits and Tenths Act of 1534 forbade the payment of ecclesiastical taxes to the papacy, redirecting them to the crown (Maitland 1941, 511).

Layton and Thomas Legh in the diocese of York, Coventry and Lichfield and listed those monks from each monastery who confessed to immoral conduct or other notable crimes (Shaw 2003). Though Hoyle (1995, 295) suggests that the visitations were conducted in order to garner the 'most salacious and outrageous allegations of monastic ill-discipline, immorality and superstition,' Bernard (2011, 398) asserts that there appears to be no consistent campaign of 'black propaganda,' and in 70% of the surveyed monastic houses, no monks admitted to criminal or immoral acts. The only charterhouse that was recorded in the extant *Compendia* was Mount Grace[8], which lists Thomas Barker and Richard Davis as wishing to leave the religious life (TNA SP 1/102, f. 16).

The results of the *Valor Ecclesiasticus* led to discussions in Parliament as to what could be done to reform the monasteries and culminated in the Dissolution of the Lesser Monasteries in 1536 (Bernard 2011, 399). However, of the 419 houses valued under £200, only 243 were suppressed, indicating that the goal was reformation, not the wholesale dismantling of the religious orders (Bernard 2011, 400). A change in the attitudes of Henry VIII and his councillors seems to have come following the Pilgrimage of Grace in the Autumn of 1536, which directly challenged the king's authority, and led to some abbots being executed as an example to others. Furthermore, two monks of the London Charterhouse, John Rochester and James Walworth, who had been sent to the Hull Charterhouse, were condemned on charges of treason, likely as a reaction to the Pilgrimage of Grace. The two men were executed in May 1537. A total of eighteen Carthusian monks were executed between 1535 and 1541, to serve as an example for any other monastic communities failing to cooperate with the Crown. In Europe, this treatment of holy Catholic men provoked outrage and demonstrates quite how significant the dissent of the Carthusian martyrs was[9].

Despite the fate of the eighteen Carthusian monks who had refused to swear the Oath of Supremacy, there was still much disinclination to surrender the monasteries when the time came. At Hinton, in Somerset, the requirement that the charterhouse should be *voluntarily* surrendered led to the monks dissenting by claiming that the monastery was not theirs to give but a house of God (Bettey 1989, 88). Horde, the prior, eventually surrendered Hinton in 1539, insisting that if the commissioners ordered him to surrender, he would but 'otherwise his conscience would not suffer him willingly to give it over' (TNA SP 1/142, f. 155).

At those houses where the prior had been executed in 1535 (London, Beauvale and Axholme), the commissioners found the communities pliable to their demands, most probably due to the forced appointment of a prior who could be relied upon to surrender the house quietly. However, the monks were not always in agreement; two monks and a lay brother from Axholme took it upon themselves to write to the prior of Sheen Charterhouse complaining of their prior's willingness to accept the suppression of the monastery (BL Cotton Cleop. E/IV, f. 113). The outcome of this complaint is unknown since no return letter from the prior of Sheen survives.

The Reformation in Scotland, and consequently, the closing of the Scottish monasteries did not immediately follow the Dissolution of the Monasteries in England. Although James V was advised by Henry VIII to follow the same pattern as himself, reaping the wealth of the monasteries to benefit the royal exchequer, James refused to betray the Pope and the Catholic Church, so instead the monasteries slowly declined (Hamilton Papers I, 29-33; Greene 1992, 181). This decline was primarily due to the situation south of the border, as Scotland was partly influenced by the actions in England, as can be seen in recruitment to monasteries; no new monks were received in Scotland from 1560, and the remaining inhabitants of the houses died off (Barrell 2000, 245).

The decline was also due to the Scottish practice of installing 'commendators' in place of abbots or priors. The commendators were essentially administrators, and usually had strong links to powerful noblemen, abusing their position of power to redirect monastic funds to the lord without paying any duties (Greene 1992, 181; Barrell 2000, 247). Thus, the monasteries slowly disintegrated, their incomes having been stolen. The consequences of this were that by the time of the Reformation, only a few genuine monks were still in office, rather than a commendator, although one of these was Adam Stewart, the prior of the charterhouse at Perth (Cowan 1982, 34).

However, in May 1559, John Knox, the leading figure of the Scottish Reformation, preached in St John the Baptist's church in Perth, inciting the congregation gathered there ('The Lords of the Congregation of Jesus Christ') to strip the altars of the church and attack religious idols (Reid 1973, 31). The congregation then proceeded to sack the priories and the charterhouse of the town (Reid 1973, 31). Donaldson (1960, 7) has noted that the charterhouse was attacked only because of its location within the burgh, and because the other friaries were being sacked, not because it was necessarily corrupt. Despite this, the charterhouse was spared complete destruction; although the interior fittings were completely cleared, the main fabric of the house remained, and it was not formally suppressed until 1569 (Cowan 1982, 190).

---

[8] Legh also visited Hull, but no record exists in the Compendium Compertorum. This information is garnered from a letter written to Cromwell dated 10 February 1536, which reads 'I have been at Mountgrace and Hull, and find them there and in all other places ready to fulfil the King's pleasure' (TNA SP 1/102, f. 22). The charterhouse at Axholme was intended to be visited, but Legh instead sent a servant to deliver and receive the signed documents acknowledging the Royal Supremacy. The proctor of the monastery informed Cromwell of the situation in a letter dated 15 January 1536 (TNA SP 1/101, f. 85).

[9] A later letter from Dr Ortiz to Empress Isabella tells that the 'heads of the holy cardinal of Rochester, the holy Thomas More, and another holy Carthusian Martyr were set up at the gate of London. Rochester's head was always fresher, although the others were turning black' (BL Add. MS 28588, f. 47).

2.4 The Aftermath of the Dissolution and the Re-use of Carthusian Buildings

Following the Dissolution, and under a cloud of discontent, some Carthusian monks including Maurice Chauncy[10], fled England towards the end of 1546 (Thompson 1930, 496). The monks fled to the charterhouse of Val de Grace of Bruges, in the Netherlands, where they renewed their professions as Carthusians, and to where a number of other English Carthusians also escaped over the next couple of years (Thompson 1930, 498).

The charterhouse at Sheen had been sold to Edward Seymour, Jane Seymour's father in 1542, who began the conversion of the former monastic buildings into a manor house (Coppack and Aston 2002, 145). However, in 1550, he was deprived of his position as Lord Protector of England under Edward VI, and in January 1552 was executed for felony, so the remodelling was never completed (Coppack and Aston 2002, 145). On the accession of Mary I in 1553, a number of monasteries were refounded, including the charterhouse at Sheen (Thompson 1930, 504-505; Haigh 1993, 226). Maurice Chauncy was named Prior of the refounded charterhouse, and fifteen former Carthusians joined Chauncy to reestablish the Carthusian presence in England (Knowles 1959, 223). The charterhouse was, however, short-lived, as it was once again suppressed when Elizabeth I ascended the throne on the death of Mary in 1559 (Coppack and Aston 2002, 145). The re-suppressed monks returned to Belgium, where they were again welcomed into the community at the charterhouse of Val de Grace (Thompson 1930, 511). By 1568, they had found a separate residence in Clare Street, Bruges, where the English Carthusians settled in a charterhouse they named Sheen Anglorum, and this house of exiles remained extant until the eighteenth century (Brantley 2007, 44; Thompson 1930, 512).

The post-Dissolution activity at the charterhouses, the discussion of which will follow, gives essential context as to the impact on the buildings and the survival of material culture. Where at Sheen the monks left to be replaced by secular inhabitants and then returned, the material remains will likely reflect in some ways these changes, especially as secular construction had begun before the monks returned. If demolition occurred after the suppression of a house, it tended not to be the complete destruction of the building but instead aimed at making the buildings uninhabitable, so that the monastic community could not return (Doggett 2001, 166). This included removing lead from the buildings, as it was a valuable commodity that could be sold on. Archaeologically, this leaves evidence in the hearths that were used to melt down the lead before it was removed from the site.

The ways in which the charterhouses were rebuilt for new uses vary, but all the charterhouses had some part of them converted into a residence by the end of the seventeenth century (Coppack and Aston 2002, 137). At Hinton, the monastery was sold to Sir Walter Hungerford, but when he arrived at the property, he found that the surveyor, Sir Thomas Arundell had taken it upon himself to demolish and remove most of the fabric of the church (Guinn Chipman 2013, 20; Coppack and Aston 2002, 139). It then passed through many hands, but eventually, at the end of the sixteenth century, a house was built against the northern precinct wall, overlooking the old monastic precinct (Thompson 1896, 344). Similarly, at Witham, Ralph Hopton, who acquired the house after its suppression, converted and adapted the existing fabric of the conventual buildings to the north of the cloister into a manor for himself (Wilson-North and Porter 1997, 83).

The London Charterhouse, perhaps because of the difficulties the monks had caused the Crown and its position in the capital, remained in the ownership of the Royal Commissioners, and Henry VIII granted a licence on 12 June 1542 to John Bridges and Thomas Hale to use the church to store the king's nets, hales and pavilions (TNA E 315/235, f. 115b). The Venetian Bassano family of instrument makers is also known to have lived in some of the old cells before they were sold to Sir Edward North in 1545 (Lasocki 1985, 117). North built himself a mansion following the general layout of the charterhouse, and the cloister garth remained (Harrison 1991, 5). After North's death, the house was bought by Thomas Howard, 4th Duke of Norfolk and second cousin of Queen Elizabeth I. Howard continued the remodelling of the charterhouse, renaming it Howard House, and on his death, it was passed to his son.

The oddly high survival rate of the buildings at Mount Grace Priory is due wholly to Sir James Strangways, who acquired the property in 1541 (Coppack and Aston 2002, 143). He already had a sufficiently large house, and so had no desire to convert the monastic buildings; his only interest was the land attached to the monastery (Coppack and Aston 2002, 143). It was not until 1653 when Thomas Lascelles bought the priory that the Guest House was converted into a house, but mostly, the monastery was untouched (Coppack and Aston 2002, 143). Strangways was not the only new owner who became the absentee landlord of a monastic estate, utilising the land only for the income it could provide (Doggett 2001, 168). In these cases, the surviving structures were often plundered for building materials by locals, as the stone could be burnt for lime and turned into mortar, or simply reused to build houses.

---

[10] Maurice Chauncy (c.1509-1581) was a monk of the London Charterhouse, who swore the Oath of Supremacy in 1535, thereby avoiding the fate of many of the other London monks. After the Dissolution, Chauncy fled to Bruges with many other English Carthusians. When Mary I reinstated Sheen Charterhouse in 1555, Chauncy returned and was made prior, although this was short lived. Elizabeth I's accession to the throne in 1559 exiled the monks once again, and they returned to Bruges, where Chauncy was made prior in 1561. Chauncy wrote of his experiences of the Dissolution in *Historia aliquot nostri saeculi Martyrum in Anglia* (Mainz, 1550), which offers an eyewitness account of the horrors which befell the London Charterhouse. The volume was intended to inform the rest of the order of the fate of his fellow monks (Sargent 2004).

2.5 Conclusions

The efforts of Hugh of Lincoln were crucial to the success of the community at Witham, and in cementing the Carthusian Order in England. Though the first foundation at Witham was slow to flourish, by the beginning of the fifteenth century, a total of eleven charterhouses had been founded, culminating in the royal foundations of Sheen and Perth. The suppression of the monasteries resulted in a sudden end to Carthusian monastic life, the partial destruction of some of the Carthusian houses, and the later sale of the properties to secular owners. Most were later converted to residences.

Though the post-Dissolution activity of the charterhouses is not explicitly addressed within the scope of this study, there are significant benefits to be gained from understanding the ways in which structural changes were made, giving insight into the historical footprint of the buildings and helping to refine interpretations of medieval material culture. This knowledge is vital for archaeological investigation, as it has a crucial bearing on how much information can be gleaned from the material culture and building earthworks[11]. Furthermore, the preservation of the sites depends on the ways in which the new owners chose to use them, Mount Grace, for example, is the best-preserved charterhouse because the secular owner had no use for it and left it to decay.

---

[11] The material culture of the charterhouse is discussed in further detail in chapter 6.

3

Church, Cloister, and Cell: The Inner Charterhouse Complex

This chapter focuses in detail on those areas of the monastery which were most frequented by the monks and puts in greater context the material culture previously discussed. Where the monks spent almost all their time either in the cell or the church, with the cloister acting as an access route between these two buildings, it is advantageous to examine these areas in greater detail, investigating both the architectural and archaeological aspects.

3.1 Overview of the Charterhouse Complex

The charterhouse took much inspiration from the Desert Fathers (Dunn 2003, 3), and for MacCulloch (2009, 391), the Carthusian Order was a reinvention of the Eastern monastic tradition. This reinvention is manifested in the importance of seclusion to the monks, seen as essential to monasticism, and through the silence that follows seclusion, an attainment of inner peace and stillness, allowing communion with God (Dixon 2009, 59; Belisle 2003, 57; 90). Isolation was not necessarily synonymous with closed off; France (1996, 26) asserted that solitude allowed the monk to be open to God, and to influences that are unavailable to lives in the secular world. Silence was crucial for prayer, but also for listening and reflection with God (Belisle 2003, 100). The layout of the charterhouse complex was structured in order to guarantee isolation and seclusion for the monks. This isolation-focussed architecture demonstrates a specific building plan and forethought as to the landscape of the surrounding area to ensure the monks could be as well provided for as possible.

Dimier (1999, 186-188) identified that architecturally, the charterhouse was divided into three main areas, the first consisting of the cloister and cells, the second, the communal buildings, the church, refectory, chapter house and kitchen, and finally the maintenance buildings, including the stables, granges, and workshops. This simple method of categorising the buildings of the charterhouse indicates the level of privacy, decreasing as one leaves the great cloister, travels through the communal buildings, and enters the area of the maintenance buildings.

Del Espino Hidalgo and García Fernández (2014) researched zoning in charterhouses in greater detail as a method for investigating how members of the community could access various areas of the monastery. They found that the rules which govern the Carthusian way of life could determine the shape of the charterhouse, as a certain level of isolation needed to be achieved by a series of walls which prevented access to certain persons (Del Espino Hidalgo and García Fernández 2014, 3). In common for all charterhouses was a layout where the monks' housing and conventual buildings were arranged around the Great Cloister. These zones constituted the 'silent' areas. The lay brothers' housing, workshops, guests' housing and what Del Espino Hidalgo and García Fernández (2014, 4) term the 'public area' can be grouped as non-silent service areas. The monks' housing was largely separated (with a few exceptions) from the non-silent area by the conventual buildings, which reduced the amount of disruptive noise that could be heard by the monks in their cells. Del Espino Hidalgo and García Fernández's model is illustrated in figure 3.1, as applied to the charterhouse at Mount Grace. The zoned layout shows how the laity and visitors were kept as separate as possible from the monks, by means of the inner court, lesser cloister, and great cloister, in which access could be strictly regulated. Though similar to the plan described by Dimier (1999, 186-188), Del Espino Hidalgo and García Fernández increased the complexity of the charterhouse zones, including guest housing, and areas such as the inner court which could in some cases be accessed by the laity. This method of classification accounts for visitors to the charterhouse and housing for the lay brothers (which is neither a communal building nor situated around the great cloister) and identifies more specifically where various types of buildings were situated in the complex.

In a further investigation into the charterhouse layout, Elke Nagel (2015) identified an architectural pattern at charterhouses in France, Italy, Switzerland and Germany, based on the dates that they were built, which grouped them into six phases (table 3.1). Nagel's phases can also be used to categorise the British and Irish charterhouses. The earliest house, Witham, fits into the Consolidation phase, defined as houses founded between 1115-1203. These houses were characterised by a small overall size, and often narrow shape due to the topography of the landscape ruling the design of the monastery (Nagel 2015, 11; 23). There are strong similarities between Witham and La Verne, France, both excellent examples of this narrow design, and the houses maintained an apostolic 12 cells. Hinton and Kilnalahanin belong to the second phase, that is, the First Adaption Phase, comprising charterhouses founded between 1203-1340. This phase features a more flexible plan and organic layouts, with less pragmatic alignment of the conventual buildings (Nagel 2015, 13). The Certosa di Firenze Galluzzo, Italy, and Hinton Charterhouse share a number of similar features, the square cloister, an increased number of cells, and more oddly-shaped cell gardens. The great majority of the British charterhouses (Beauvale, London, Hull, Coventry, Axholme, Mount Grace) belong to the First Representation Phase, founded between 1340-1408. Nagel (2015, 16) characterises these houses as those that were accompanied by founders'

Communal Solitude

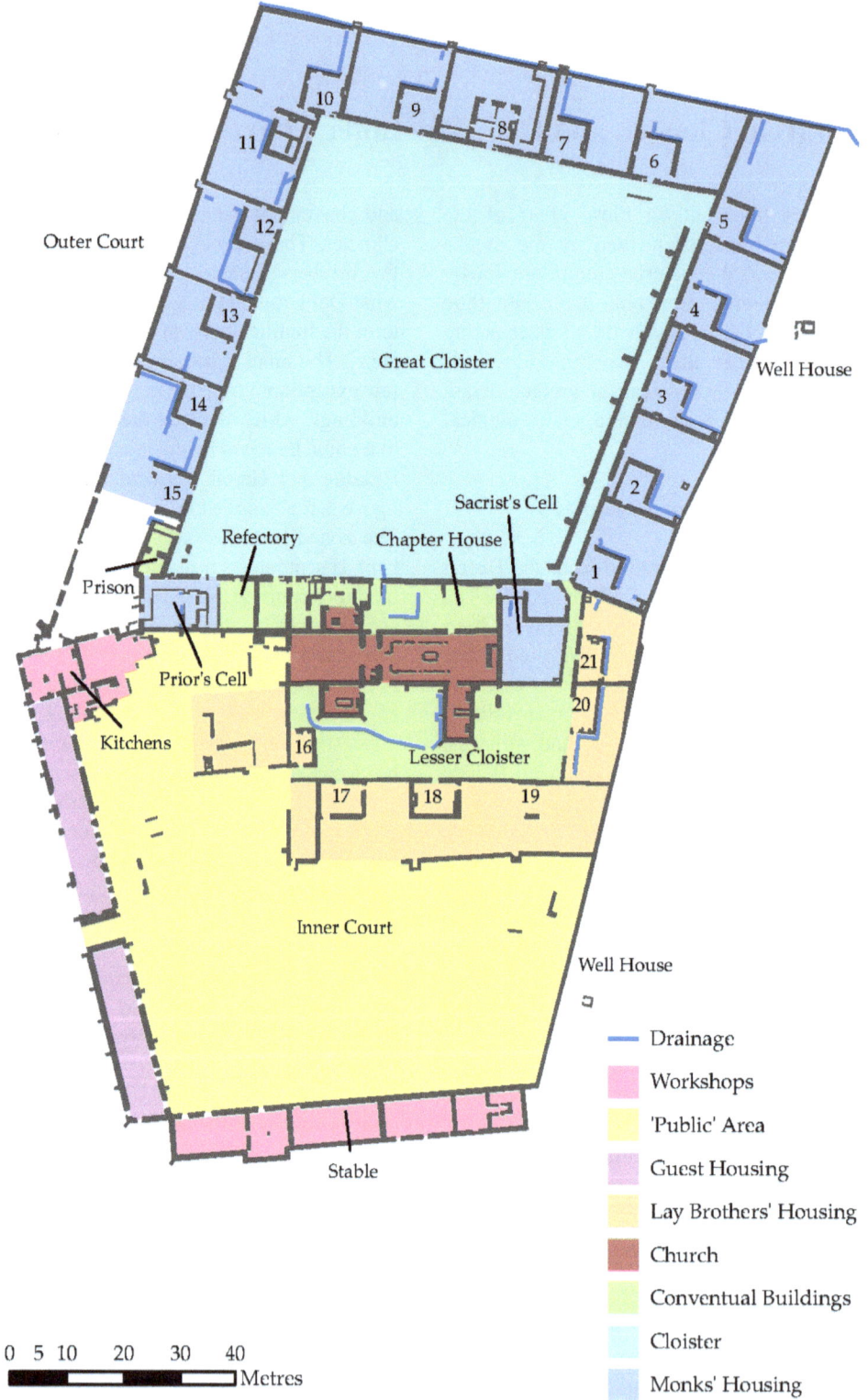

Figure 3.1. Zoning plan of Mount Grace Priory, based on the methodology of Del Espino Hidalgo and García Fernández (2015) (Map after Coppack and Keen 2019, 358).

wishes, and thus became more externally visible, with a complex layout and an obviously intentional design from the outset. The French house of Villeneuve-lès-Avignon demonstrates this design, featuring a precinct wall, similar to that of London Charterhouse, which indicates the growing popularity of the Carthusians, and their need to maintain solitude from the secular world. Although this method of phasing building styles can be useful for the charterhouses, Nagel only examined houses close to La Grande Chartreuse, in Eastern France, Southern Germany, Switzerland and Northern Italy. In trying to adapt this method for the English houses, some issues occur. First, Sheen and Perth do not fit into Nagel's phasing system, as she did not consider any building activity that took place between 1408 and 1450, and yet, Sheen was built in 1414, and Perth in 1429. Nagel's next phase (Second Adaption

Table 3.1. Nagel's (2015) phasing of medieval to early modern charterhouse constructions, with the addition of how British and Irish charterhouses fit into the categories.

Phase	Characteristics	Example house
Foundation Phase (1084-1115)	Remote, inhabitable landscape Layout follows topography of landscape	La Grande Chartreuse
Consolidation Phase (1115-1203)	Small overall size Pragmatic alignment of conventual buildings Long narrow layout	La Verne, Portes, Witham, Saint-Hugon
First Adaption Phase (1203-1340)	Remote location More organic layout, less pragmatic Flexible approach to planning	Pomiers, Hinton, Kilnalahanin, Firenze Galluzo
First Representation Phase (1340-1408)	Increase in patronal influence Intentional design for whole layout Regularly sized cells and gardens Extra buildings to screen cloister	Villeneuve-lès-Avignon, Pontiagnano, Basseville, London, Beauvale, Hull, Coventry, Axholme, Mount Grarce
Second Adaptation Phase (1450-1498)	External visible churches Large guesthouses Wide-spread layouts	Padova, church of Pavia
Second Representation Phase (1585-1633)	Complex baroque layout Decorative elements Larger cloisters and cells	Lyon, Bosserville

Phase) began in 1450 (Nagel 2015, 19), but based on the characteristics of this phase, including a large, externally visible church, castellated walls, and grand gatehouses, the last two of the British charterhouses would appear to be more in keeping with the First Representation Phase, as previously discussed (Nagel 2015, 16; 19). The Second Adaption Phase includes houses such as the Certosa di Pavia, built by the Visconti family of Pavia, and featuring a spectacular church façade. These phases can show strong homogeneity amongst charterhouse building plans, but there are flaws in the method if one is to use it for houses across Europe. That there is a definite pattern to the architectural design indicates an evolution of a Carthusian layout that could be applied to different environments, but which maintained basic similarities. It is also worth considering the different needs and styles of the countries in which these houses were built. A house in northern England, for example, is going to require a greater degree of shelter from wind, rain and snow than a contemporary house built in southern Italy, and this is demonstrated in the difficulty of fitting each house into Nagel's phasing.

The walls of the monastery fulfilled both a spiritual and psychological role in Carthusian life. Their main function was obviously to physically delineate space, and for the external precinct wall, to keep the monastic complex secure (Popović 2007, 52). Psychologically, however, the walls represented an exclusionary boundary of the 'other,' ensuring secular persons could not invade the monastic space, but also ensuring the monks' seclusion (Dey 2004, 358; Horn 1973, 15). The external wall protected the monastery as a whole, a second wall screened off access to the chapter house, church, refectory and other conventual buildings (Bales 2001, 264). Guests to the house would have likely been given access to the church but would not have been allowed to enter the Great Cloister. At the London Charterhouse, the guest accommodation was located in the Little Cloister with the lay brothers' quarters, where they could visit the church, but were highly restricted in their movement towards the monks' cells. The chapter house, church and refectory themselves acted as a barrier to the cloister and monks' cells, whose walls protected their inhabitants (Bales 2001, 264).

This demarcation between secular and religious was also represented through the senses. The burning of incense in the church, for example, which Hamilton and Spicer (2005, 7-8) have suggested 'set the divine apart from the smells of the world,' also constituted a sacrificial offering that could drive away evil spirits from the church. Bad smells were associated with the Devil and Hell, whereas pleasant smells evoked good things, so the use of incense to fill the church with a sweet odour became symbolic of sanctity, prayer and the divine (Woolgar 2006, 118-119). Likewise, the ringing of church bells was seen to drive away demons and signified to all those in hearing range of the sound of sacred events, such as the elevation of the host during Mass (Hamilton and Spicer 2005, 8). Within the charterhouse, the day was punctuated by bells as signals for the beginning of each of the religious offices, and for the laity in the local area, therefore defined the sanctity and devotion of the monastery in contrast to the secular world. Hamilton and Spicer (2005, 7) also suggested that bells were intrusive, and were illustrative of one monastic house's control over a particular area, in this case, the Carthusian desert.

Spiritually, walls and boundaries signified the intentional withdrawal from the secular world to solitude, the communal isolation of the Carthusian Order (Webb 2007,

12). However, the charterhouse was not isolated only in this way, the monastery as a whole was divided from the secular world, the monks were isolated from the rest of the lay community, and finally, each individual monk was isolated from each other (Del Espino Hidalgo and García Fernández 2014, 2). This can be seen as a series of increasingly smaller concentric circles of access, with the individual monk central, as seen in figure 3.2.

With concern to the secular world, the laity was always prevented where possible from visiting the charterhouse. Charters of La Grande Chartreuse indicate that women and armed men were prohibited from entering the Carthusian desert, and a guard house was built at the entrance to the desert to ensure that no unwanted visitors could enter the site (Dubois 1965, 189). The Carthusian Statutes (21:1) also specifically prohibited women from the monastery, stating 'We do not allow women to enter our boundaries at all, knowing that… [no man] could escape the caresses and cunning of women'. With the Carthusians' need for solace, allowing lay persons into the charterhouse invaded that silence, and prohibited the proper conduct of the monks' religious devotion.

To investigate how easily people could gain access to various spaces within a cell, Nicola Aravecchia (2001) used Space Syntax Analysis to investigate the fourth-century hermitages at Kellia in Lower Egypt. Space Syntax Analysis is a technique which analyses the configuration of space and can be used to create access plans that show how many rooms or areas one must pass through to reach a specific location (Hillier 2014, 19; 21; Aravecchia 2001, 29). The diagrams created from this method illustrate the flow of people through a building, and the relative difficulty of access is measured by depth, that is, the number of steps it takes to reach each room (Richardson 2003, 374-375). Often, those rooms with a higher depth measurement are of high value or status, but the direction of access as well as the number of access points can also denote its status or function (Fairclough 1992, 353). A room with few access points is likely to be more secluded than one which can be entered from more than one room. For the Carthusian Order then, this method can be used to demonstrate the level of isolation each individual monk was afforded, according to the depth measurement of each individual cell. Any potential journey would have also been regulated by locked doors or guarded entranceways, which forbade certain persons from entering the most isolated areas of the monastery (Aravecchia 2001, 30). The tool is often used in town planning, where it can analyse how pedestrians navigate urban transportation systems but also access routes through museums and shopping malls. In archaeology, the method has been applied to a range of different sites but has rarely been used to examine medieval monasteries.

In order to demonstrate a number of possible Carthusian configurations using Space Syntax Analysis, three access plans have been created, one for Mount Grace Priory, a rural house, one for London Charterhouse, an urban house, and one to demonstrate access within the cell[1]. These three plans offer the opportunity to examine issues of control and seclusion in the charterhouse. The plans for London and Mount Grace indicate a high level of regulated access to the cells. At Mount Grace (figs. 3.3, 3.4), a visitor would be required to pass through the outer court, gatehouse, inner court, little cloister, a passageway, and the great cloister before reaching only the door of a monk's cell (cells 1-15, 22-23). Based on the access plan, this constitutes a depth measurement of 8 spaces and interestingly, although to be expected, the prison[2] is the most inaccessible, with access only via the Prior's cell. Within the monks' cells (figs. 3.5, 3.6), further restriction is encountered; the oratory is the most regulated area. That it was the place for silent and private prayer agrees wholly with its seclusion, as the holiest area of the monk's cell. At the London Charterhouse (figs. 3.7, 3.8), an urban site, a similar level of restriction was ensured, with a gatehouse restricting access from the West Smithfield cemetery to the Carthusian inner court. From the inner court, it was possible to reach one of the chapels of the church, that of St Anne and the Holy Cross, a western extension of the nave, which allowed women to be able to hear mass, but prevented them from entering the

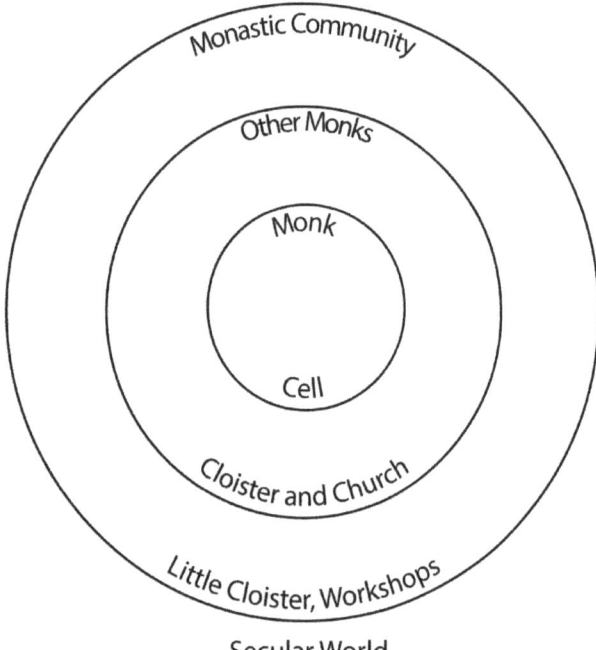

Figure 3.2. Diagram illustrating areas of access in the charterhouse.

---

[1] These plans are based on Aravecchia's (2001) methodology for justified access plans of Qusur el-'Izeila 23 at Kellia. Each space (building, open area, passage) is represented by a box labelled with its name. Access routes from each space are indicated by a line leading to the next space.
[2] The prison was used to hold Carthusian monks who were not conforming to the order, and the miscreant monk would often be sent to a different charterhouse. The Chartae of the General Chapter tells of a monk from the Hull Charterhouse who had been imprisoned at La Grande Chartreuse for a number of years by 1423, and the prior of Hull was urged to travel to the motherhouse to collect the monk (LPL MS 413, f. 48v; Hogg 1987, 64). By 1425, the monk was still languishing in prison, and the prior of Hull had been threatened with reduced rations of beer and wine if he did not collect the prisoner and pay the cost of keeping him there (LPL MS 413, f. 58r; Hogg 1987, 65).

Church, Cloister, and Cell: The Inner Charterhouse Complex

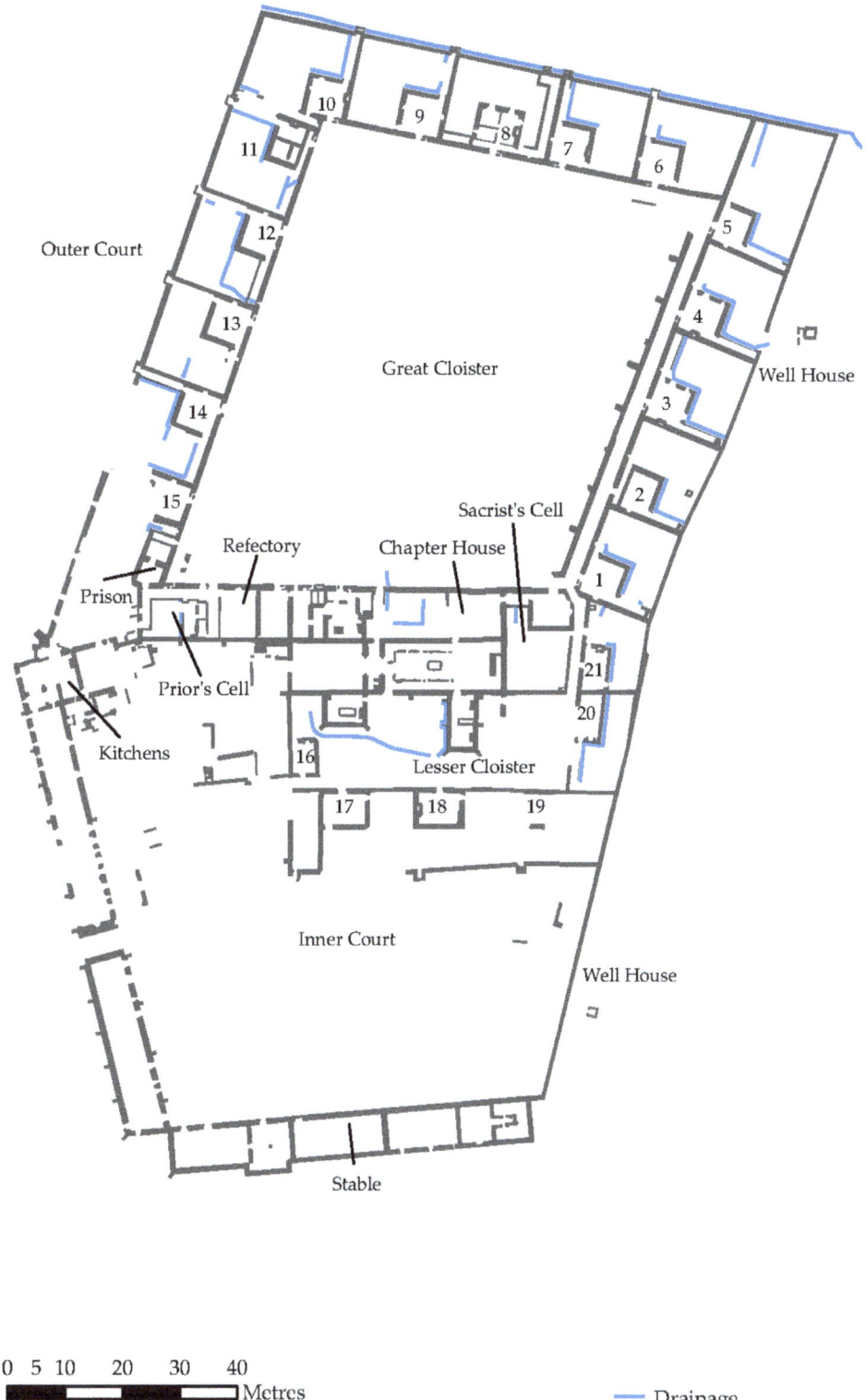

Figure 3.3. The layout of Mount Grace Priory, indicating drainage routes and numbered cells (after Coppack and Keen 2019, 299).

church proper, as there was no access to the church from the chapel (fig. 3.7) (Barber and Thomas 2002, 32). This chapel was consecrated in 1405, but within a few months, women had been excluded from it by the 1405 Carthusian Visitation (St John Hope 1925, 43; TNA LR 2/61, ff. 12v-13). Men were still allowed to attend the monastic church, however. This chapel was located by excavation in the period following the Second World War, proving that an eastern wall was built to segregate the women from the rest of the monastic church.

The application of Space Syntax Analysis to a medieval monastery has illustrated how useful the tool can be in exploring accessibility in a religious institution. Though some of the results were unsurprising, such as that the cell was one of the most heavily guarded areas of the monastery,

Communal Solitude

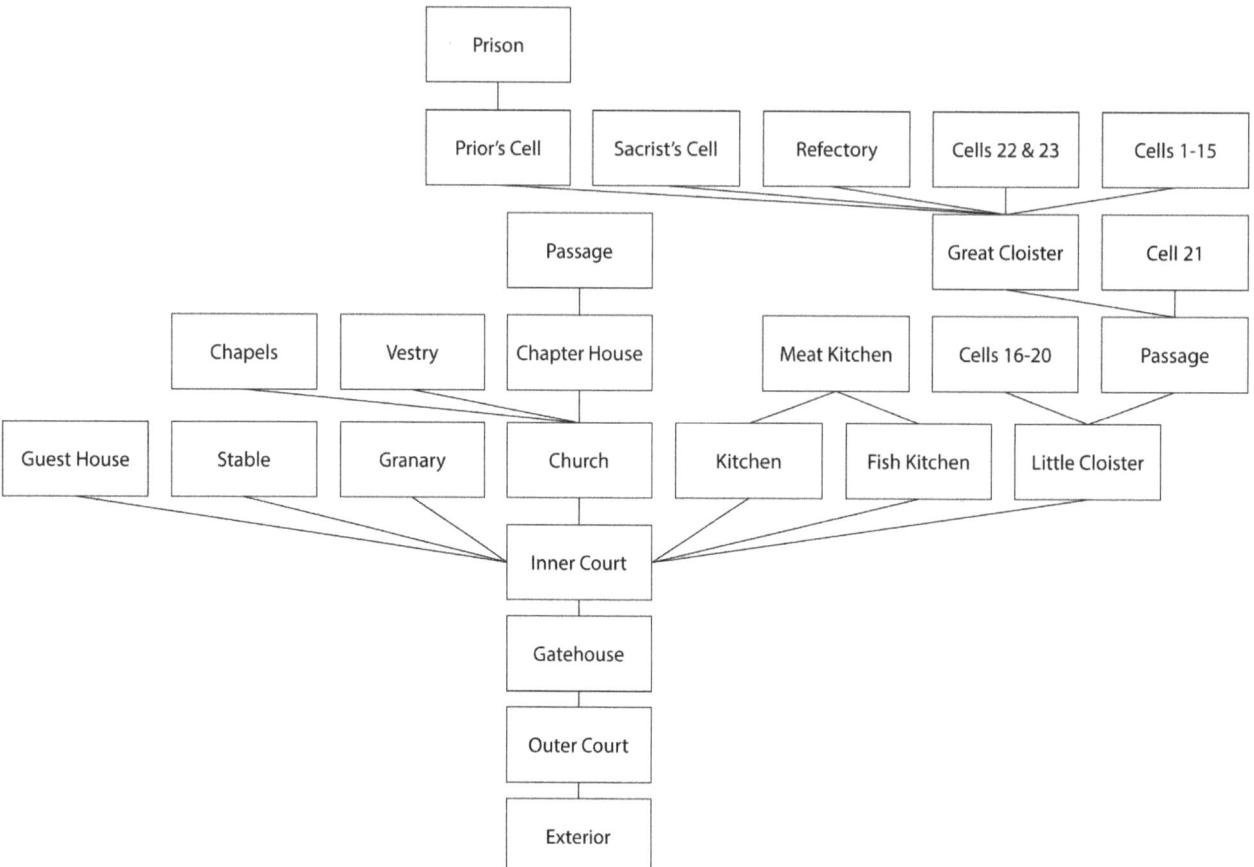

Figure 3.4. Space Syntax Analysis access plan for Mount Grace Priory, a rural charterhouse.

the method indicates that in both urban and rural settings, access to even the little cloister was restricted, and external visitors would not have been able to easily enter buildings such as the church or chapter house.

3.2 Previous Excavations and Resistivity Surveys

This section will highlight the two charterhouses that are the focus of this research, Witham and Hinton, and where possible, focus on the friaries of these houses. As these two monasteries were the only British charterhouses to feature separate upper and lower houses, they offer a singular opportunity to examine the layout of the friaries and give a background to the primary research conducted in the course of this study which will be discussed in greater detail in chapter 7. Though a brief discussion of previous archaeological work at the charterhouses was discussed in chapter 1, a more in-depth exploration of previous scholarship is vital to inform further investigation. The assertions made by late nineteenth- and early twentieth-century historians are able to give meaning to anomalies in resistivity plots and have also informed later discussions of the sites.

3.2.1 Witham Charterhouse

In 1918, the Dean of Wells, Rev. Armitage Robinson suggested that the site of the charterhouse may lie where the Wyndham Mansion had once stood, based on his study of the Foundation Charter of Witham Charterhouse and a Perambulation made in 1244 (Armitage Robinson 1918, 15, 24). Specifically, the phrase *ad parcum monachorum ipsorum*, which appeared to relate to the field named 'New Building Ground' in a sale map of 1813 (Armitage Robinson 1918, 24).

Until 1890, it was believed that the church at Witham Friary was the centre of the main charterhouse, rather than the chapel of the lay brothers. Henry Gee (1890) first noted that the word 'Friary' reflects the use of the area for the frères, asserting that the site belonged to the lay brothers, not the monks. This theory was further promulgated by Cook in 1904, who noted that the name of Witham Friary comes from the French *frèrie*, and had been corrupted in various forms, Frery, Frary, over the years (Cook 1904, 24). Cook (1904, 25) also documented the only other remaining Friary building, the dovecote, which was discovered in 1902 when it was turned into a parish room, and the plaster was chipped off to reveal the nesting holes for the monastery's birds. This building is currently used as the office of an architectural firm, but the nesting holes can still be seen (fig. 3.9).

From Gee (1890), Cook (1904) and Armitage Robinson's (1918) assertions T. F. Palmer was able to identify parch marks in the grass at Witham Hall Farm, which appeared to form a quadrangle and what he defined as a number of small rooms (Palmer 1921, 91). In 1921, a group led

Church, Cloister, and Cell: The Inner Charterhouse Complex

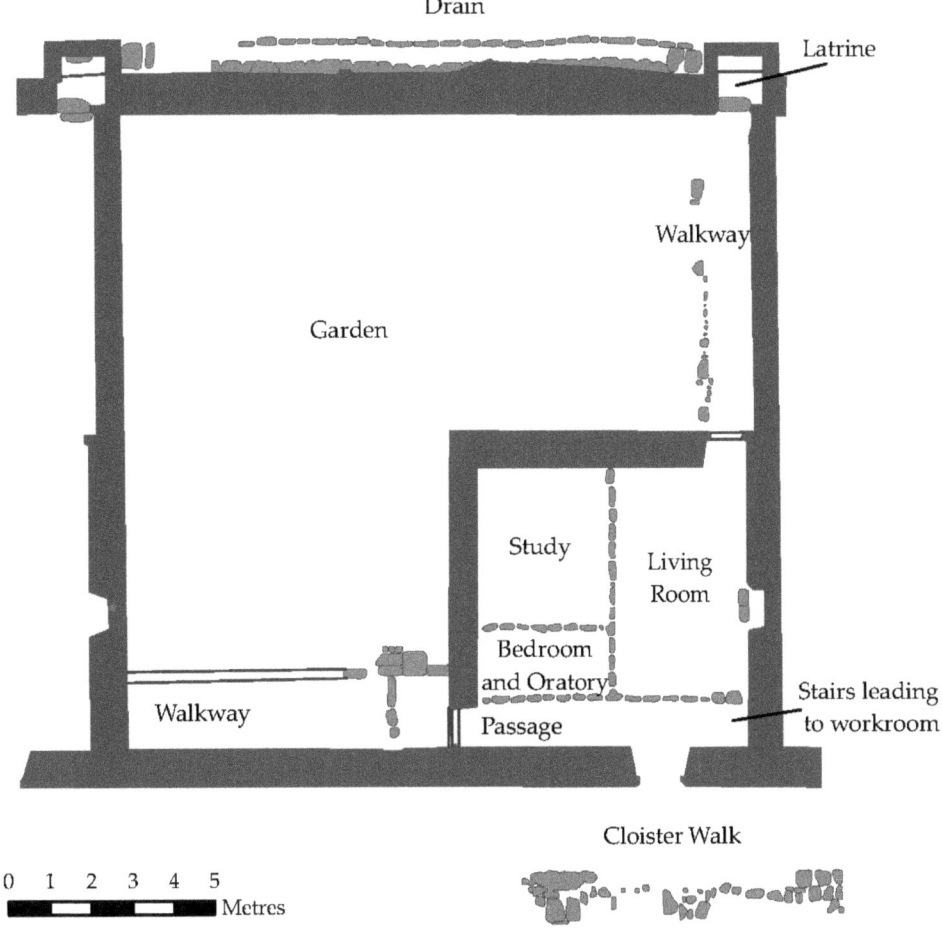

Figure 3.5. The layout of Cell 13 at Mount Grace Priory, an example of the monks' cells. This illustration shows the bricks found *in situ* during excavations at the site and indicates the division of space within the cell (after Coppack and Keen 2019, 141).

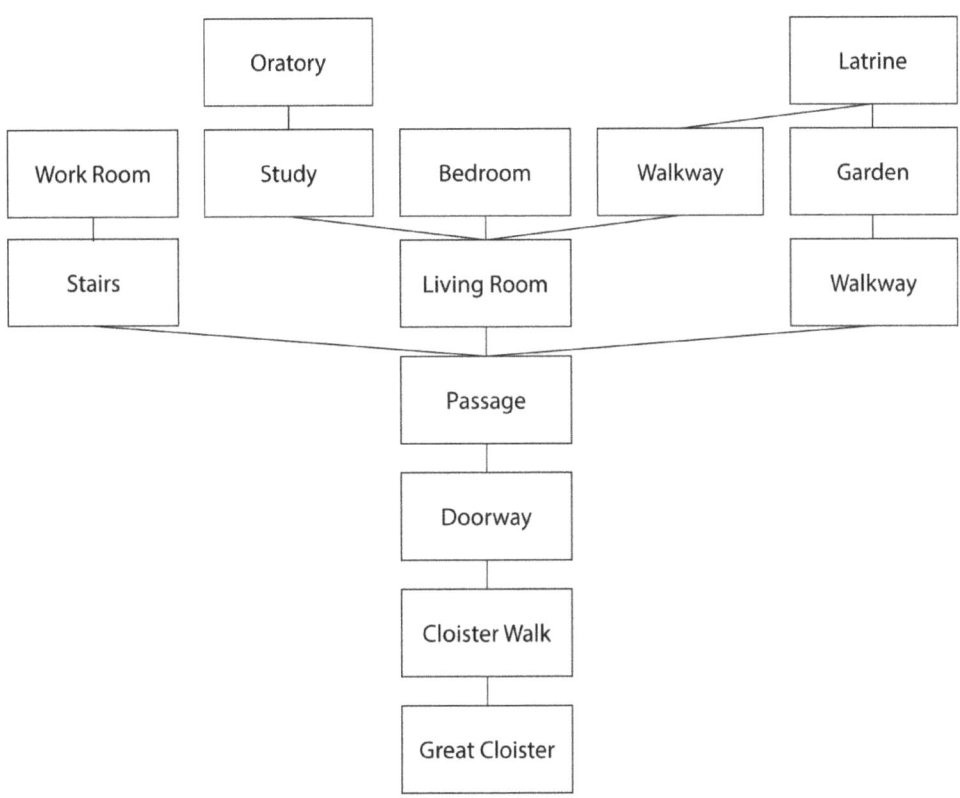

Figure 3.6. Space Syntax Analysis access plan of a Carthusian cell, based on cell 13 at Mount Grace Priory.

Communal Solitude

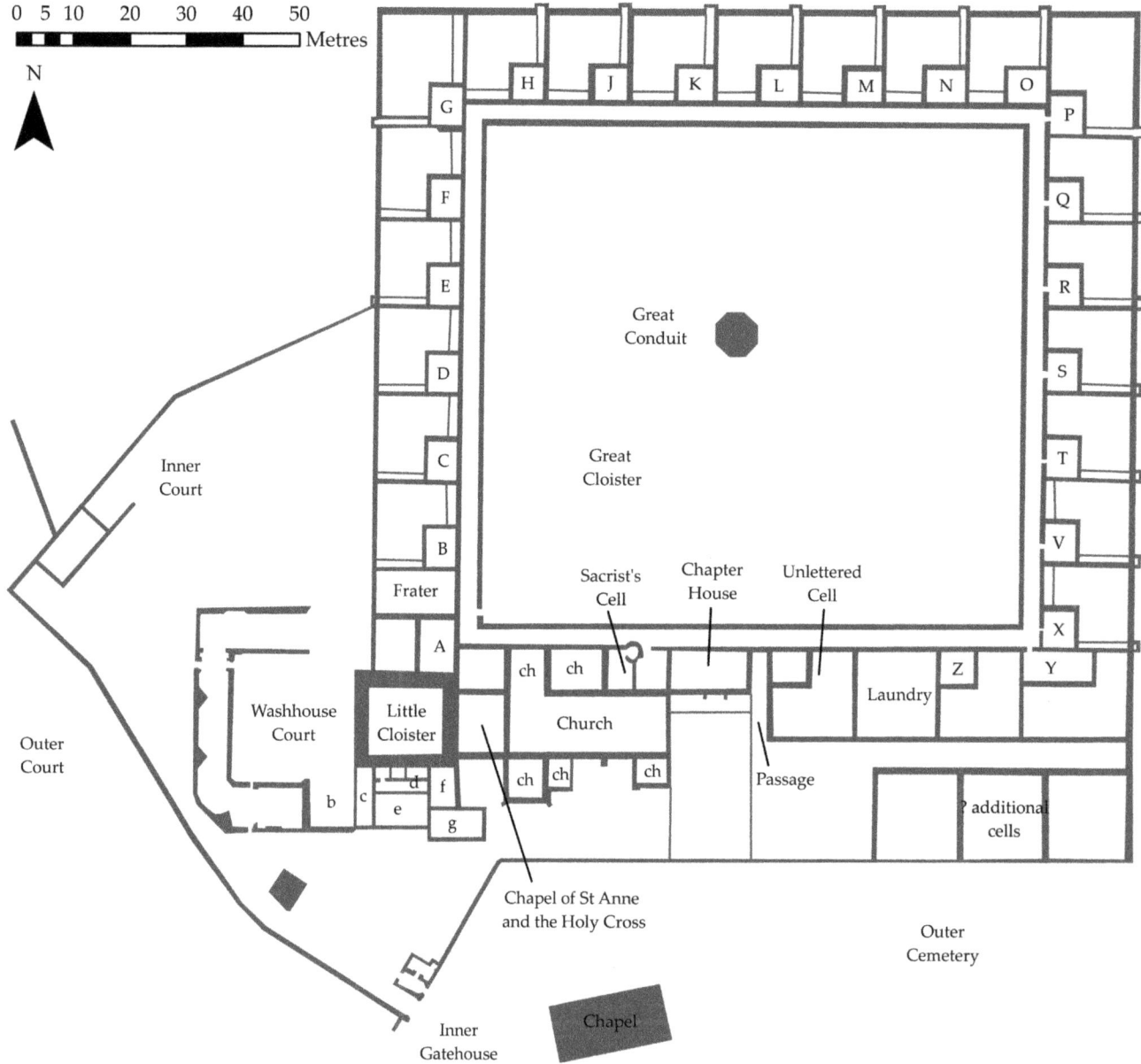

Figure 3.7. Layout of the London Charterhouse (after Barber and Thomas 2002, 38-39).

by Palmer conducted a small excavation consisting of two trenches cutting into the edges of the quadrangle (Palmer 1921, 91). The investigation uncovered the wall foundations, roof tiles, and glazed floor tiles, some *in situ*, which may have been the remains of the cloister alley (Palmer 1921, 92). Nothing else was recovered, and no further attempts were made by the party to excavate the site, but the excavation did confirm the view that the field held the remains of the Carthusian monastery.

Based on Palmer's findings, the Wells Archaeological Society excavated the site from 1965 to 1969. Using the evidence from the 1921 excavation and aerial photographs, the flat rectangular area in the field was thought to be the cloister garth, and thus, the first trenches were concentrated on understanding these features (Hogg 1977, 123; Reid and Barlow 1966, 6-7). This was somewhat complicated by the almost continual occupation of the site from the monastic period until the early nineteenth century, where the destruction and decay of post-Dissolution structures obscured the original monastic remains (Hogg 1977, 123). In addition, the finds from the excavation indicate this occupation also, including a wine flagon fragment with the arms of the Wyndham family, thirteenth-fourteenth century floor tiles, a silver sixpence dated to 1572, a silver penny dated circa 1300, a halfpenny from 1672 and a post-medieval glass bottle seal with the initials W. H., thought to belong to a member of the Hopton family (Reid and Barlow 1966, 7; Barlow 1968, 10).

The 1966 excavation consisted of a total of 24 trenches, as well as a number of sondages (Burrow and Burrow 1990, 149). All except one were focused on the northern part of the cloister and conventual buildings, with the remaining trench used to establish the southern limit of the cloister alley.

Figure 3.8. Space Syntax Analysis access plan of the London Charterhouse, an urban Carthusian monastery.

The subsequent excavation report (Burrow and Burrow 1990, 179) notes the odd shape of the inferred cloister location, with its 'dog leg' in the north-eastern corner, but describes it only as 'unusual', and does not suggest that perhaps the excavators had been wrong in their assumption. In fact, the interpretation shows that largely, the location of the cloister alley is built on conjecture. None of the other British charterhouses had a cloister with an odd corner such as this, and as it has been shown previously that the Carthusians maintained a consistent building style and plan, it is unlikely that the inferred location of the cloister is correct.

The earthwork survey carried out by the RCHME (1994) gives a good overview of the site and clearly shows the site of the cloister as a large, flattened, rectangular area of land, south of the railway line. The conventual buildings to the north appear as several small linear earthworks, and the site of the Beckford mansion to the south of the charterhouse site is also visible as an irregular-shaped earthwork, although the other post-Dissolution buildings do not appear to have manifested as earthworks. There is also some evidence of the garden created during the occupation of the site by the Wyndham family, in the linear earthworks leading to the east, away from the railway.

GSB (Gaffney 1994) utilised the earthwork survey to target the area of the cloister and the buildings to the north of it for resistivity survey. These surveys enabled the correction of some of the inaccuracies of the 1965-1969 excavation, including the odd 'dog leg' part of the cloister. The Church was found to be located in the northern part of the cloister, joining this corner. This amendment gives the shape of the cloister a more conventional, rectangular shape, as would be expected (Gaffney 1994, 2).

3.2.2 Hinton Priory and Friary

No excavations have been conducted at the lower house of Hinton, at Friary, but in the 1950s Hinton Priory was investigated by the then owner, Major Philip Fletcher. He and his sons excavated the site over a series of summers from 1950 to 1959 and were able to uncover the majority of the area of the cloister and surrounding buildings. By 1959, the entire layout of the priory buildings surrounding the cloister had been located (Fletcher 1958), allowing it to be compared to other sites such as Mount Grace Priory in North Yorkshire. This comparison established that archaeologically, the split houses (separate upper and lower houses) do differ from the joined houses (monks and lay brothers housed in the same complex), in the size of the buildings, and the size of the priory overall. As studies in the layout of charterhouses were in their infancy at the time, the result was of vital importance, with accurate evidence to determine the size and shapes of various buildings of the priory.

At Hinton, the geophysical survey conducted by GSB largely confirmed what Fletcher had excavated in the 1950s. The advantage of the resistivity survey over the excavation, however, was that it was able to be conducted inside the walled garden, the centre of the cloister, revealing what appears to be the paths or small walls of a post-Dissolution garden (Gaffney 1995b, 1). It is likely that this is contemporary with the manor house, as immediately after the Dissolution, the cells were utilised for housing livestock (Fletcher 1958, 76-77). The survey was also able to shed light on the areas of land north of the refectory and chapter house, revealing a complicated series of linear features, which appear to indicate the northern buildings of the little cloister. Similarly, the area immediately to the north-east of the chapter house appears to feature some sort of rectangular buildings (Gaffney 1995b, 2), which may have been joined to the chapter house during the life of the priory. The data was somewhat distorted by modern constructions, such as driveways, and water pipes, as well as the use of the site in the past as an orchard (SRO DD/FL/8), but overall the general overview of the priory has been well maintained. The Friary was not included in the survey project.

The most recent investigative work at Friary was completed in October 2012, by the Bath and Camerton Archaeological Society (Hawke 2015). The research comprised a small-scale resistivity survey on the area immediately to the east of a house known as Woodman's Cottage and produced some interesting results (Hawke 2015, 4). The field where the survey was conducted is known locally as 'Church Field' (Hawke 2015, 2), and it is for this reason that the investigation was targeted in this area. In the northern part of the survey area, two large areas of very high resistance were located, both on an east-west alignment, the most northerly area having a long, linear shape, in keeping with the design of a simple Carthusian church, as at Witham Friary. As this survey did not cover the whole area available, and the processing makes the plot difficult to read, the site at Friary has been resurveyed as part of this study, and the following sections have been researched in order to provide some context to the features identified on the subsequent resistivity plot.

3.3 The Carthusian Church: Use, Expansion and Decoration

The church was used only for Matins and Vespers on a daily basis, and also for Mass on Sundays and festival days. The rest of the night offices were celebrated individually in the cell. As a result of this, the Carthusian church was small and sparsely decorated, styled more like a parish church than that of a monastic house (Coppack and Aston 2002, 47).

The Carthusian church, in its simplicity, was always rectangular shaped, at least in its original form (Vrána 2006, 77). What can be reconstructed of the church at Witham is demonstrative of this regular design, and likewise the still extant lay brothers' church at Witham Friary is a simple single-aisled building with an apsidal chancel. The church at Hinton appears to have had no modifications made to it during its life as a religious site and retained the most original form of all the English charterhouses (Coppack and Aston 2002, 49). Commonly, extensions were made to the nave as this allowed the accommodation of more people, or more chapels, facilitating increased lay benefaction. The church at Beauvale Charterhouse was expanded within a generation of its foundation, indicating changing needs either of the monastic community or of its lay patrons (Coppack and Aston 2002, 50). Coppack and Aston (2002, 51) have suggested that the expansion of the church at Coventry (an addition of 13.4m to the east) was prompted not by the increased needs of the monastic community, but by the augmentation of patronage as well as offering space for burial within the church. At Coventry, 41 inhumations were excavated during archaeological investigations. Coppack and Aston (2002, 53) reasoned that expansion in all the later English charterhouses was in order to create space for lay burials, meaning that more reliance and influence was placed upon the lay benefactors and patrons of the charterhouse than may have been deemed suitable by the Carthusian Order. Further to this is the evidence of the inventory recorded by Drs. Thomas Legh and Francis Cave in 1539 during the Dissolution (TNA E 117/12/22). The items taken from the church include a 'vestment of white velvet wythe an Angel of Gold embroidered and set wythe pearls' (TNA E 117/12/22) and a large amount of plate which exceeds that which was thought to be proper according to the Carthusian Statutes (C.C. 40:1) and again indicates the degree to which the laity was involved in the daily running of the charterhouse, as these were more than likely given as gifts, rather than bought by the monks themselves (Coppack and Aston 2002, 53).

The increase in chapels outside the chancel was promoted by the desires of the laity to have masses said for the dead and by the increased desire for burial within the monastic church. At Mount Grace, three side chapels were established in expansions to the church, described as burial chapels by Coppack and Aston (2002, 58), which featured a tomb and at least one altar. While two of the chapels were accessed from the nave, the last was accessed only via the presbytery, which may indicate a higher status individual. Certainly, burial in the monastic church was restricted to those individuals who were willing to provide a substantial donation in return for the privilege (Coppack and Aston 2002, 68). As has already been discussed, the London Charterhouse expanded its church to the west in order to include a chapel for solely female visitors. The evidence for additional chapels within the monastic church is indicative of how reliant the community was on lay benefaction, as the churches were expanded substantially in order to accommodate the desires of the laity, and not for the benefit of the monks. The chapels of St Michael and St John the Baptist, and St Jerome and St Bernard were founded by Sir John Popham in 1453-4 at the London Charterhouse, in order that he might ensure a perpetual chantry for himself, as his tomb was also placed opposite the figure of St Michael in the chapel of St Michael and St John the Baptist (Knowles and Grimes 1954, 57-58). Popham was accepted into the fraternity of the charterhouse in 1460, which increased the spiritual benefits available to him after his death in 1466 (TNA E 326/8775; Rowntree 1981, 378).

In the charterhouses inhabited by both monks and lay brothers in the same complex (all those founded after Hinton in 1222), there was a necessity to share the monastic church for worship. In these cases, a choir screen divided the nave, segregating the choir monks from the lay brothers (Lindquist 2003, 181; Soden 2001, 161). This method of separating the monks and lay brothers seems to have ceased after the foundation of Beauvale Charterhouse when the division between the two areas was created by a transept passage in the nave (Coppack and Aston 2002, 51). Later churches also sectioned off the presbytery or chancel with a pulpitum (Rodwell 2012, 164).

3.4 The Cloister

The cloister acted as an area of mediation, dividing the areas of habitation and the conventual buildings, but also connecting these areas via the cloister walk (Irvine 2011, 42). Kinder (2002, 131) described it as a 'crossroads of the inner abbey', providing access to various different parts of the monastery. The cloister garth was also often used as the monastic cemetery, making it a place of remembrance as the monks would have to pass through it every day. It is for this reason that many lay benefactors requested to be buried under the cloister walk, it being the closest location to the monastic cemetery, and with the belief that resting beneath the paving where the monks walked every day would provide them with greater spiritual assistance in their journey to heaven. Excavations at London Charterhouse just after the Second World War (Knowles and Grimes 1954, 46) revealed memorial slabs in the cloister walk, with settings for brasses, which was later suggested by Barber and Thomas (2002, 25) to indicate burial beneath the floor of the cloister alley. Without the name brasses, it would be very difficult to discover the names of the deceased at the London Charterhouse, but the necrology of Nieuwlicht Charterhouse in the Netherlands, which lists the location of all burials in the monastery, includes members of the laity who were buried in both the Great and Lesser Cloisters (den Hartog 2018, 281). An example from the necrology reads:

> next to the Sacrist's cell, Jacob Sloyer, once a citizen of Utrecht, was buried beneath the stone, he has an engraving in the wall above him. With him in the same tomb is buried John Sloyer, his son, and his wife; after this, before the door of the Sacrist, Henry Sloyer and his daughter Joan Sloyer, then John Sloyer, son of Henry Sloyer.'[3] (van Hasselt 1886, 370; own translation)

The necrologies of the English charterhouses do not survive, but the example from Nieuwlicht indicates strong ties with the local community, especially since a number of deceased members of the same family were buried in the same area of the cloister alley, acting almost like a family burial plot or mausoleum.

For the Carthusians, the size of the cloister was determined by the number of cells that needed to be accommodated around it. As Coppack and Aston (2002, 97) noted, Mount Grace's cloister for 17 monks was twice the size of the cloisters at Fountains and Rievaulx, which accommodated at least 100 monks, simply because each of the cells and gardens needed space around the cloister. The size of the cloisters at the British and Irish houses comparatively accommodated between 12 and 30 cells. Sheen was the largest, and the original intention was to build a house for 40 monks, but the monastery was actually constructed for 30. As it was difficult to alter the layout of the cloister after its construction, where there was a need for more cells, some more interesting solutions had to be created. At Mount Grace, cells 22 and 23 were located on the first floor above cellars along the southern cloister walk. Neither had a garden and were much smaller than the original cells (Coppack and Aston 2002, 83). Likewise, at Hinton Charterhouse, cells 10 and 11 were created by splitting one cell in half, and cell 15 was added to the north west corner of the cloister (Fletcher 1958). These additions show that although the prescribed number of monks was 12, the monasteries were obviously sufficiently popular to require further cells to be added, especially the cells at Mount Grace, which were so small that there was no space for a work room or private cloister, and they were timber-framed (Coppack and Aston 2002, 83).

The cloister stood at the heart of the monastery, from which all of the most important buildings for religious life could be reached. The cells were situated along three sides of the cloister, and the remaining range housed the other essential conventual buildings – the church, refectory, chapter house, library and often, the prior and sacrist's cells. This was almost an extension of the idea of

---

[3] 'juxta cellam sacriste, Jacobus Sloyer, quondam civis Trajectensis sub petra tumulatus existit, habens sculpturam in pariete supra se. Apud quem in eodem sepulchro postea sepultus est Johannes Sloyer, filius eius, et uxor eius; postea, ante januam sacriste, Henricus Sloyer et filia Johannis Sloyer; deinde Johannes Sloyer, filius Henrici Sloyer.'

the cell, furnishing it with everything a monk could need so he would not need to leave it unnecessarily. Likewise, the cloister housed all the buildings required, so that the monk would not need to depart from the sheltered area into the noise and bustle of the outside world (Kerr 2009, 21).

Bales (2001, 265), who researched spatial interactions at La Certosa di Calci in Pisa, Italy, noted that the Carthusian cloister with the central communal cemetery represented for the monks 'the heavenly Jerusalem or paradise'. Likewise, the Great Cloister is referred to in the Nieuwlicht necrology as *Magna Galilea*, and the Lesser Cloister as *Parva Galilea* (van Hasselt 1886, 370; 379), in clear reference to the Sea of Galilee, where many of Jesus' miracles occurred[4]. The appropriation of this name for the cloister suggests that it was indeed seen as a paradisiacal environment for the monks, from which one had access to their own miniature paradise – the cell.

3.5 The Cell

The Carthusian cell was built on two floors, the ground floor housing the bedroom, oratory, study and living room, with a workshop on the first floor. Excavations at Mount Grace Priory (Coppack and Keen 2019) found evidence for sockets cut into the stone walls which would have held the stairs leading to the first floor. The cell was bounded by a small garden where the monks could grow vegetables and herbs and gave them access to the outdoors. Food was provided through an L-shaped hatch in the cloister wall, where a lay brother would place meals, along with any other necessary items requested by the monk that day (Brantley 2007, 37). This set-up was exactly like the design of the fourth-century hermitages at Kellia, with the exception that these cells were conjoined, and arranged around a central cloister, instead of being placed haphazardly without specific design as at Kellia (Signori 2014, 33). Cells of different charterhouses, particularly those in England, tended to be of the same size; while this comparison can only be made from excavated houses (therefore excluding Axholme, Sheen, Perth, Kilnalahanin and Hull), there seems to be no discernible difference in the size of cells from houses with 12 monks to those with 24. The cells at London (a double house), for example, were approximately $6m^2$ internally, in a $14m^2$ garden, and at Mount Grace, the cells were approximately $6.4m^2$ internally in a $14.5m^2$ garden. Beauvale and Coventry featured similarly sized cells and gardens[5]. This is, therefore consistent with the assertion made by Coppack and Aston (2002, 47), and discussed above[6], that the size of the cloister was altered in order to accommodate the size of the cells, not vice versa. There is, however considerable difference in the layout of the interior cell building. Beauvale and Mount Grace share an almost identical layout, similar to that of London's cells, and not too far removed from the cells at Coventry. This style features a large living area, with one or two smaller rooms leading off from it, and a corridor or lobby separating the internal rooms from the cloister wall. Hinton's layout, however favours one larger main room, with an L-shaped pentice adjoining a lobby area. Although the cell divisions were not established at Witham, it is likely that they were similar to those at Hinton. The cells presented here are representative layouts, and there was of course variability from one cell to the other, which may have been affected by the position of the cell around the cloister, or the period of time it took to build all of the cells.

An adherence to solitude was maintained by ensuring that no two individual cells were conjoined, safeguarding against any contact between the monks outside sanctioned hours. As the cell was usually situated in the corner of the square garden, this meant that some cells, such as Cell 8 at Mount Grace Priory, featured two passageways from the cell to the garden, and in order to maintain seclusion, the cell had to be placed central to the garden, rather than in a corner (Coppack and Keen 2019, 90; Thompson 1930, 175). There were a few differences between the cells of the monks and those of the lay brothers. First, the lay brothers were not always provided with a garden, their role in the monastery often being too prohibitively time-consuming for gardening. Likewise, the lay cell only contained a single floor, without the provision of an upper workspace, as they worked in the offices and workshops of the monastery, and they were not required to remain in their cells. From the surviving lay brothers' cells at Mount Grace Priory (cells 16-21), it would appear that otherwise, they were designed in a similar way to those of the monks, with a three-roomed floor, and a latrine placed at one corner of the garden (Coppack and Aston 2002, 113). The lay brothers' cells were arranged around the lesser cloister at Mount Grace, where they were segregated from the monks and also so that they could also reach the workshops and offices easily.

Each cell was identified by a letter, a practice taken from the Desert Fathers, and documented in the London Charterhouse Water Supply map, which labels each cell A-Z, with one unlettered cell (Sargent and Hennessy 2008, 180). The letter was carved into the cell's door frame and was enhanced by the addition of a devotional verse (fig. 3.10) (Coppack and Aston 2002, 74; Sargent and Hennessy 2008, 182). Sargent and Hennessy (2008, 182-183) have suggested that this demarcated the cell boundaries and made the cell a devotional object in its own right. As the monks walked along the cloister walk to church of an evening, or met in the cloister on a Sunday, the verses would be a devotional reminder of the importance of the cell. The use of letters also anonymised the inhabitant of the cell, identifying them only by their abode rather than their person, and meant that any requests for items made could be signed with the letter of his cell (Brantley 2007, 37; Sargent and Hennessy 2008, 180).

---

[4] On the shores of the sea of Galilee, Jesus fed the five thousand (Matthew 14: 13-21), walked on water (Matthew 14: 22-33), and appeared to his disciples for the third time following his crucifixion (John 21:1-3).
[5] Beauvale's cells were around $7m^2$ internally in a $13m^2$ garden, and Coventry's were approximately $6m^2$ internally in a $12.5m^2$ garden.
[6] See section 3.4 on the cloister for discussion on relative sizes.

suggested that this lack of guidance meant that the monks could cultivate the gardens into a true wilderness. In those charterhouses founded in cities, this may have meant that they could escape from the busy surroundings outside the monastery walls. The cell gardens at Mount Grace Priory and Coventry have been excavated, which showed that although no suggestions were given as to how the garden should be presented, the monks obviously took time to make the garden a pleasurable location, with raised beds and walkways. At Coventry Charterhouse, excavations revealed a stone-lined well in the garden of Cell 3, and in Cell 1's garden, a line of edge-set ceramic tiles, which look to have lined a garden bed (Soden 1995, 61-62; Moorhouse 1991, 114). The gardens at Mount Grace featured drainage channels, paths laid out with lines of stone and provided evidence of deep-rooted plants (Coppack and Keen 2019, 111-112; 117-118). An area of the garden of Cell 10 was also suggested by the excavators to have been a grassed area, where one could look out onto the decorative garden (Coppack and Aston 2002, 90). MacCulloch (2014, 99) described the garden as a paradise, and perhaps, therefore, the decorative nature of some of the gardens pursued this ideal. Fruit pips and stones recovered from London Charterhouse have led to a suggestion that the monks may have been growing these in their cell gardens. Certainly, there was an apple orchard just south of the charterhouse, but plums, sloes and cherries could have been cultivated in the gardens (Barber and Thomas 2002, 67). This would be consistent with the deep-rooted plants observed to have been grown at Mount Grace.

3.6 Conclusions

Seclusion was a key element of Carthusian observance. The charterhouse walls demarcated specific areas that could be accessed by different members of the community and restricted the access of visitors to the site. Smells, sounds and light also contributed to this setting apart of the monastic community from the local laity, by demonstrating their devotion to the divine. Lay benefaction was a great influence on the charterhouse; the evolution of the Carthusian church was due largely to the desires of the laity for prestigious burial locations, rather than the needs of the monks. This demonstrates that despite the solitary nature of the Carthusians, in many cases they were reliant on secular society for benefaction, like any other monastic community. The secular benefaction of the charterhouses is also illustrated in the claustral burials at Nieuwlicht, which were recorded in the monastic necrology. These different examples of lay interaction indicate that the charterhouse was increasingly receptive to the desires of its patrons, especially where women were eventually allowed to be buried in the cloister. The lay benefactors also expected a certain level of commemoration, which was manifested through the claustral plaques and the additional chapels.

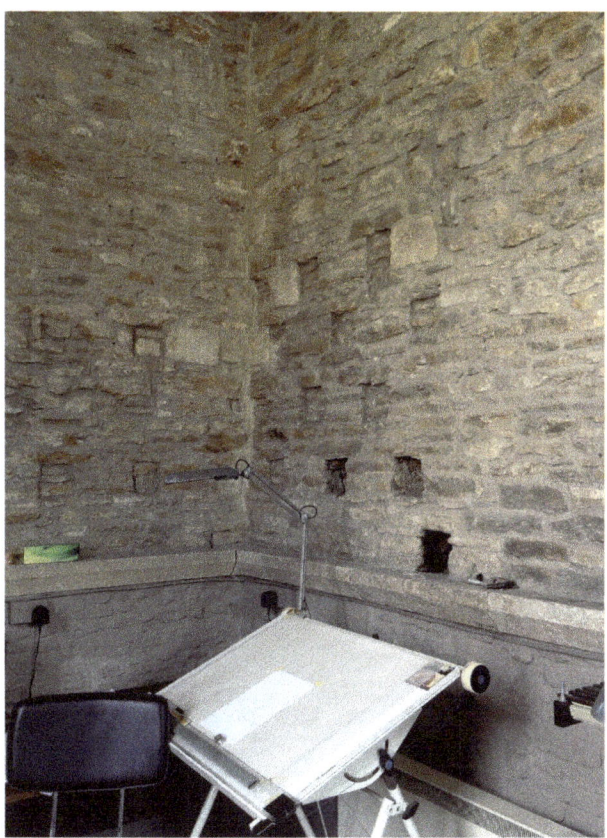

Figure 3.9. The nesting holes still visible in the Witham Friary dovecote (now used as an architect's office). © Francesca Breeden 2022.

Figure 3.10. Painted letter above a cell door at La Musée de la Grande Chartreuse. On the door of Cell A, the accompanying verse reads. 'Ayez grand soin d'aimer le Seigneur votre Dieu' (Be very careful to love the Lord your God), a verse taken from the Bible, Joshua 23:11. © Francesca Breeden 2022.

The provision of a garden for each monk meant that they were able to grow their own vegetables and herbs to supplement the meals brought to them by the lay brothers. There were no official guidelines as to what could be grown in the garden, or how the monks were to organise the space (Ritchey 2014, 194), and Ritchey (2014, 194) has

The previous excavations and research conducted at Witham and Hinton charterhouse illustrate how an understanding of the relationship between the monks and lay brothers has evolved, from confusion as to the

Communal Solitude

site of Witham Charterhouse, to the discovery that the monks and lay brothers lived in separate complexes. The layouts produced from these investigations also provide vital background information to the primary research to be discussed in chapter 7, and highlighted where further research is required.

4

Daily Life in the Charterhouse

The greatest part of a Carthusian monk's day was spent alone in the confines of his cell. Only on Sundays or Feast Days were the community allowed to come together and speak to each other. However, to understand how the surrounding landscape and buildings were used, the activities conducted by these monks throughout both a normal day and a feast day deserve consideration. This is equally true for the Carthusian lay brethren. Although they did not spend their days alone in the cell, their time was subject to a similarly strict schedule of prayer, interspersed with manual labour which was vital to the everyday running and maintenance of the charterhouse.

4.1 The Daily Schedule

The Carthusian day was organised around the monastic offices – periods of worship at specific times throughout the day. The schedule of the charterhouse and the timings of the monastic offices are illustrated in the table below (table 4.1). In between these periods of worship, the monk or lay brother also conducted spiritual exercises or manual works, which will be discussed in the course of the chapter. For the monks, only three of the monastic offices were said communally in the church, where although they were meeting together, communication was forbidden (Thompson 1930, 25). All other offices were conducted alone in the small oratory that was provided within the cell. The lay brothers were led in worship in the church for all of their offices (C.C. 42). The manual work they conducted in between worship would have differed depending on their occupation[1].

The daily schedule ran thus: at around 11 pm, a bell was rung to wake the monks and signal to them that they should begin the Matins of the Blessed Virgin, which were said in the cell. When completed, they silently walked to the church, where Matins was continued and in which the lay brothers joined, finishing at around 3 am. At this point, the monks remained in the church and moved on to the worship of Lauds, after which they returned to their cells to sing the Lauds of the Blessed Virgin. The lay brothers returned to their cells after Matins, where they said private devotions in their mother tongue, as they tended to be uneducated in Latin. At 6 am, the monks sang Prime in their cells, and the lay brothers returned to the church, to be led in prayer by the Procurator. Between Prime and Compline, the monks conducted spiritual exercises, or manual labour, during which their thoughts were to be directed towards God at all times. The lay brothers spent the majority of the day engaged in work which benefitted the community, such as animal husbandry, cooking or making bread. At about 11 am, after Sext was said in the cell, the monks ate their only meal of the day. Following Compline at 6 pm, the monks retired to bed. The timings of the day varied slightly depending on the time of year. In the summer, a siesta was added in the middle of the day, to account for the early sunrise and late sunset (C.C. 29). Equally, during the winter, the monks had an additional meal in the late afternoon to early evening (C.C. 33:4). Sundays were again a different schedule, which will be investigated in the following section.

4.2 Prayer and Spiritual Exercises

The offices celebrated in the cell were known as the lesser offices and were conducted in the small oratory that was provided to each monk. Guigo I[2], the compiler of the Carthusian statutes in 1116, believed that solitary worship was a vital part of coming closer to God, and promoted 'mystical ascent' in a way that could not be achieved as a community (Ritchey 2014, 171). These offices were marked by the ringing of the monastery bell, signifying the beginning and end of the worship period. Those offices conducted in the Church (Matins, Lauds, Mass and Vespers) were chanted in their entirety, although the melody was simple as the monks did not meet together to practice the chants (Lambres 1970, 17; Brantley 2007, 36). Dependent on the organisation of the house, that is whether the upper and lower houses were conjoined, the lay brothers may have joined the monks in the church for worship. In this case, the choir was split by a screen which delineated the area for the monks from that for the lay brothers (Brogden 1941, 7). Although the monastic offices were always conducted in Latin, the lay brothers were taught what to say or do at specific times during the service, so that although they may not have understood the language being used, they could participate as fully as possible (Villabos-Hennessy 2008, 168). They were also required to learn the Paternoster and the Ave Maria (C.C. 43).

Where half of the Carthusian community was likely to be unversed in Latin, the Procurator led the monastic offices for the lay brothers. All of the lay brothers' worship was undertaken in the church, and they would imitate the

---

[1] Chapter 4.3 discusses occupations and the classes of lay brothers in further detail.

[2] Guigo I (1083-1136) was the fifth prior of La Grande Chartreuse, elected in 1109. It was he who compiled the Carthusian Statutes, giving guidelines to other charterhouses between 1121 and 1128, and also wrote the Meditations, which outline his beliefs in a solitary life. He was a contemporary of Bernard of Clairvaux and Peter the Venerable, both of whom exchanged letters with Guigo, and the former also visited La Grande Chartreuse in the 1120s. (Les Méditations, SC 308; Introduction to Coutumes de Chartreuse 1984, 13-16).

Communal Solitude

Table 4.1. The daily schedule for both Carthusian monks and lay brothers. After Thompson 1930 and 'Un Chartreux' 1984, 46.

	Monks	Lay Brothers
23:00	Matins of the Blessed Virgin in Cell	
23:30	Matins in Church	
03:00	Lauds in Church Lauds of the Blessed Virgin in Cell	Private Devotion in Cell
06:00	Prime in Cell Spiritual Exercise	Prime in Church
07:00	Adoration in Church	
07:15	Conventual Mass	
08:00	Private Mass in Cell Terce in Cell Reading, Study, Manual Labour	Terce in Church Work
11:00	Sext in Cell Dinner	Sext in Cell Dinner
13:00	None in Cell Manual Labour	None in Church Work
15:30	Vespers of the Blessed Virgin in Cell	Work
15:45	Vespers in Church	
17:00	Prayer, Reading	Vespers, Supper
18:00	Compline To Bed	

genuflections and movements made by the Procurator (C.C. 42:1). The lay brothers' statutes from Sheen Charterhouse (transcribed by Pask Matthews, 1930, 1931) give specific instructions as to how many Paternosters the lay brothers were to say, which ones with genuflection, and at what times. This allowed the lay brother to participate in the monastic offices without needing a full understanding of Latin. For the 50 psalms chanted by the monks at Vigils, the lay brothers instead said Paternosters (Pask Matthews 1930, 211-212; C.C. 43:2). The statutes also ensured that even if the Procurator was absent, the lay brothers could still worship: they should say three Paternosters and Ave Marias with genuflection for each of the offices (Pask Matthews 1930, 217).

As the laity and lay brothers were taught the required liturgical passages, rather than reading them, it is a common belief that they were unable to engage properly with and understand the religion to which they adhered (Dauphin 2001-2002, 58; Gottschall 2014, 9; Baldwin 2016, 44). However, Madigan (2015, 300) argues that the capacity to listen and retain knowledge was far greater than our abilities today, and some lay folk were able to recite great passages of the Bible and religious literature. In this sense, through what Swanson (1995, 79-80) called 'passive literacy,' the illiterati were able to gain the same understanding and knowledge by listening to religious readings as they would from reading the Bible. 'Illiterate' in a medieval understanding may also have meant being unable to read and write in Latin, rather than being unversed in the vernacular language (Bäuml 1980, 238). Caie (2004, 128) cites examples of widowers joining religious orders during and after the Black Death, who are labelled 'illiterate' due to their lack of Latin knowledge. Lay people were not expected to be as well versed as the clergy in religion, and although some may have wished to devote themselves further to devotional study, those who did not would not be sinning; it was enough to be present at church, and to follow the mass (Tanner and Watson 2006, 400). By the late fourteenth century, a number of instructional pamphlets, such as the *Lay Folks' Mass Book* (Lydgate n.d.), were circulating amongst the laity. These guides showed the common people how to navigate the rituals of the Mass, which prayers to use and the actions of the clergy which indicated various parts of the Mass (Swanson 1993, 79).

In the early days of the Carthusian Order, Mass was only taken on vigils and feasts, in keeping with how the Desert Fathers were thought to have worshipped, and lay brothers were only allowed to take communion once a month (Lockhart 1985, 38; King 1955, 19). It was thought that too many Masses (and therefore opportunities to be amongst other monks) would be a distraction from a monk's relationship with God (C.C. 14:5). Guigo I emphasised that the Carthusian vocation was to solitude and silence, insisting 'we believe that nothing is more laborious in the exercises of regular life than the silence of solitude and rest', and cited the example of Jeremiah from the Bible[3] (C.C. 14:5). In Guigo I's Praise of the Solitary Life (C.C. 80), he writes that in the Bible, Jacob sends his family away in order to be alone, and it is only in this way that he can see God face to face[4], emphasising how important it is for the Carthusian monk to avoid all temptation to leave his cell unnecessarily. Despite this, after 1222, a daily conventual Mass was established, and the 1259 Statuta Antiqua fixed this in the daily schedule (King 1955, 20).

On Sundays and Feast days the normal schedule of the day was changed slightly. Following Prime, instead of the usual spiritual exercises, the monks held chapter and then gathered in the church for the blessing of holy water, which the lay brothers also participated in (C.C. 7:3-4). After this, they sang Terce, and celebrated the Mass, except during Advent and Septuagesima (C.C. 7:5). The Mass was followed by a short interval where the monks took the holy water back to their cells, and then returned to the church to sing Sext, later proceeding to the refectory to eat dinner together, albeit in silence (Thompson 1930, 37; C.C. 7:8). Immediately after dinner, the monks congregated in the church to say None, and the community was finally allowed to break their silence when they came together in the cloister to talk about 'useful things'[5], and to ask the Sacristan for supplies such as ink, quills, parchment, and books to be read or copied (C.C. 7:9). On Sundays, the monks ate a second meal after Vespers.

The monastic liturgical calendar for all orders was split up into different levels of feast days, which dictated how the feast was to be celebrated. The most important were solemnities, which celebrated important events in the life of Jesus or his mother Mary, as well as other important saints or mysteries of faith such as the Trinity (Liturgy Office, 13). Beneath solemnities were feasts, which were further split into Feasts of Twelve Lessons, and Feasts of Three Lessons, the former being the more important (Liturgy Office, 13). Feasts celebrated lesser events in the life of Jesus, Mary or an apostle, or were used to commemorate major saints. Lesser saints were commemorated by memorials, the lowest ranking of feast days (Liturgy Office, 14). The community was only allowed to meet together and converse on Sundays, chapter feasts and solemnities. The number of chapter feasts and solemnities was restricted. By the end of the fifteenth century, only 54 were celebrated by the Carthusian Order (Brogden 1940, 10). This ensured that the monks were not obligated to leave their cells too often, which as already discussed, was to be avoided where possible.

To further emphasise the monks' devotion to austerity and a clear path to God, the church was sparsely furnished, 'in the Church we do not have ornaments of gold or silver, with the exception of the chalice and reed which are used for taking the Lord's Blood. We do not have wall hangings or carpets' (C.C. 40:1). The empty church ensured that the monks could not be distracted from the task at hand. This was a clear distinction between the Carthusians and other monastic orders, who, especially at the Dissolution, were accused of their wealth and opulence, not befitting ones who had given themselves over to a life of poverty[6].

When the Carthusian monks were not at worship, they were instructed to conduct themselves in spiritual exercises (C.C. 29:3). These exercises would have been activities which strengthened a monk's spiritual resolve, such as reading and studying devotional texts (Cunningham and Kusukawa 2010, xiv). The statutes indicate that each monk was permitted to borrow two books from the library at a time for personal reading and for copying[7] (C.C. 28:3). A number of Carthusian monks wrote their own devotional texts, which were subsequently circulated throughout the Carthusian Order and secular society. One of these was *The Quadripartite Exercise of the Cell*, written by Adam of Dryburgh, a monk of Witham, which instructed the Carthusian monk on the importance of solitude in the cell and the four parts of religious exercise: 'reading, meditation, prayer and action' which would bring him closer to God (Pat. Lat. 153, col. 828C). He further expounded on being cautious in speech, even when the monks are allowed to talk, and avoiding 'foolish, false, and quarrelsome words' (Thompson 1930, 358). Texts such as this emphasised to the monk the spiritual importance of their silent life, and how they could become closer to God. However, they also functioned as an important tool for members of secular society who wished to reach the divine and attain spiritual salvation (Schirmer 2005, 349).

4.3 Manual Works

The role of the Carthusians in circulating devotional material was inextricably linked to manual labour; a compulsory part of the daily schedule that ensured the monks would not become idle. This was also called purposeful work, as the activities conducted were intended to be useful to the community in some way, rather than manufacturing something for its own sake. This understanding had its roots in scripture, Colossians 3:23-24 reads: 'whatever you do, work heartily as for the Lord and not for men, knowing that from the Lord you will receive the inheritance as your reward.' This activity was also seen as vitally important in the battle against the Devil[8] and to avoid the temptations that arise through

---

[3] Jeremiah 15:17, 'I did not sit in the company of revellers, nor did I rejoice; I sat alone, because your hand was upon me, for you had filled me with indignation.'
[4] Genesis 32: 22-24, 'The same night he arose and took his two wives, his two female students, and his eleven children, and crossed the ford of the Jabbok. He took them and sent them across the stream, and everything else that he had. And Jacob was left alone.'
[5] Here, 'useful' refers to spiritual importance, not utility.

[6] The vestments of the church are discussed in further detail in chapter 5 (see 5.3), with evidence from the inventory taken at the Dissolution. Allen (2012) has discussed the decorative Carthusian misericords in Italy, and while the misericord definitely forms part of the Carthusian liturgy, they would not necessarily be decorated. Without any surviving examples from England, it is impossible to ascertain the level of decoration, if any.
[7] See Chapter 6 for further discussion of the material culture of reading and writing in the charterhouse.
[8] This refers to Jesus' temptation by the Devil in the desert: 'Then Jesus was led up by the Spirit into the wilderness to be tempted by the devil' (Matthew 4:1).

idleness (Gilchrist 1995, 157). Hanna (1994, 92) further identified that labour provided 'spiritual excellence' for an eremitical lifestyle, preventing one from lapsing into a fantasy world, as is possible when in permanent isolation.

A significant number of Carthusian monks worked as copyists, or were involved in book manufacture in some way, as Guigo I writes: 'we teach copy work to nearly everyone we receive, if possible' (C.C. 28:2). Each cell was equipped with all items needed to function as a one-person scriptorium (Gilbert 2014, 371). Furthermore, writing and copying gave the monks an outlet which could not be provided in speech: 'by our hands we preach the word of God, as we cannot by our mouths' (C.C. 28:3). In this way, the Carthusians could reach the outside world, and be of spiritual benefit to secular society through their writing. In a number of cases from the Sheen Charterhouse, a Carthusian monk copied, or translated devotional texts into English for the nuns at Syon Abbey, across the Thames, as already noted above (see section 2.2; Bodl. MS Laud Misc. 517; GUL MS. Hunter 136). Most importantly, in manual labour, the monk was to turn his thoughts always to God, no matter what vocation he chose, and the labour itself should be for the glorification of God alone (Bellitto 2001, 79).

Adam of Dryburgh's *The Quadripartite Exercise of the Cell* emphasised this train of thought and further gave advice to the monk, noting that manual labour prevents idleness (which is hostile to the soul), and provides useful recreation (Pat. Lat. 153, col. 881B). By keeping the body busy, the mind was free for contemplation and prayer (Caner 2002, 40; Leyser 1984, 56; Jasper 2004, 27). According to Adam, the work to be done was at the discretion of the prior and could include binding, illumination, copying, correction, or adornment of books (Pat. Lat. 153, col. 881D). This is significant in that the work the monks were doing was not fuelled by their own desires, but by the needs of the monastery, and they were at all times serving a greater good. It also suggests that although the monks were specifically trained in copying, they could in some cases turn their hand to another facet of book manufacture, when needed.

The type of work a lay brother may have been tasked with was dependent on the specific type of lay brother. There were four classes of laity in the charterhouse: the *conversi*, the *redditi*, the *donati*, and the *mercenarii*. The differences were in the types of vows the brother took or their ties to the charterhouse. The *conversi* were, essentially, lay monks, and could be seen as the 'true' lay brother. They took religious vows, wore habits (although in brown, not white), were restricted to the charterhouse in their movements, and spent their days largely in silence, though continued to conduct tasks such as cooking and baking within the precinct (Thompson 1930, 41-47). The *redditi* and *donati* were largely similar, with a few slight differences. The *redditi* took vows like the *conversi* and wore the same habit but were distinguished by not having beards (Thompson 1930, 124). They conducted obediences (manual labour) as the *conversi* did but tended to handle the external affairs of the monastery and would go out to the granges. The *donati* were the oblates of the Carthusian Order; they were not professed members of the community, but by choice gave themselves to the service of the charterhouse through a civil contract instead of vows (Thompson 1930, 123). They were also allowed to leave the monastic precinct, and like the *redditi* were in charge of external affairs. The *mercenarii* were hired, secular labourers, who worked the land of the granges under the leadership of the *donati* or *redditi* (Thompson 1930, 115).

For the lay brothers, therefore, much of their time was taken up by manual labour, although this was not restricted to one vocation. Some of these vocations would have been solely the domain of the *conversi*, whereas others could have been taken on by the *redditi* or *donati*, such as those which required leaving the charterhouse, generally concerned with livestock or agriculture. The Statutes (46-50) list five different vocations as possibilities for the lay brother: the cook, baker, shoemaker, master of agriculture and master of shepherds. By the end of the fifteenth century, when the Lay Brothers' Statutes for Sheen (BL Add. MS 11303) were written, this list had expanded to ten different jobs. These were a cook for the upper house, a butler for the upper house, a cook for the lower house, a baker, shoemaker, smith, gardener, carpenter, master of husbandry, and master of shepherds (Pask Matthews 1930, 222-226; 1931, 112-116). Not only do the statutes list these jobs but they also give specific counsel to the reader as to how these occupations were to be carried out, and how the holder should comport themselves whilst in those roles. For example, the gardener was the keeper of the garden and the bees and was given a special house where he could keep tools and seeds. He was to weed the herbs and dress the garden and was given help when needed. Where there was no gardener, the cook was to take on this role (Pask Matthews 1931, 113-114). Similarly, the baker was provided with a suitable amount of grain for the year and was charged with drying and grinding it into flour. He was excused from Matins on baking days and was also in charge of sprinkling holy water around the lay brothers' cells, which was carried from the upper house (Pask Matthews 1931, 112). The obediences of the lay brothers were vital in keeping the monastery running, rather than as an exercise to avoid idleness, but they were equally expected to turn their thoughts to God throughout their work and understand that their work too, was for the glorification of God, in the maintenance of a religious house.

4.4 Meals

From examining manual labour, the discussion now turns to the food and drink of the monastery. The Carthusian view of food tended towards seeing it as only a necessity, rather than a luxury or something to be enjoyed (Jotischky 2011, 43). It sustained life, but that was its sole purpose. This perspective has its origins in the early Christian hermitic lifestyle, and especially the Desert Fathers

(Jotischky 2011, 98). They believed that by depriving the body of food and sleep to a certain degree, the body and mind could be separated, and thus one could more closely commune with God (Dunn 2003, 16). This was supported by passages in the Bible such as Luke 6:25, which reads 'woe to you that are full now for you shall be hungry' and Luke 12:22-23: 'do not be anxious about your life, what you will eat, nor about your body, what you will put on. For life is more than food, and the body more than clothing.' The Desert Fathers further believed that abstaining from meat would inhibit certain desires in the body, such as hunger and lust, which were a further barrier to divine salvation (Dauphin 2001-2, 58).

Likewise, the Carthusian monk abstained from meat completely, eating a pescatarian diet (Hogg 1991, 11). When the Consuetudines were written in the early twelfth century, the monks fasted three times a week on Monday, Wednesday and Friday, eating only bread and drinking only water, with salt allowed if desired. This was later reduced to fasting once a week (Hogg 2014, 38). On Tuesdays, Thursdays and Saturdays, the monks cooked their own vegetables, which consisted of a mixture of green beans, peas and broad beans, with raw herbs and fruit when available. Wine was provided by the cook, but was always watered down, and was to be drunk only with dinner and supper (Hogg 1991, 12). In 1250, the General Chapter decided that preparing meals was cutting into the monks' prayer time too much, and therefore they would only prepare their own meals once a month (Boutrais 1934, 180). However, the practice was abolished altogether a few years later in 1276, and the monks relied entirely on the lay brothers to bring them their meals (Boutrais 1934, 180). From 1259, the Carthusians were allowed a pittance, which was a bequest of food provided by patrons, on Mondays and Wednesdays, which were two of the three fasting days (Harvey 2006, 218). This usually consisted of two eggs or the equivalent per monk, per pittance, which would be added to the normal meal of soup and vegetables (Hogg 1980, 134). Gradually, the pittance was expanded to two eggs plus the equivalent of fish or cheese, although the General Chapter in 1413, 1426 and 1448 gave ordinations that the size of the pittance should be controlled, as certain monasteries were allowing the monks too much food (Hogg 1980, 134). During Advent, however, the monks were not allowed to consume any dairy products, and therefore cheese and eggs were removed from the pittances. On Sundays after Supper, the monks received a small tort of black rye bread, which as a cheaper and coarser alternative to wheat bread, served to remind them that they were Christ's Beggars (Thompson 1930, 38; Brown 2011, 144). A document dated 13 October 1535 (TNA SP 1/97, f.132) describes the daily meal of the Carthusians in London between Sunday 10 October and Wednesday 13 October, during the charterhouse's occupation by the king's commissioners:

> Sunday at dinner: every monk had furmentye, a hot pie of lampreys, and three eggs; the lay brothers, salt fish and cheese. Monday: monks and lay brothers alike had pottage of herbs, plenty of Suffolk or Essex cheese, and three eggs. Tuesday: furmenty, oysters, and a piece of ling for each monk and lay brother. Wednesday: pottage of herbs, a great whiting, and two eggs; for the lay brothers, pottage, oysters, and a whiting to each man.

Ling and whiting were both cheap, white ocean fish, similar to cod, and salt fish was preserved cod or herring, also a cheap commodity. Pottage was a thick stew or soup made by boiling vegetables, and 'furmenty(e)' was made by boiling cracked wheat, to which milk was added, and then sometimes spices and currants, similar to a sweet porridge. However, the lamprey, a fish similar to eels, although not in the same family, was widely eaten by the upper classes during the Middle Ages, and thus suggest an occasional luxury on the part of the monks, perhaps for the Sunday feast. Lampreys do, however, live in rivers and ponds, so could have been easily cultivated by the monks, although no record exists to suggest this.

In the cloister wall of each cell, there was an L-shaped hatch where the monks received their meals and pittances each day. The hatch was so shaped to ensure that there was no contact between the monk and the lay brother delivering the food. Behind the cell, the monks were provided with a small garden, where they could grow vegetables and herbs for themselves to supplement their meals, but they also had covered walkways to allow them to take exercise (Jotischky 2011, 98; 132). Additionally, in the cell was a piped supply of fresh water, which the monks could use for cooking, cleaning, and drinking (Coppack and Aston 2002, 117). At sites such as Mount Grace, the water was sourced from springs in the hillside to the east and piped through well houses to each of the cells (Coppack and Keen 2019, 294-5). This ensured a pure source of water, which would be safe to drink, and fulfilled the needs of the monks' ascetic fasting days when only water was permitted.

When a monk was ill, he still abstained from meat, which was unlike any other religious order (Henisch, 1976, 2; Gribbin 2001, 200). Even in those orders that forbade the consumption of meat, this rule did not apply to the sick (Harvey 1993, 39). Because of this avoidance, the majority of the Carthusian monks' protein was gained from fish. The excavations at Mount Grace Priory found a large number of fish remains in the kitchen and south-west cloister area (the servery for the refectory), which reveal somewhat the nature of the Carthusians' pescatarian diet (Irving and Jones 2019, 334).

Fish remains were recovered from all monastic occupation phases at Mount Grace and are representative of kitchen processing waste. In many cases, the articulated skeleton was collected, indicating that fish were being brought to the site whole, and prepared in the kitchen (Irving and Jones 2019, 340). The species of fish consumed at the priory varies across the three phases of occupation, but there is an overall predominance of eel, haddock, whiting and herring, all of which are marine species (Irving and Jones 2019,

338). Although this may appear odd, given that Mount Grace had a well-stocked series of fishponds within its precinct, and it was 30 miles from the sea, Harvey (1993, 47) has already shown that marine fish were the typical species consumed by not only monastic communities but also upper-class domestic households. Cod and herring in particular formed the bulk of the fish consumed, whether fresh or preserved, throughout the country in the Middle Ages (Serjeantson and Woolgar 2006, 107). Bond (1988, 74) found that at Bromholm Priory in Norfolk, 17% of the food expenditure was on herring. As Bromholm was a Cluniac house, and the inhabitants would have also therefore eaten meat, one could expect a higher percentage of fish consumption from a Carthusian house. Gribbin (2001, 201) has suggested that the fishponds' supply of freshwater fish was a luxury, perhaps eaten on feast days, but generally regarded as an emergency store of food, rather than everyday sustenance. The monks at Mount Grace, therefore, were purchasing fish from a nearby port, as the community at Fountains Abbey purchased fish from Yarm (Irving and Jones 2019, 338).

Despite the prevalence of marine fishes, the evidence of the fish remains indicates that the monks consumed a wide variety of species, including turbot and sturgeon. Shellfish were also highly represented, with mussel shells found in the highest numbers, followed closely by oyster shells, which is in keeping with assemblages from other monastic sites nearby, such as Kirkstall Abbey (Irving and Jones 2019, 565; Moorhouse and Wrathmell 1987, 152). Documentary evidence from the Benedictine St Swithun's Priory in Winchester shows the purchase of oysters was a regular occurrence, and that of mussels, cockles and whelks less so (Bond 1988, 79). Remains of freshwater fish, most of the Cyprinidae family (different species of carp) were recovered at Mount Grace, although not in similar amounts to the marine fish (Irving and Jones 2019, 339). This is in line with the prevalent theory that freshwater fish were kept for special occasions and were cultivated in the monastic fishponds (Irving and Jones 2019, 340). Carp appears to be the principal stock kept in fishponds, due to its easy maintenance, as well as good nutritional value (Bond 1988, 93). One of the most interesting conclusions arising from Irving and Jones' (2019, 341) discussion of the Mount Grace piscatorial assemblage is understanding what constitutes 'fish' to the Carthusian community. In the kitchen, across all three phases of occupation, fragments of seal bones (*Phocidae*) were found (Irving and Jones 2019, 341). Although monastic rules generally forbade the consumption of quadrupeds, the Carthusians did not eat fowl either, but it would appear that marine mammals were suitable for consumption under the very broad category of 'fish'. These types of marine life may also have been restricted to consumption on special occasions or feast days only, as only six fragments of seal skeleton were recovered, and therefore do not represent a major part of the everyday Carthusian diet. The market at Coventry is reported to have sold porpoise among other fishes, suggesting that it would have been available to the Carthusians there, and was not necessarily an unusual

foodstuff (Dyer 1988, 30). The case at Mount Grace was not isolated. Bernáldez Sánchez and Bazo Carretero (2013) in a zooarchaeological study of the charterhouse of Santa Maria de las Cuevas in Seville found remains of shells from freshwater turtles. In total, 54 complete or partial shells of *Mauremys leprosa* (Spanish pond turtle) and *Emys orbicularis* (European pond turtle) were recovered from a sixteenth-century layer in the prior's cell (Bernáldez Sánchez and Bazo Carretero 2013, 2578). The authors suggested that the shells were evidence of the prior entertaining guests, as the assemblage was isolated within the monastery, which seems a reasonable assumption, and demonstrates the importance of ensuring guests were fed and treated in a manner befitting their station whilst staying in the community.

4.5 Silence

Silence and solitude were the cornerstones of Carthusian life. Through silence, one could commune with God, and hear His word; it was not intended to isolate, but to provide the opportunity for reflection and to strengthen one's faith (Belisle 2003, 100). Nissen (2008, 210) has noted that although the Carthusians were seeking seclusion from the outside world, their 'solitude was not void', it was communion with God, a 'solitary togetherness'. At a time when people tended to always be in a group and seeking solitude could be seen as a sign of lunacy, the Carthusians made silence a safe haven, rather than a threatening position where one was subject to the wiles of mystical creatures who roamed the wilderness (Nissen 2008, 205). Where the Cistercians and Cluniacs used sign language to communicate with one another, the Carthusians refused to utilise any alternative method of communication (Gilbert 2014, 371). The community was warned against idle chatter, meditating on how each and every careless word spoken would be accounted for on the Day of Judgement (MacCulloch 2014, 99).

The importance of silence was highlighted in the Statutes of the Carthusian Order, where Guigo wrote of the inextricable link between a monk and his cell: 'the cell is necessary to his salvation and life, as water is to fish and the shepherd to his sheep' (C.C. 31:1), suggesting that the Carthusian monk would not manage well outside the cell, and further emphasising the need to be ensconced in solitude. This refers to the words of St Anthony the Hermit, who wrote of the solitary life in the 4th century: 'Fish, if they tarry on dry land, die: even so monks that tarry outside their cells or abide with men of the world fall away from their vow of quiet' (Waddell 1962, 81). The cell was uniquely the monk's domain, no one, save the prior (and only with express permission) was to enter a monk's cell, thereby preserving the solitude of the eremitic lifestyle. The cell functioned not only to ensure silence for the monk but as a boundary of separation from the outside world, which could distract from the overall goal of communing with God. In theory, there was very little contact with secular society, although urban charterhouses such as London likely felt obligated to maintain a level of secular patronage and involvement due to the situation of their foundation[9] (Luxford 2011, 267). However, the Statutes of 1259 maintain that external solitude was only the first step. Internalised solitude, or purity of heart, allowed God to permeate all areas of the monk's life and encouraged him to pursue endeavours only if they glorified God (Statuta 4.2).

As already noted in discussing the schedule of Sundays and feast days, the monks were allowed to break their silence when they met together in the cloister to speak on important spiritual subjects, avoiding the aforementioned careless words. The rule of silence applied to all members of the charterhouse, including the lay brothers. There were certain instances when members of the community could communicate. For example, when two or more monks were working on the same manuscript, they were permitted to speak briefly in reference to the work (C.C. 32:1). The lay brothers were bound to keep silence completely from Compline in the evening to Prime the following day, and the conversi who were appointed to an obedience were allowed to talk amongst themselves 'of profytable & necessarye thynges', or to the brother in charge, but were forbidden from speaking with the monks, any secular visitors, or brothers from another obedience (Pask Matthews 1930, 220-221; C.C. 45). They were further bound to remain silent during meal times and on Sundays and feast days, much like the monks (Pask Matthews 1930, 220). As will be discussed in the following section, the silence of the monastery could be broken in times of grief.

4.6 Death and Memory

When a member of the Carthusian community was dying, the prior, with some other monks, laid him on a bed of consecrated ashes, and all the monks gathered together to say a litany (C.C. 13:2). When the man died, he was washed and clothed, then laid on a bier and carried into the church, where the community continued the psalmody (C.C. 13:3-5). If there was time to celebrate the Mass first, the burial would take place that day, if not, on the following day. On the day of the burial, the monks were not required to keep to their cells or their silence, but came together in consolation, and took two meals together (C.C. 14). The grave of a monk was marked with a simple wooden cross, with no name to indicate who lay there. It is possible, however, that a record of the order of burials in the monastic cemetery was kept by the prior, as was the case at Nieuwlicht Charterhouse in the Netherlands (den Hartog 2018, 290-291). The date of the monk or lay brother's death, with his name, would be written into the martyrology, a book which contained the feast days of the saints (C.C. 14:2). Following the burial, a daily Mass was said for the next thirty days in the individual cells of the monks, and a conventual Mass would be said on the yearly anniversary of his death (Thompson 1930, 40). Guigo states that both monks and lay brothers were treated the same in death, there was no difference in the liturgy or actions of the day, and only the garments of the deceased were different (C.C. 14:3).

The first thirty days after death were the most important for prayer, as this time was seen as when the soul was in greatest desperation and most likely to be influenced by the Devil (Finucane 1981, 45). The prayers said after death were seen to speed the soul to heaven, and ensured that the spirit would be at peace as soon as possible. Prayers and good works done on earth could temper the fires of purgatory, and shorten the time the soul spent there, both before and after death[10] (Kreider 1979, 41; Rousseau 2011, 3). Marshall (2002, 7) summarised that as the dead did not ascend directly to heaven, but lingered, purging their sins, those remaining on earth, therefore, felt an obligation to ease the deceased's suffering in Purgatory.

As Purgatory was such a terrifying prospect for medieval society, great store was set by the intercession of religious persons in praying for souls both deceased and living. The enclosed religious orders in particular were seen as having the most effective intercessory powers, and increasingly following the Black Death, the Carthusians, due to their austere lifestyle, became patronised by a greater number of lay persons. A cursory glance at the data collected from wills (fig. 4.1) shows that there was a sharp spike in the number of bequests to charterhouses between 1325 and 1399, which may be attributed to the change in devotional practices post-Black Death. In patronising or founding a charterhouse, the lay person often stipulated specific conduct of the monks, such as praying for certain souls, saying a particular number of Masses or other spiritual duties. For a number of the post-Black Death charterhouses, such as London, the monastery was founded not by one single person, but by a syndicate of persons, each founding one or more cells. Wines (2008, 70) has suggested this was a 'cost-effective' method of ensuring intercession by the Carthusians, without spending a great deal. However, there were other reasons for founding a Carthusian cell. The prayers of the Carthusians were seen to be the most effective means of intercession, and their austerity, therefore, attracted the wealthiest benefactors (De Weijert 2015, 261). Across Europe, charterhouses were founded by royal and wealthy benefactors, marking the value placed on the solitary life of the Carthusian (MacCulloch 2014, 115). Three of the British charterhouses were founded by royal patrons: Witham, by Henry II, Sheen by Henry V, and Perth by James I of Scotland. Bernard (2012, 190) has also highlighted the opinion of Henry VII, who believed that the Carthusians' austerity exceeded that of any of the other orders, a 'spiritual aristocracy'. The cell essentially functioned as a chantry chapel, the inhabiting

---

[9] As each cell had been founded by various secular benefactors, and the charterhouse relied on lay patronage, the laity appears to have been allowed a greater level of access to the London Charterhouse than in other English Carthusian houses.

[10] A sermon written by John Fisher in 1532 stated that 'the fyre of Purgatory is more grevouse than any maner of payne that can be sene in this worlde, or felte, or yet thought.' (Fisher 1532, sig. C2). However, the deceased's stay in purgatory could be shortened: 'But every daye of penaunce that is done here shall stande there in sted of an hole yere' (Fisher 1534, sig. A2).

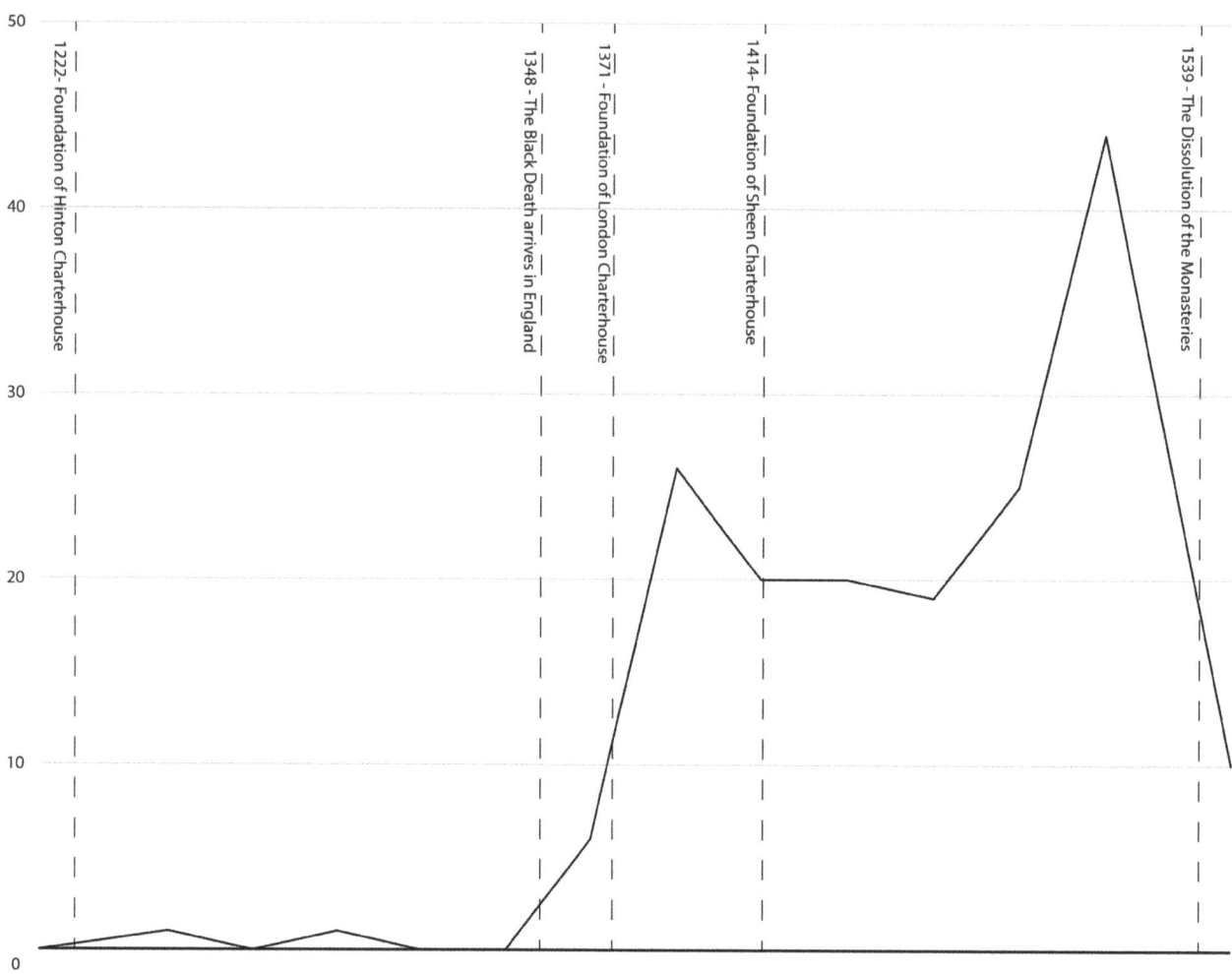

Figure 4.1. Graph illustrating the increase in the number of bequests to charterhouses between 1200 and 1539.

monk bound to say Mass for the soul of the founder in perpetuity. When the monk died, another would take over the intercessory prayers. Stöber (2007, 16) noted that the rising cost of intercession prevented many members of the public from founding a whole monastery, but the donation of one cell gave the benefactor the same benefits without the high price. Their donation meant that their names would be written in the necrology of the house, which recorded the gifts donated (De Weijert 2011, 147). De Weijert (2015, 264) noted that every charterhouse would have been required to keep a necrology, but none of the British or Irish charterhouses' necrologies are known to have survived. The example from Nieuwlicht in the Netherlands demonstrates how the record was kept and gives an inventory of the liturgical vessels among other items that were donated to the house, not only on the death of a donor but also during their lifetime (De Weijert 2011, 160). Bijsterveld (2007, 189) asserted that donations to monastic houses constituted a 'spiritual trade,' the donor being compensated with divine rewards for giving alms. A biblical verse reiterates this, reading, 'And everyone who has left houses or brothers or sisters or father or mother or children or lands, for my name's sake, will receive a hundredfold and will inherit eternal life' (Matthew 19:29).

Analysis of a number of wills written during the late Middle Ages from across the country shows that people were specifying the types of intercession they required on their death. This ranges from a simple Mass or obit (taking place on the anniversary of death) to trentals (a series of thirty Masses) and Placebo and Dirige, specific parts of the Office for the Dead (Swanson 2009, 362-363; Duffy 2005, 368-369). Not only were the types of intercession specified, but some more wealthy patrons required the Carthusian monks to say 1000 Masses immediately following their death, in the belief that this would limit the amount of time spent in purgatory. Specific types of intercession allowed members of lower social groups to have access to spiritual intercession and gain association with a religious house (Brown 2003, 123). Where it was possible to purchase a single obit or mass, this type of salvation became more accessible to those who would otherwise have had no memorial. Interestingly, of the wills analysed, the will of John Hayne, dated 28 August 1493, gave 3s. 4d. to 'Frary'[11] (Somerset Wills 311-312). This

---

[11] The part of the will dealing with 'Frary' reads: 'to be buried at the entrance of the cloister of the house of the BM of Wytham in Selwode, of the Carthusian Order. To the principal Carthusian House in France 6s. 8d. To the house of Wytham 40s with a silver goblet. To the church of Frary

would be either Witham or Hinton Friary, coming from the Somerset Wills, but no other examples currently exist exhibiting a specific bequest to the Carthusian lay brothers rather than to the charterhouse as a whole. Unfortunately, the will did not specify what the lay brothers were to do with the money given to them, it may have simply been a gift, but was more likely a request for them to pray for his soul in some manner.

Analysis of wills further indicates the familial ties which may have influenced the decision to leave bequests to the Carthusians. The de la Pole family (fig. 4.2) were frequent donors to the Hull Charterhouse. Michael de la Pole, 1st Earl of Suffolk founded the charterhouse with the money put aside by his father, William de la Pole (1302-1366) for a religious foundation. Both William and his wife Katherine were buried in the charterhouse, Katherine's will stipulating that she was to be buried in the choir of the church (Test. Ebor. I, 119). Michael's sister, Blanche, married Richard le Scrope (1327-1403), who gave 10 marks to the house on his death (Test. Ebor. I, 272-278), and his brother, John, gave £20 for improvements to the building when he died in 1405 (Test. Ebor. I, 338-339). Other members of the family continued to patronise the Hull Charterhouse; both of Michael and Katherine's sons, and two of their grandsons either gave money for trental masses or requested burial in the church (Test. Vet. 189-190; Test. Ebor. I, 372-373; North Country 8-9; 50-1). This familial tie to the benefaction of a particular house can be seen also in the Mowbray family (fig. 4.3). Thomas de Mowbray, 1st Duke of Norfolk, and father-in-law to Michael de la Pole, 3rd Earl of Suffolk, founded the Axholme Charterhouse, and his son John continued to patronise it, requesting burial in the church on his death, and for the bones of his father (who had died and was buried in Venice) to be returned to the charterhouse (North Country 36-39; Archer 2008). The earliest example of familial benefaction is from Henry II's foundation of Witham Charterhouse; his illegitimate son, William Longespée founded the Hinton Charterhouse, with his wife Ela, 3rd Countess of Salisbury (fig. 4.4). Their youngest son Nicholas, bishop of Salisbury, left 10 marks to the house on his death in 1297 (Eng. Epis. Acta 37, 515-519). However, there was not always a continued loyalty to a particular house. None of the families of the founders of Beauvale, Coventry (fig. 4.5), Mount Grace and Sheen chose to leave bequests to those houses after their deaths. This of course does not mean that the families did not make donations during their lives, but as the necrologies of the British houses do not survive, it is difficult to establish patronage during the lives of the donors. As Bernard (2012, 200-201) also noted, descendants of founders in the fifteenth and sixteenth centuries were increasingly unlikely to continue patronage of a specific house, and monastic foundations were decreasing.

Of the 184 wills analysed during this study[12], 29 also requested burial in the church or cloister of the charterhouse[13] (fig. 4.6). Burial in the cloister (which was the monastic cemetery) was forbidden by the twelfth-century statutes, but the Carthusian General Chapter had agreed that founders and prelates of the house could be buried there (Luxford 2011, 265-266). Evidence from the Nieuwlicht necrology also indicates that non-Carthusian burial did occur within the monastery (De Weijert 2015, 266). The burials were likely to have been in the alley of the Great Cloister, rather than the garth itself, but this location placed the deceased in a location that the monks walked through every day, where they could be reminded to pray for the dead (De Weijert 2015, 267). By the end of the sixteenth century, the London Charterhouse was burying other individuals as well; Luxford (2011, 268) has suggested that there must have been at least 100 'non-Carthusian burials in the church, cloister and chapter-house'. Although no evidence has been found to prove this happened at other charterhouses, requests were made in wills to be buried at the charterhouses of Hull, Mount Grace, Witham and Axholme (North Country 8-9, 36-39, 50-51; Reg. Test. II, 211b; Somerset Wills 41-42; Test. Ebor. I, 119, 325-327; Test. Ebor. II, 166; Test. Ebor. IV, 172-173; Test. Ebor. V, 155-157, 271-272; Test. Vet. 189-190). Only monks and lay brothers could be buried in the Great Cloister garth, and this was further segregated at Nieuwlicht to partition the monks and conversi, buried to the south, from the donati, buried to the north (De Weijert 2015, 266). The church served as a burial location for the most important benefactors, namely the founders and their families, but the chapel, chapterhouse, Great Cloister alley and Little Cloister accommodated all other non-Carthusian burials (De Weijert 2015, 266). The segregation of men and women is highly visible in the claustral burials here. De Weijert (2015, 267) found that within the Great Cloister alley, of the 140 burials, 100 were men and only 40 women. Conversely, in the Little Cloister, 74 burials were female and only 14 male. This is one of the ways that the charterhouse was able to accommodate women when they were technically excluded from the charterhouse (De Weijert 2015, 267). The Little Cloister was the most public area, and therefore did not necessarily contradict the rule. When the rule was later relaxed, women were able to be buried in the Great Cloister. Analysed wills also showed that of the 184 bequests made to the English charterhouses, 87% were from male benefactors (fig. 4.7). Similarly, 83% of the burial requests made were from men, which indicates that women were less likely to propose burial in the charterhouse and when they did, most commonly it was because their husbands were already buried there.

Donations to the charterhouse were also taken during the life of the donor. Tiles recovered from the Coventry Charterhouse indicate an important political situation that was evolving at the time of the charterhouse's foundation

---

13s 4d if it be possible, otherwise 6s 8d. To the servants of the house Whitham 14s' (Somerset Wills, 311-312). This establishes definitely that he intended the bequest to the lay brothers, and not to one of the houses of Friars in nearby Bristol or Bridgwater.

---

[12] See appendix for full details of wills examined in this study
[13] A full list of burial requests to charterhouses can be found in Rowntree 1981, 369-372.

Communal Solitude

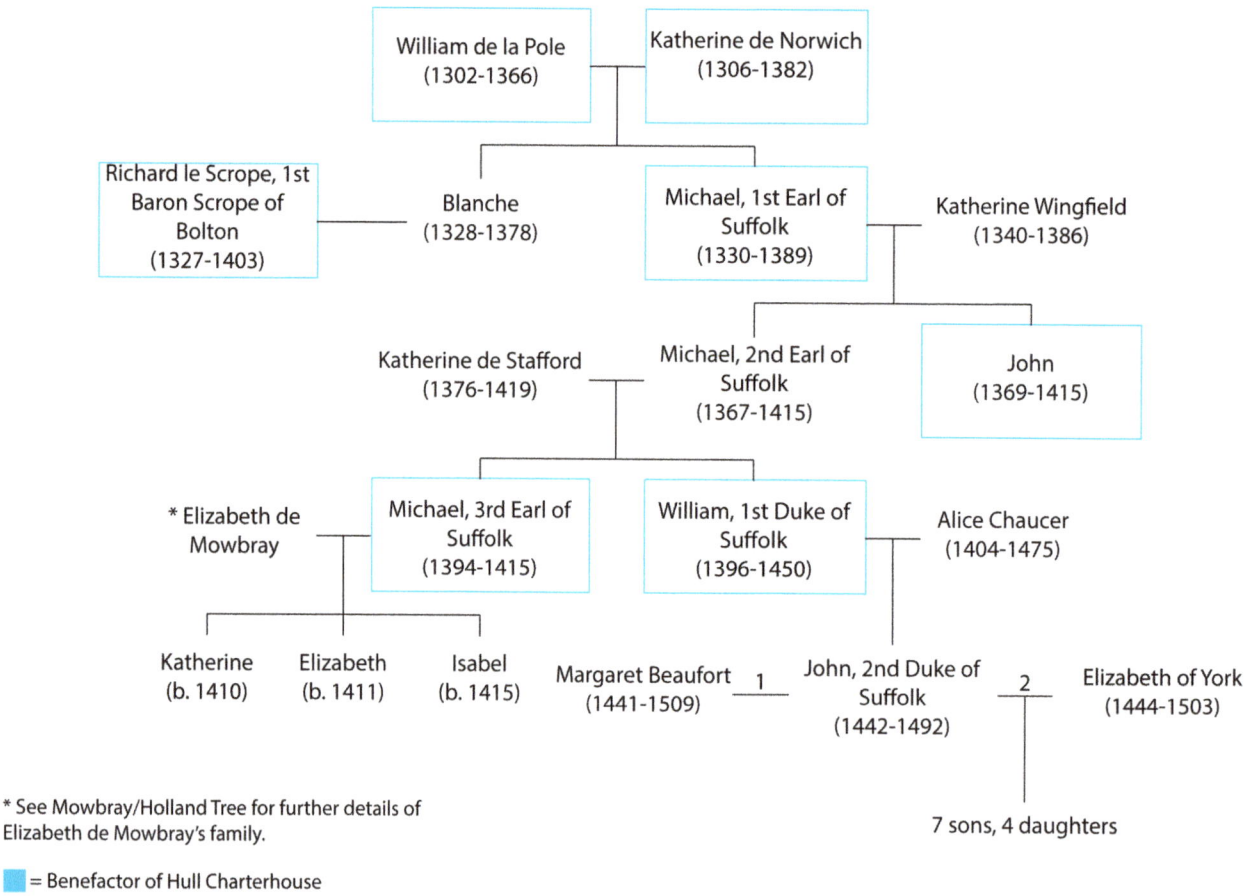

Figure 4.2. The de la Pole family tree, fourteenth-fifteenth centuries.

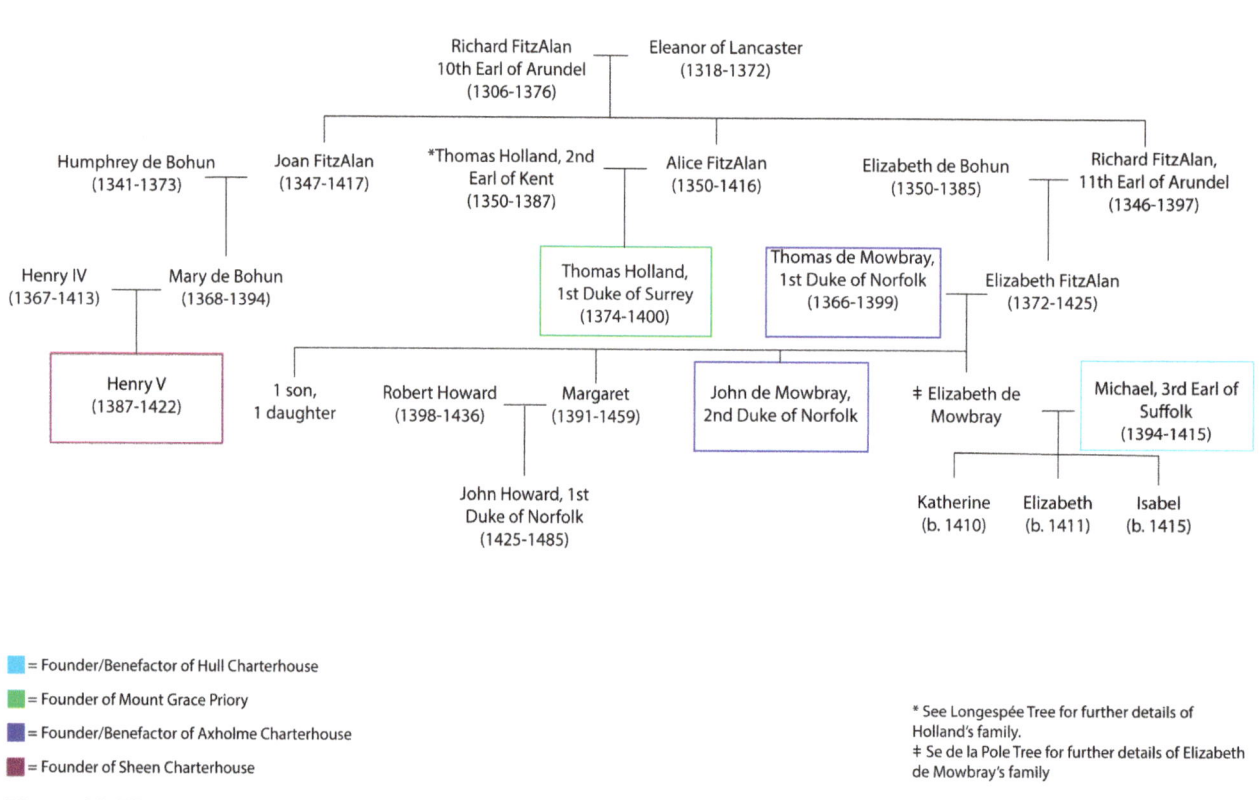

Figure 4.3. The Mowbray-Holland family tree, fourteenth-fifteenth centuries.

Daily Life in the Charterhouse

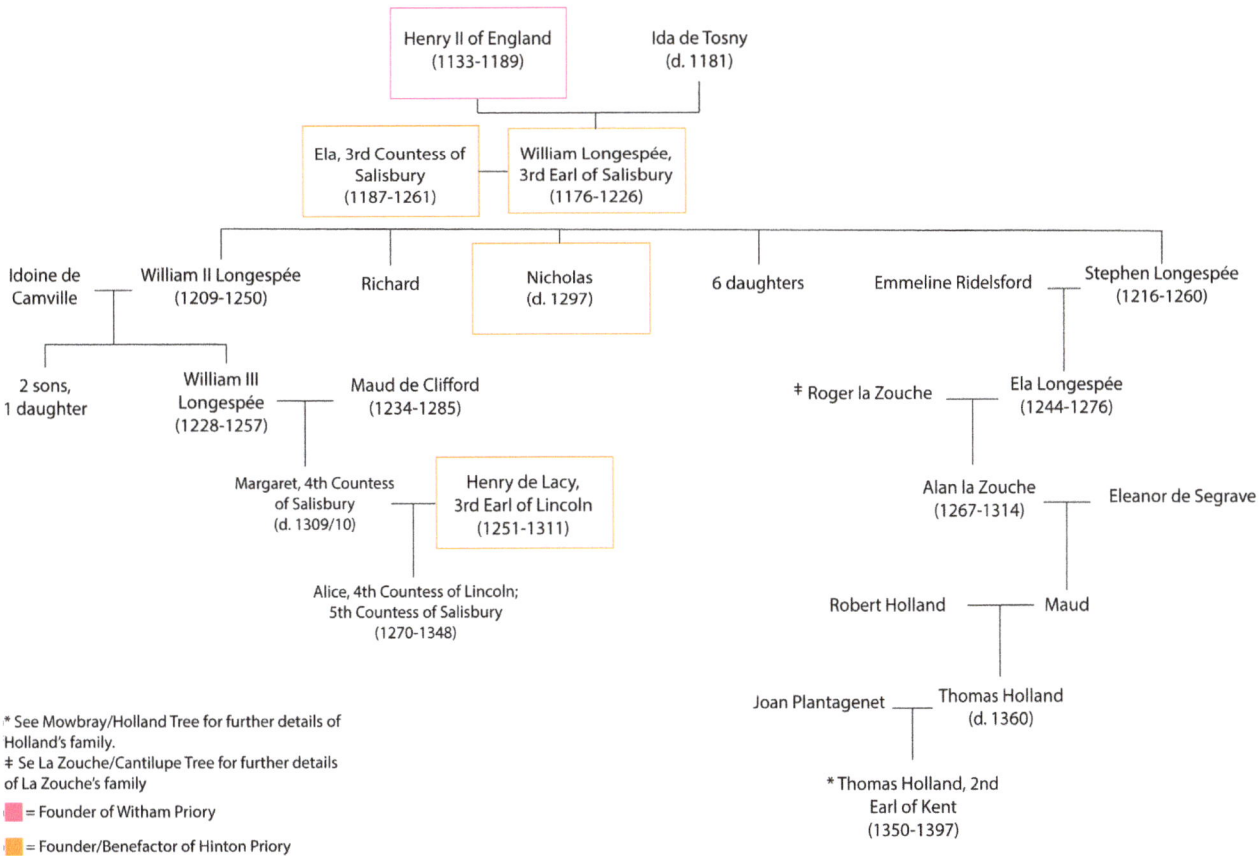

Figure 4.4. The Longspée family tree, twelfth-fourteenth centuries.

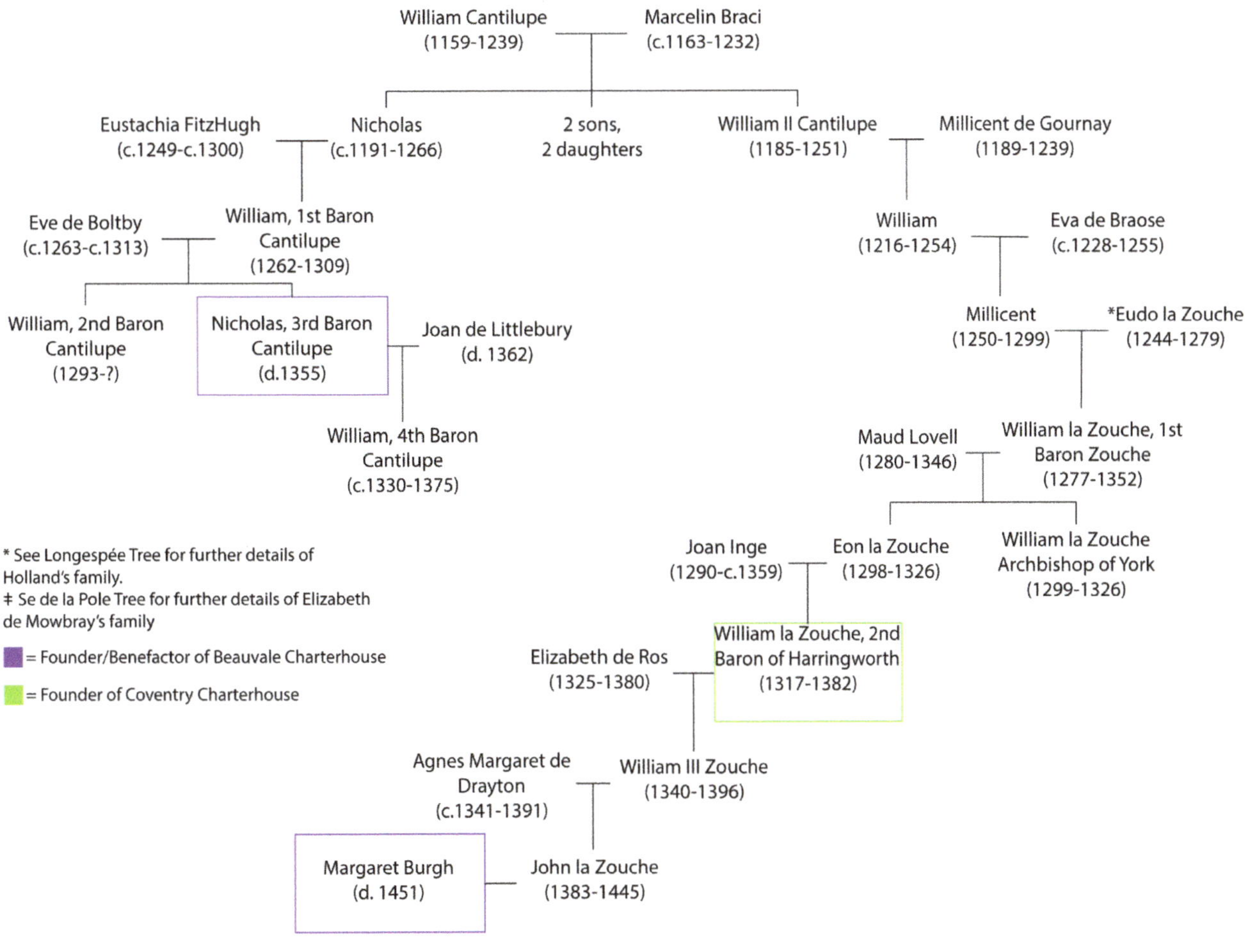

Figure 4.5. The La Zouche-Cantilupe family tree, twelfth-fifteenth centuries.

Communal Solitude

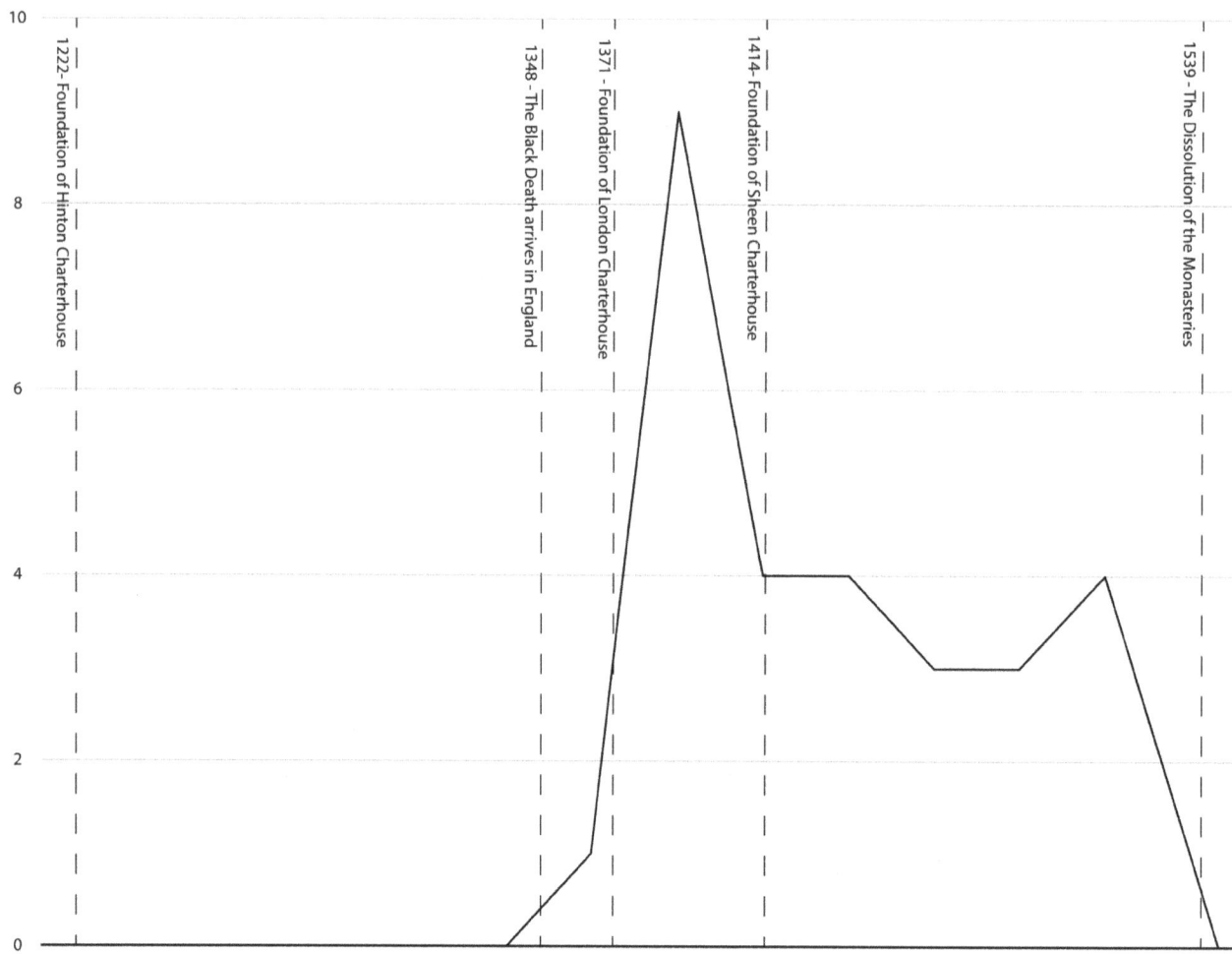

Figure 4.6. Graph illustrating the number of burial requests made to charterhouses from 1200 to 1539.

in 1381. Of the 382 decorated tiles that were recovered, 20% were armorial, and thus represented a specific person or family, which as Soden (1995, 163) rightly points out, is a high percentage given that very few (if any) people other than the monks would have seen these tiles. Although an odd method of memorial and benefaction, the tiles may have fulfilled a similar function to the claustral burials at Nieuwlicht, whereby the monks were reminded to pray for their souls as they walked around the cloister. Among others, represented in these tiles are John Burghill, Bishop of Coventry and Lichfield from 1398-1414, and John Onley, the Mayor of Coventry in 1396 and 1418 (Soden 1995, 103-104). It is thus evident that from its foundation, Coventry was regarded as an important religious house, worth investing in. In addition to this, three of the Lords Appellant[14] are represented in the heraldic tiles of the charterhouse: Thomas de Beauchamp, Henry Bolingbroke and Thomas de Mowbray. Thomas de Beauchamp, Earl of Warwick (1369-1401) gave £20 for the construction of cell 7 and is represented in seven of the recovered tiles (Soden 1995, 103). The marriage of Henry Bolingbroke (the future Henry IV) to Mary de Bohun in 1381 is seen in 23 commemorative tiles of differing designs (Soden 1995, 103). Lastly, 7 tiles featured the arms of Thomas de Mowbray, Duke of Norfolk and also the founder of Axholme Charterhouse (Soden 1995, 104). That the Lords Appellant chose to patronise a religious house that Richard II claimed to have founded, indicates the political (albeit inadvertent) role of the Carthusians in the late fourteenth century.

4.7 Conclusions

The daily life of the Carthusian was one of routine, following strict and austere rules which allowed the inhabitants of the house to commune individually with God. This life of austerity was represented by sparsely decorated buildings that demonstrated the community's dedication to a life of poverty. The lay brothers too were subject to a strict ordering of time, and restrictions on when they could and could not speak. The *conversi* in this way were essentially unprofessed monks, and the occupations which were available to them provide context for the recovered material culture associated with lay areas of the monastery, such as the kitchens, stables,

---

[14] The Lords Appellant were five nobles who in 1387 sought to restrict Richard II's rule and to compel the king to agree to a trial of five of his favourite courtiers, which resulted in the Merciless Parliament of February 1388 (Tuck 2011, para. 1). For further discussion of the Lords Appellant and their role during the reign of Richard II, see Goodman, A. 1971. *The Loyal Conspiracy: the Lords Appellant under Richard II*. London: Routledge.

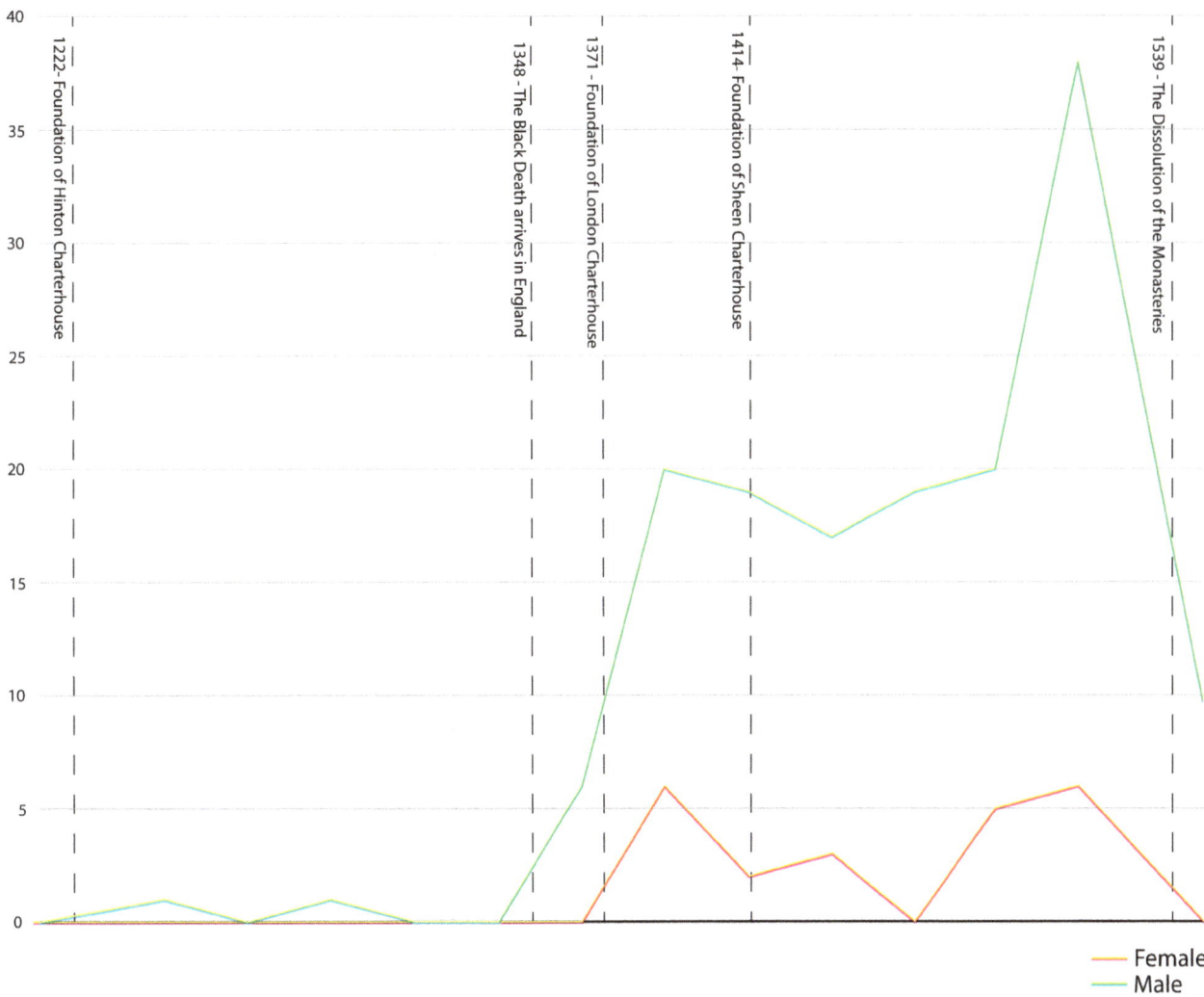

Figure 4.7. Graph illustrating male and female bequests to charterhouses from 1200 to 1539.

workshops and lay cells. That the Carthusian monks were involved in book manufacture is also represented in the material culture assemblages of book fittings, writing implements and illumination materials[15]. The ways in which the Carthusians were governed by these rules, and how it affected their access to, and interaction with, the buildings around them are of vital consideration before understanding the built environment of the charterhouse, which will be examined in chapter 5.

Understanding the circumstances of death and memory at the charterhouse means that the archaeology can be better contextualised. The Nieuwlicht necrology, for example, allows individual burials to be named and indicates how claustral burials, both monastic and lay, were zoned. This, and the evidence from English wills gives insight into familial benefaction and the ways in which a patron may feel tied to a specific religious institution due to the circumstances of their ancestors' benefaction. The evidence from English wills also shows that altered devotional practices after the Black Death were in part manifested in an increased number of bequests to charterhouses. Men were six times more likely than women to leave bequests to the charterhouses in their wills, and nearly 5 times more likely than women to request burial in a charterhouse. Lay benefaction also influenced the structural expansion of the monastery and therefore provides the opportunity to examine the archaeological footprint of these changes.

---

[15] The material culture is further discussed in chapter 6.

5

The Wider Landscape of the Carthusian Precinct

The local environment of the charterhouse was of great importance for the Carthusians, to whom the wider landscape outside the monastery walls was known as the desert. Dunn (2003, 3) suggests the desert as the location of true religion, where poverty and silence were the most important aspects of life. Biblical references to the desert or wilderness invariably describe it as a frightful place, '...the great and terrifying wilderness, with its fiery serpents and scorpions and thirsty ground where there was no water...' (Deuteronomy 8:15); 'He shall dwell in the parched places of the wilderness, in an uninhabited salt land' (Jeremiah 17:6); 'who led us in the wilderness, in a land of deserts and pits, in a land of drought and deep darkness, in a land that none passes through, where no man dwells?' (Jeremiah 2:6). These images reinforced the understanding that the monks were sacrificing their lives to live in isolation, with the faith that it would bring greater salvation on the Day of Judgement. The wilderness was a common theme in monastic life, particularly for anchorites and hermits. Dyas (2005, 21) illustrated the importance of this theme in that it evoked a 'sense of alienation and deprivation, of struggle for survival, of being on a dangerous spiritual knife-edge posed between the horror of eternal condemnation and the hope of redemption'. In this way then, the silence and isolation of the charterhouse challenged the monks to confront their situation in order to become closer to God.

5.1 Siting of the Charterhouse

The solitude of the Carthusian precinct created the illusion of a desert wilderness, which indicates the importance of the idea of isolation, as suggested by Arnold (2013, 56). This was reinforced by foundation stories which bolstered a myth that the monks were living an entirely isolated life, fleeing to the desert from the evils of the world. The myths provided a common theme that connected the community together and helped to delineate their lives from other religious or lay groups (Remensnyder 1995, 3). This was a phenomenon experienced across many, if not all, medieval religious orders. Janet Burton's (2006, xxxiii) introduction to Byland and Jervaulx's foundation histories reported that Cistercian narratives follow typical conventions, emphasising a strong spiritual leader in the abbot, the encounter of a desert or wilderness site, and how the monks overcome their struggles through divine intervention. This formula can be similarly applied to Carthusian foundation histories, evidenced through Adam of Eynsham's description of the establishment of Witham Priory. He discusses how Henry II offered the Carthusians a site in the Royal Forest of Selwood which was in his control entirely, and which he could therefore empty of inhabitants for the religious community (a desert or wilderness site). The king, however, was not forthcoming with funds to build the monastery (a struggle), and when Hugh of Avalon arrived from La Grande Chartreuse (a strong spiritual leader), the monks were living in huts (another nod to the desert site). The monks overcame their struggle through the leadership of Hugh, who ensured a steady stream of funding for the construction of the site, through his intellect and spiritual faith (*Magna Vita* II, vi).

The theme of isolation and solitude is prevalent throughout the foundation stories of the Carthusians, which refers back to the original flight to the desert by the Desert Fathers. The silence of the Carthusians also evoked the 'horror of solitude,' but was not unique to the Carthusian Order, being a cornerstone of the Rule of St Benedict, and as such, a key element of monastic life in general (Milis 1992, 138). Within the Cistercian Order also, this concept persisted, encapsulated by William of Thierry describing Clairvaux:

> There was a sense in which the solitude of that valley, strangled and overshadowed by its thickly wooded hills, in which God's servants lived their hidden lives, stood for the cave in which our father St Benedict was once discovered by shepherds — the sense in which those who were patterning their lives on his could be said to be living in a kind of solitude. They were indeed a crowd of solitaries. Under the rule of love ordered by reason, the valley became a desert. (*Vita prima Bernardi* trans. Matarasso 1993, 31).

The solitude of an uninhabited location was ideal for the charterhouse in the same way as it was for the Cistercians. In this place, they could challenge their faith in the same environment (as they saw it) as Jesus had when he was tempted by the devil in the wilderness.

The monks had a number of requirements for the location of the charterhouse. In order to create the 'desert' required, a site had to be found which could be cleared of people to afford the monks the solitude they desired. Dixon (2009, 55) highlighted three main factors in creating solitude: geographical isolation, silence, and social isolation. The rural Carthusian desert fulfilled all of these ideals, and the individual cells furthered silence and social isolation. This was the case at Witham, as previously discussed, where the Carthusians had sufficient space to create an inhospitable landscape to call their wilderness (Coppack and Aston 2002, 27). Alexander of Lewes, who joined the community whilst Hugh of Lincoln was prior, disliked the silence and successful isolation of the area so much that he described it as 'a place of horror and empty solitude' (quoting Deuteronomy 32:10), and promptly deserted the Order[1] (*Magna Vita* II, xi).

The sites were not chosen randomly. Often, as is the case for many monastic establishments, the charterhouse was founded at an already religious site. Witham was given a church originally owned by the Augustinian canons at Bruton, the London Charterhouse was established around Sir Walter Manny's chapel for the plague dead, and the priory at Axholme was established on the site of a pre-existing chapel to the Virgin Mary, known as the 'Priory in the Wood' (TNA E 135/9/15, f. 8). Though Dixon (2009, 55) suggested that solitude requires geographical and social isolation, Merton (1999, 96) wrote, 'as soon as a man is fully disposed to be alone with God, he is alone with God no matter where he may be — in the country, the monastery, the woods or the city'. This understanding meant that the Carthusians could still maintain their solitude even though they were situated in a busy, noisy city; geographical isolation was not necessarily a requirement in the cases of the urban charterhouses.

A number of charterhouses were built in cities during the Middle Ages, despite the crowded topography of these areas. London (1370), Amsterdam (1392), Venice (1422), Florence (1345), Cologne (1334), Paris (1257), Perth (1429), and Antwerp (1324) are just a few of the cities whose inhabitants included Carthusian monks. By and large, their precincts tended to be situated outside the city walls, a nod to the desired isolation of the Order, but also likely due to the crowded urban space. By the time these monasteries were founded, space inside the city was at a premium, and thus the only spaces really available for the charterhouses were outside the city walls (Brown 1985, 79; Johnson 2014, 176). The charterhouses at London, Paris, Perth, and Cologne were established on the edge of the city proper and were slowly subsumed into the urban environment over the years through population increases and the natural expansion of the cities. The houses at Hull and Coventry were founded just outside the city, which gave them slightly more privacy and isolation than that of London, for example, but the influence of the locality on the monastery was still evident. The bequests of land and property, as will be examined later in this chapter, illustrate strong regional ties to specific city-based charterhouses, indicating the Carthusian influence on the local laity, and equally the reciprocal influence on the monastic community itself[2]. Excavations at London Charterhouse (see Chapter 6 for more detail) found material culture which suggested that local people were allowed entry to at the very least, the outer court (Barber and Thomas 2002). It would be fair to suggest that neighbouring religious houses would also be of influence to the charterhouse, particularly in cities. The London Charterhouse was situated next to the Priory of St John of Jerusalem and St Mary's Clerkenwell to the west, and the Priory of St Bartholomew-the-Great and St Bartholomew Spital to the south (fig. 5.1). The water supply had to be run through the land of St John's, for which an agreement was arranged. The monks at Mount Grace maintained spiritual ties with the Cistercians of Jervaulx, as did the Charterhouse at Axholme with Roche Abbey, and the Sheen Charterhouse with the nuns of Syon (Cross 2008, 231), whereby devotional texts were exchanged, and discussion of common religious themes held via letters. In the case of one George Lazenby, a monk of Jervaulx, the refusal of the monks of Mount Grace to agree with the King as Supreme Head of the Church inspired him to do the same, resulting in his execution for treason in August 1535 (Cross 2008, 231).

Though the ideal location for the charterhouse was a rural area, devoid of people, and in an inhospitable environment, it was by no means the typical location. As Foreville (1973, 19) asserted, both Witham and the French charterhouse at Liget were surrounded by inhabited areas, despite attempts to clear the area, as it was impossible to close off the religious community entirely from the secular world. The forest areas which they inhabited became the desert, 'Europe's version of the Hebraic desert wilderness' (Schama 1996, 227), and provided the monks with an environment in which they could further withdraw from the world, becoming closer to God (Arnold 2013, 46-47). It was impossible to cut the community off entirely from society, especially in locations where the laity had previously occupied the area. This was the situation at the London Charterhouse, where there was much public opposition to the foundation of a monastery in an area that was considered to be a public open space, and where the laity believed they had the right to attend the church and visit the cemetery (Barber and Thomas 2002, 70; Knowles and Grimes 1954, 21-22). The church of St Mary without Aldersgate, or the Pardon Chapel, was established by Sir Walter Manny to serve the plague cemetery, and was, therefore, considered a public building which should not have restricted access (Harben 1918). When the land of West Smithfield was given to the monks to build their charterhouse, the Pardon Chapel was appropriated as the church of the monks, preventing lay access. Likewise, the burial places of members of the local community became equally restricted, causing upset to the locality.

Solitude and isolation were not the only advantages of a woodland retreat. Schama (1996, 227) notes that from at least the seventh century, the siting of a monastic house in forested areas stemmed from a need to 'take advantage of the thriving natural economy', and not necessarily to withdraw from the secular world, although this was not discouraged. The theory that a monastery could be sited based on the proximity of natural resources is evidenced in the Carthusian use of water within the monastery, as will be discussed in the following section.

5.2 Water Management

Related to the choice of location for the charterhouses, is how the Carthusians utilised nearby resources, and more specifically, water sources. The singular layout

---
[1] 'locum horroris et vastae solitudinis' (*Magna Vita* II, xi).
[2] See Chapter 3 for discussion of lay benefaction and influence.

of the Carthusian house and the necessity of providing fresh water to each of the cells meant that many of the Carthusian sites were chosen for their good water supply and drainage. For example, Witham Priory sat between the River Frome and another tributary, which allowed it excellent access to fresh water, but also provided a method of drainage for the site (Coppack and Aston 2002, 30).

The Carthusian Order was unique in its method of distributing water to the monastery, as their liturgy stipulated fasting on bread and water only, instead of the ale traditionally drunk by monks (Coppack and Aston 2002, 117). This meant that a source of fresh water had to be located close to the house, and often had a vital bearing on the choice of location of a site. A nearby spring could provide potable water for drinking, but also had to be sufficiently strong that enough pressure could be built up to transport the water to and throughout the monastery. With the introduction of individual garderobes in each cell, there also needed to be a method of flushing, whether by diverting a stream or by the use of another spring. The systems were not always integral from the beginning; at Mont-Sainte-Marie in Gosnay, France and Mount Grace Priory, at least partial water management systems were included in the original building plans, but the Charterhouse in London utilised wells for fresh water for 60 years until a spring was found, and always used cesspits for waste disposal (Bonde and Maines 2012, 633; Coppack and Aston 2002, 124; Bowlt 2003, 121). Likewise, the earlier houses at Hinton and Witham had piped systems added later, although they were sited close to rivers for waste disposal. The differences in the topography of each site and the access to water had a bearing on the layout of each house. Although every charterhouse was built on the same basic layout, they were altered depending on their situation. Consequently, the cloister could be located in any direction relative to the church, and the claustral layout did not need to remain square. The ability to provide water to each cell had a huge bearing on how the house was built.

At London, the water supply was also routed to secular establishments. A contemporary water supply plan from 1430 indicates that after supplying the charterhouse, water was pumped to four taverns outside the precinct walls, and the springs also supplied the nuns at St Mary Clerkenwell (Greene 1992, 115; Magnusson 2001, 18, CM MP/1/14a). Furthermore, the supply required an agreement from the house of St John of Jerusalem at Clerkenwell, to allow the pipes to be run across their land, indicating a level of inter-monastic discussion and interaction. The level of complexity placed upon a piping and drainage system illustrates the importance of water to the Carthusian Order for maintaining solitude and preventing any need to leave the cell. A similar situation is found at Mount Grace Priory, where the water was supplied by three spring houses set into the hills surrounding the priory. Each of the springs supplied a different area of the priory via lead pipes and settling tanks, ensuring a clean source of water that had not been compromised by waste products (Magnusson 2001, 60). This meant that the priory had one source for drinking water, one for flushing the drains which ran under the monks' latrines, and one which fed the fishponds and drove the mill (Coppack and Aston 2002, 30). Coppack and Aston (2002, 30) have suggested that this continuous supply of water so close to the monastery was one of the prime reasons why the site was chosen, as often water was piped over some distance in order to ensure a fresh source.

5.3 Topographic Analysis: Using LiDAR to assess landscape changes

Topographic analysis of the Carthusian sites can give greater detail as to the landscape surrounding the monasteries. LiDAR (Light Detection and Ranging) data can be used to reveal archaeological features, in the same way that earthwork surveys do, but at a much faster speed. LiDAR will be discussed here to analyse the potential of the Carthusian sites for further archaeological exploration, highlighting areas that are likely to yield interesting geophysical and archaeological results.

Airborne LiDAR is a remote sensing technique that uses a laser beam to scan the topography of a landscape (Airborne Laser Scanning – ALS), detecting measured variations in height (Devereux *et al.* 2005, 651). In archaeology, the technique can be used to calculate heights and to reveal landscape features that are invisible in aerial photographs (Crutchley and Crow 2009, 4-5). The best available LiDAR data for the case study sites is currently at 1m resolution.

There are some points to be aware of when using LiDAR data. Paramount is that LiDAR visualisations are still only visualisations, and cannot replace a physical field assessment, as LiDAR can only record limited types of archaeology (Doneus *et al.* 2008, 891). The data created by LiDAR must be field-verified and should not be used as the sole method of investigation (Fisher *et al.* 2017, 3). It is also important to stress that LiDAR investigations can only show above-ground anomalies. It does not detect buried features, and therefore cannot be used in the same way as geophysical surveys.

For the Carthusian sites, the best techniques for visualising the landscape were determined to be the Cluster and Swiss Hillshades, as these methods illustrated the widest range of features, and utilised both directional and complex illumination. Cluster hillshading is a method of relief shading which defines small-scale features through differential lighting across a landscape (Veronesi and Hurni 2015, 121). This makes it a useful tool for identifying archaeological areas of interest, which tend to be small-scale. Swiss hillshading uses a blue to yellow colour ramp to differentiate between areas of lower and higher terrain (Pingel and Clarke 2014, 228; Kennelly 2008, 569, 575; Jenny and Hurni 2006, 198-200). This gives emphasis to ridges and valleys and can highlight major topographic features. The combination of both visualisation techniques allows for a more complete view of the landscape, maximising the number of features that can be highlighted.

Communal Solitude

Figure 5.1. The London Charterhouse in the context of other religious houses in London.

For the site of Witham Friary, there were no visible features. This is likely due to the spatial resolution of the LiDAR data, at 1m resolution, it is not detailed enough to pick up on such small-scale features, especially in a built-up area such as the village. Equally, as there are only a few small open areas of land, it is possible that even a higher resolution LiDAR dataset would not be able to reveal any pertinent features.

The LiDAR visualisations for Witham Charterhouse (fig 5.2), on the other hand, depict a number of interesting features. The central cloister is prominent, and as can be seen from the Swiss hillshade, the southern part of the cloister was ploughed at some point, which explains why the previous geophysical survey had difficulties identifying features in this area of the site. When viewed in this way, it is possible to make connections between the alignment of the cloister with the alignment of an outer boundary, which may delineate the precinct of the upper house.

By overlaying the geophysical survey undertaken by GSB on top of the LiDAR data (fig. 5.3), it is possible to identify a number of further features. Where the resistivity survey located the area of the cloister garth (also visible in the LiDAR), it was also possible to pick out the cloister walk from a large amount of high resistance material revealed there. The edge of this material correlates with linear features in the LiDAR, which seem to delineate the edge of the cloister walk where the doors to the monks' cells would have been. Parallel to this, the LiDAR has also revealed the back wall of the monks' cells, which indicates the length of each cell. Previously, only one cell in the north west corner had been excavated, and the resistivity survey was able to distinguish only a few cells on the western side of the cloister. There is some correlation between the earthworks to the north east of the cloister and the results revealed by the resistivity survey, but largely, any topographic remains of the conventual buildings have been destroyed.

On a wider scale, there are a number of earthworks which can be attributed to the landscaping of the site in

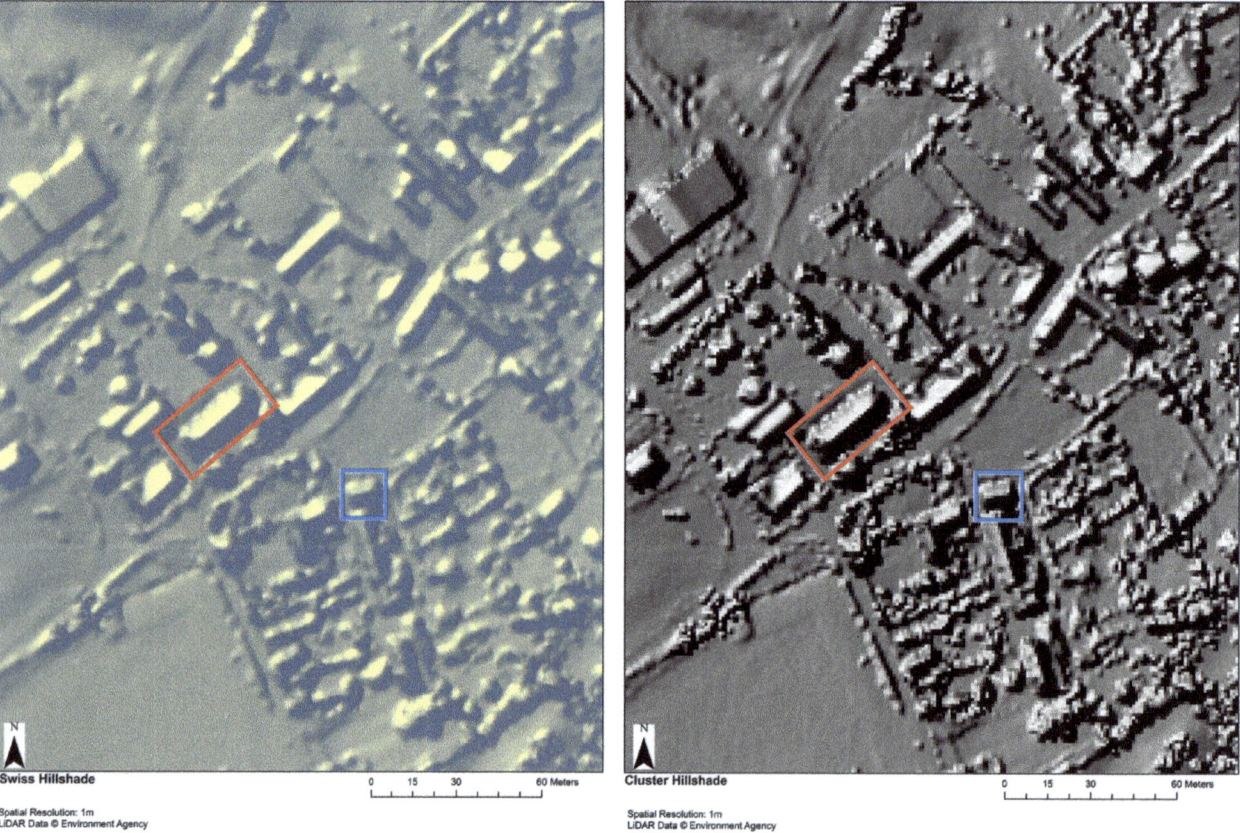

Figure 5.2. Swiss and Cluster hillshaded LiDAR at Witham Charterhouse. The church (red) and dovecote (blue) are outlined.
Contains public sector information licensed under the Open Government Licence v3.0.

the seventeenth to eighteenth centuries to create a formal garden for the mansion built by Wyndham in the mid-seventeenth century[3] (fig. 5.4). The Wyndham mansion itself is difficult to identify but would appear to have reused the area of the conventual monastic buildings as its footprint. The Beckford mansion, on the other hand, is clearly visible in the LiDAR to the south west of the main priory site, with what may be a formal garden to the south of the earthworks, although it also appears that efforts were made to join the Beckford mansion to the formal gardens of the Wyndham mansion, based on the long linear earthwork features in the LiDAR data.

The LiDAR data for the site of Hinton Priory confirms the features which the geophysical survey also locates (fig. 5.5). It is possible to identify the outer south and eastern walls, and part of the western outer wall, as well as a number of dividing walls indicating the extent of each cell. The linear shape of the earthworks to the west of the priory may indicate historic field boundaries, especially as a number of the linear features run perpendicular to the current hedgerow. However, this is the area of the monastic fishponds, so it is possible that the linear features represent irrigation channels or the fish pond boundaries. To the south east of the priory site, a long curving feature seems to represent a dried-up river bed, which likely fed into the River Frome, to the east of the priory. This would have been a convenient location for any wastewater from the Priory to empty, where it would be quickly and easily carried away.

In combining the LiDAR data for the priory with the resistivity survey results conducted by Geophysical Surveys of Bradford, the earthworks correlate well with the resistivity anomalies. The LiDAR also indicates a number of features outside the range of the resistivity survey, particularly the linear features on the eastern and southern extents of the survey. These may indicate the presence of an external boundary wall, especially as the features run parallel with the known outside walls of the cells. A linear feature to the north of the main priory site may also be identified as the northern extent of the priory buildings, but this is not certain, although it does match with a linear feature located by resistivity survey.

The LiDAR data for the site at Hinton Friary provides a better overview of the area than the corresponding data for the Witham Friary site (fig. 5.6). It is possible to identify a number of interesting features in the area of the hamlet. The eastern-most field contains a number of parallel, linear features, which likely represent ridge and furrow from previous ploughing efforts. To the west are many short linear earthworks, which likely represent geological features, due to the steep angle at which this area lies. The area in the middle surrounding Woodman's Cottage has revealed more short linear earthworks, which may be representative of buried monastic buildings. This area has been surveyed as part of the current research, and so the LiDAR data will be assessed with the resistivity and magnetometer results to provide an overview of the remaining features at the site.

Only three of the other British and Irish charterhouses are suitable for any analysis employing LiDAR, Sheen Priory, in Richmond, Axholme Charterhouse, in Lincolnshire and Mount Grace Priory in North Yorkshire. The reasoning behind this is that for Beauvale, no LiDAR data is available and in Hull, London, Coventry, and Perth, the sites of the charterhouses have been built over, so no earthwork data remains to be examined. Finally, the site of Kilnalahanin in Co. Galway was reused by the Franciscans only 80 years after its foundation as a charterhouse, and therefore the remaining earthworks relate to the Franciscan occupation of the area, not the Carthusian.

For Sheen Priory, the site has become rather confused after its conversion to a golf course in 1892. The Cluster Hillshade provides the most detailed view of the site; a rectangular feature to the south of the site may represent the remains of the cloister (fig 5.7). The visualisation has also picked up what may be the boundary wall for the inner court, running N-S to the east of the site. It is difficult to pick out any other potential archaeological features, due to later land use.

The interpretation from the GSB geophysical survey (Gaffney 1997) shows some details of Cloake's (1977) conjectural plan match up with buried remains, but largely there are no earthwork remains to support either plan. The reuse of the site as a golf course has likely flattened any earthworks which could have been visible, and the immediate post-Dissolution occupation of the site by Lord Lisle is likely the cause for the scant buried remains (Gaffney 1997, 2).

At Axholme (fig. 5.8), it is possible to distinguish the back walls of the monastic cells, as they back onto the watercourse running around the site. The earthworks for other conventual buildings north of the cloister may also be identified, although the exact layout of these is undetermined. The resistivity interpretation from the GSB survey (Gaffney 1995a) makes it possible to identify a potential cloister garth and a continuation of the moat-type watercourse running north around the cells. The earthworks are, however, sparse, and although the LiDAR here is an interesting addition to other data, it could not be used as a sole prospection technique, as has been already observed at Witham and Hinton. Likewise, the LiDAR data available for Mount Grace Priory (fig. 5.9) is able to provide an interesting view of the landscape and topography surrounding the house, but the resolution is not high enough to give more pertinent results regarding buried features relating to the monastery itself. This method of investigation does allow for an understanding of how the Carthusians exploited the land, such as how water was re-routed around the monastery, which will be discussed in further detail in the following section.

---

[3] See Chapter 7 for further discussion of the post-medieval remodelling of Witham Charterhouse (section 7.2)

Communal Solitude

Figure 5.4. LiDAR at Witham Charterhouse with location of post-Dissolution buildings added (after Burrow & Burrow 1990; RCHME 1994). *Contains public sector information licensed under the Open Government Licence v3.0.*

Figure 5.3. LiDAR at Witham Charterhouse with resistivity survey data added (after Gaffney 1994). *Contains public sector information licensed under the Open Government Licence v3.0.*

The Wider Landscape of the Carthusian Precinct

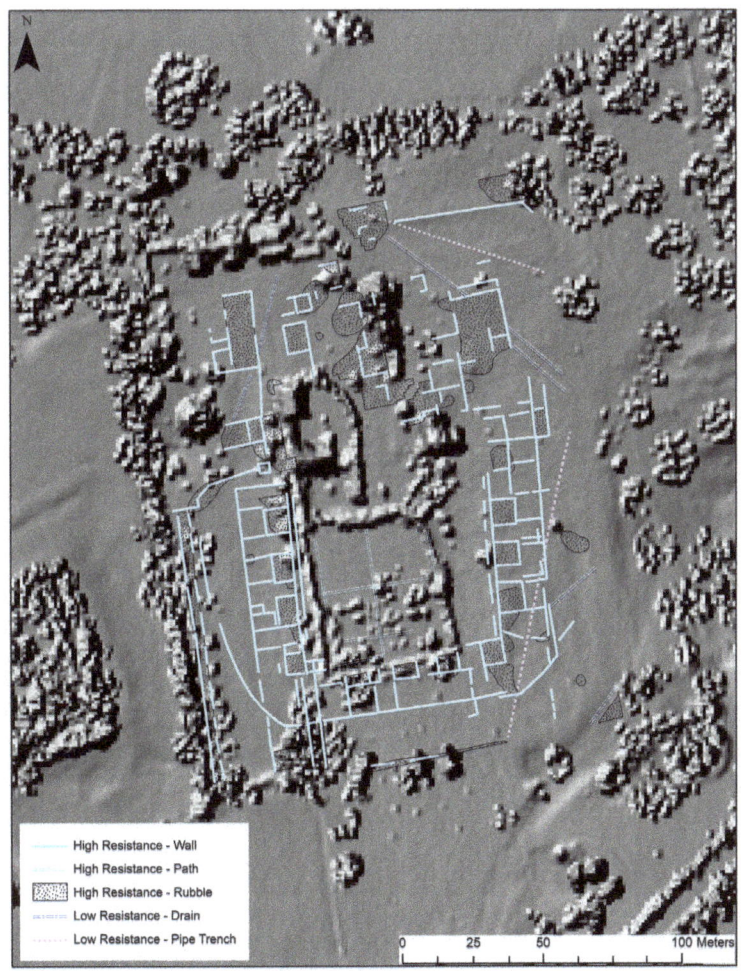

Figure 5.5. Cluster hillshade LiDAR at Hinton Priory with resistivity survey data added (after Gaffney 1995b). *Contains public sector information licensed under the Open Government Licence v3.0.*

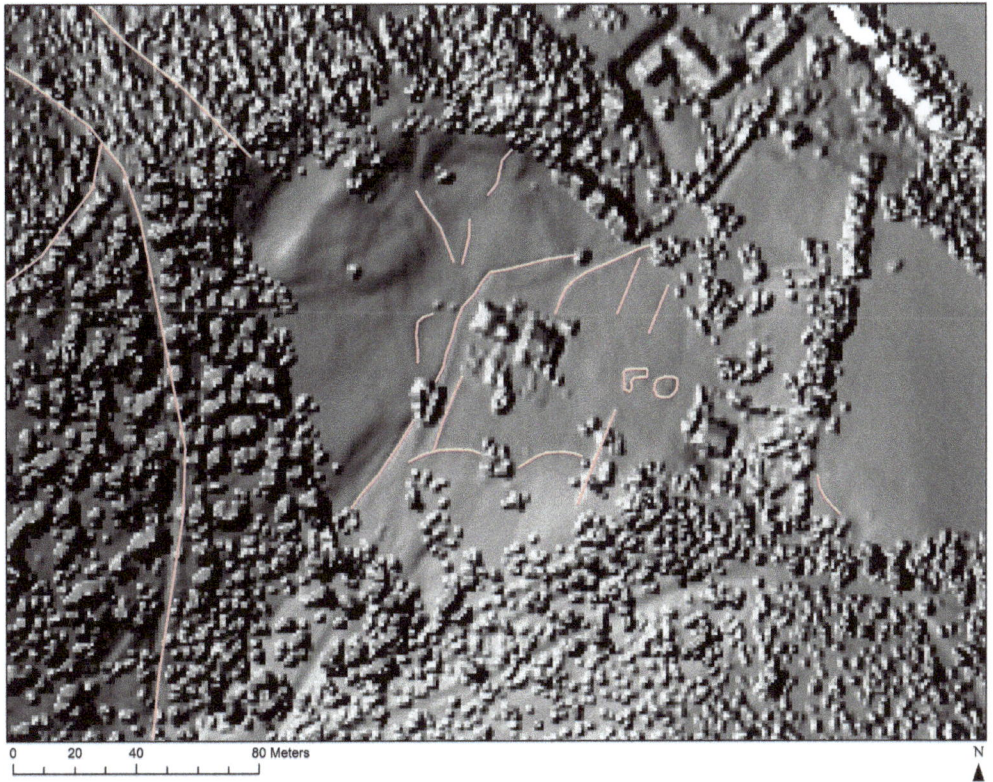

Figure 5.6. Cluster hillshade LiDAR at Hinton Friary, with additional interpretation. *Contains public sector information licensed under the Open Government Licence v3.0.*

Communal Solitude

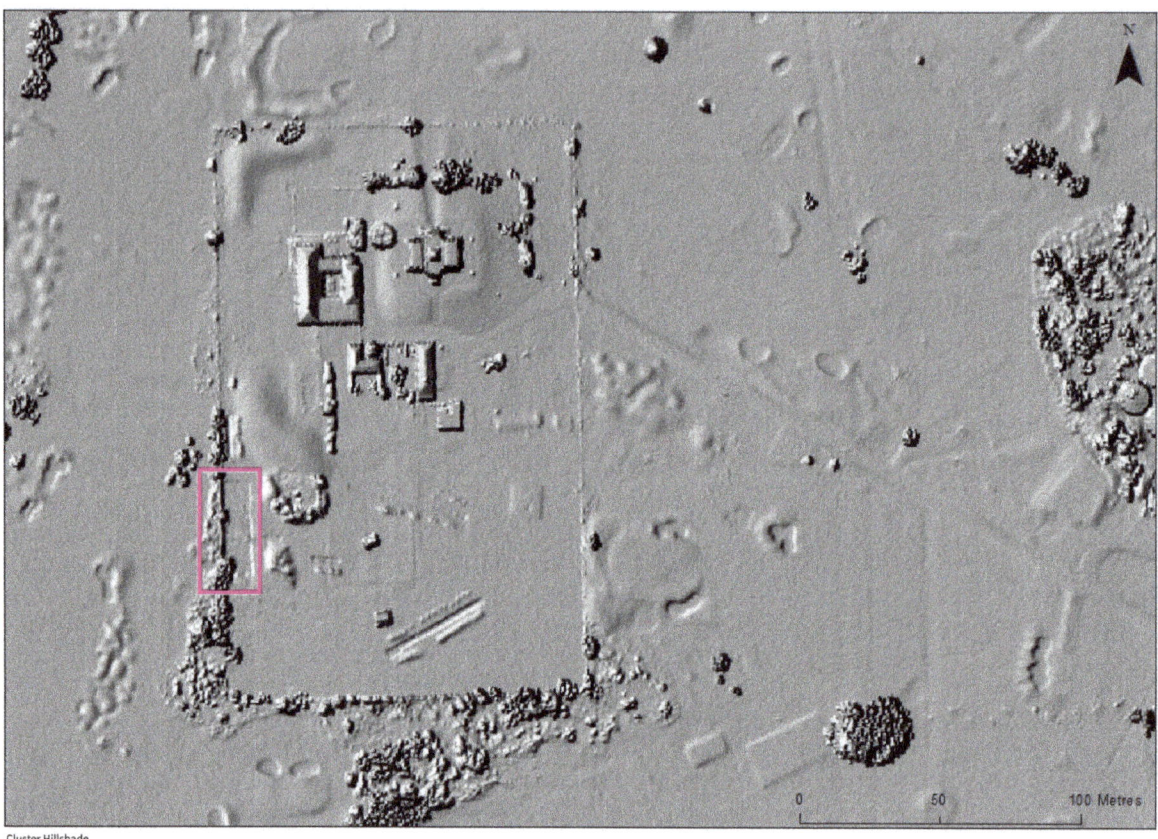

Figure 5.7. Cluster hillshade LiDAR at Sheen Charterhouse. The possible location of the northeast corner of the charterhouse complex is outlined. The conversion of the site to a golf course in the late 19th century has obscured any possible earthworks. *Contains public sector information licensed under the Open Government Licence v3.0.*

Figure 5.8. Swiss hillshade LiDAR at Axholme Charterhouse. The southern and western ranges of cells are outlined in orange. *Contains public sector information licensed under the Open Government Licence v3.0.*

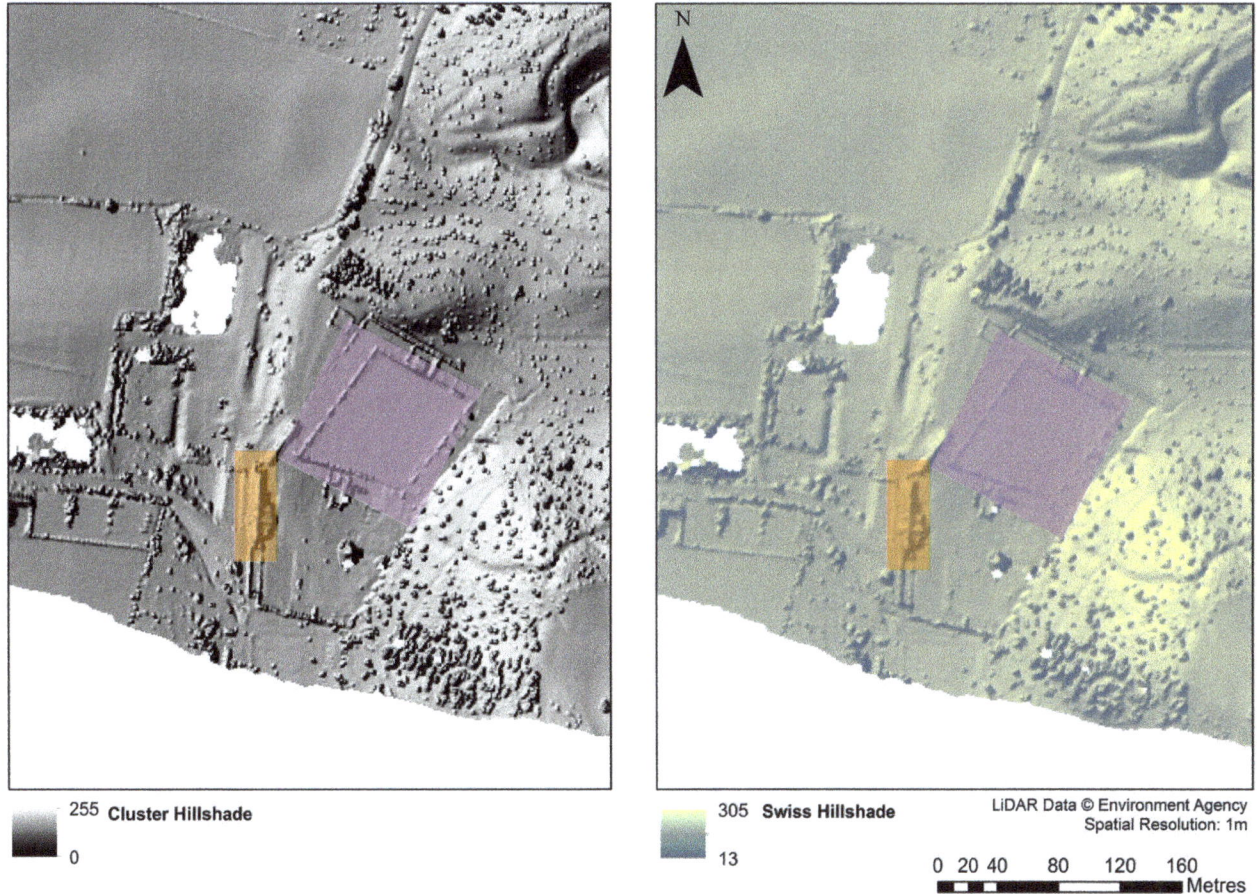

Figure 5.9. Cluster and Swiss hillshade LiDAR at Mount Grace Priory. The Great Cloister is highlighted in pink, and the gatehouse is highlighted in orange. *Contains public sector information licensed under the Open Government Licence v3.0.*

5.4 The Influence of the Carthusians on the Local Landscape

The first and most obvious influence of the Carthusians on the landscape was their clearance of the area surrounding the monastery. In order to create the isolation they desired, at Witham, the forest of Selwood had to be emptied of its inhabitants, who were compensated with land in North Curry, near Taunton (C. Wells, 352-353). This occurred within various religious orders in England, who were given licenses to assart land, which made it suitable for cultivation (Burton 1994, 237). In Nottinghamshire, Barley (1957) investigated the case of the Cistercian Rufford Abbey, whose land clearances led to the desertion of three villages, all the inhabitants being resettled elsewhere. This illustrates the power of the monasteries, and the importance they placed on keeping their lands free of lay interference.

The Carthusians' exploitation of land reached further than simply removing local inhabitants from the area of the charterhouse. Both of the Somerset charterhouses owned granges in the Mendip Hills, for Witham at Charterhouse-on-Mendip, or Hydon Grange, and for Hinton, the sites at Green Ore and Whitnell. The land at Charterhouse-on-Mendip had been mined for lead by the Romans (Fradley 2009), and in 1283 the Carthusians were granted the right to work all lead mines they found on their land, and to keep any profits arising from them (TNA C66/102, m.11), although there is scant evidence to suggest that the Carthusians ever explored this industry (Aston 2000, 148). The charterhouse in Nottinghamshire, Beauvale, leased out a coal mine they owned in Newthorpe from 1380 (Bond 2004, 341), which contradicts the desire of the Order to remain outside secular landholdings and tenancies.

The grange held at Charterhouse-on-Mendip was also used to keep sheep, although more is known about Hinton's granges. The Carthusians owned two sleights at Green Ore, and one at Whitnell, in the Mendip Hills, where they kept flocks of sheep (Brett 2012, 148). By 1538, when the prior of Hinton, Edmund Horde, sold the lease on the land to his brothers Robert and Alan, they also took on 400 sheep, although it was noted that the sleights could hold up to 1200 beasts (Brett 2012, 148). Indeed, in a 1577 dispute, one of the witnesses, a 92-year-old man, who remembered the last three priors of Hinton, recorded that the Carthusians were keeping 1000 sheep in a sleight on Mendip during the early sixteenth century (Dunning 1991, 39). The meadows at Green Ore were also used to produce hay, stored in barns at the grange, as was St John's Meadow, owned by the London Charterhouse from 1376 (McLean 1981, 51; Barber and Thomas 2002, 68). Hay was used as fuel, as well as to feed livestock, and to fill the mattresses of the monks and lay brothers. Not all of the charterhouses farmed their own lands, however. The charterhouse at Coventry was granted an indult in April 1419 to let their land to lay farmers without requiring a diocesan licence (Cal. Pap. Reg. VII, 141). The London Charterhouse owned an orchard nearby as well as a kitchen garden and fishponds, despite their city-based location. Following the suppression of the London Charterhouse, two of the commissioners, Thomas Legh and Richard Layton supervised the removal of property from the monastery and its reallocation to secular persons. This included:

> to the King's gardener for his garden at Chelsea all such bays, rosemarie grafts, &c. as were meet for his Grace's garden…To Mr. Richard Cromwell's gardener, all such bay trees and grafts…Dr. Billowse's servant had two carload of hay…Sold and delivered to Mr. Pickering by Dr. Cavys commandment all the wheat and malt in the house…To the cater of my lord Privy Seal's house three baskets of herbs…To the King's gardeners out of the orchard of the Charterhouse 3 tree grafts of all sorts…in all 91 trees…Delivered to Mr. Semer and Mr. Smyth…last 200 carps…Delivered to Foyerwyll pond to Dr. Layton 100 carps for the King's store… Delivered to Dr. Layton…a bundle of rosyers. (TNA SP 1/139, ff. 148-152)

Evidently then, the location of the charterhouse did not mean that the monks and lay brothers had to rely entirely on local produce and merchants to keep the house. They were at least semi-self-sufficient, having a fishpond, orchard and a seemingly large herb garden which would supplement their simple diet.

As the Carthusians were keeping sheep, they also needed to sell the wool somewhere. As early as 1225, the priory at Hinton had been granted permission to hold a yearly fair in Norton on the feast of St Philip and St James (30 April, 1 May, 2 May) (Brett 2002, 167; TNA C53/46A, m. 6). A total of eight grants were made to the priory concerning fairs and markets until 1353, including a weekly market on Fridays and Tuesdays, and another yearly fair on the day of the Decollation of St John the Baptist, 29 August (Brett 2002, 167; TNA C53/73, m.7; C53/80, m.15; C53/130, m. 17; C53/132, m.5; C53/133, m. 19; C53/138, m. 4). On the 27 April each year a cloth fair was held in Norton St Philip, selling woollen cloth in the churchyard and linen cloth in the George Inn (Dunning 1983, 40; Gazeteer of Markets & Fairs, Somerset). The George Inn still stands in Norton St Philip, three miles south of the priory. Interestingly, the last charter made, in 1353, allows the May fair to be extended to five days instead of three (TNA C53/138, m. 4). That the charterhouse requested a licence to hold a fair demonstrates a certain level of secular involvement and an understanding of the needs of the local community. Though the fair allowed the priory to sell the wool that was cultivated by the lay brothers at their granges, the impact of two large markets a year for the area should not be underestimated. The fairs continued despite the disruption caused by the Black Death at the end of the 1340s (Brett 2002, 167). The fairs were well known, and the priory was able to make good profits, as they charged 4*d*. per pack of linen cloth stored at the George Inn, on top of the profits from the fairs themselves, which were taken by the prior (Brett 2002, 172; Williams, Penoyre and Hale 1987, 317); the profits amounted to 60*s*. per annum as recorded in the *Valor Ecclesiasticus* in 1535 (Brett 2002, 172). Williams, Penoyre and Hale (1987, 317) noted that Somerset traded a considerable amount of wool and cloth in the fourteenth and fifteenth centuries to nearby ports such as Bristol, Southampton and London for export to the Flemish and Italian cloth markets, and therefore the Inn at Norton was well situated to take part in this trade. The George Inn also functioned as a stopping place for visiting merchants and travellers who could not be accommodated at the priory, which must have become an issue by 1375 when the Inn was built (Bond 2004, 264).

Due to their position in the Royal Forest of Selwood, the Carthusians at Witham were given special privileges by the crown. In 1251 notice was sent to 'all foresters, verderers and other bailiffs and ministers of the forest' that the charterhouse was 'quit for ever of regard' (TNA C66/62, m. 1). This grant was repeated in 1534 when the liberties of the charterhouse at Beauvale was in question, and so the prior of Witham, Richard Peers, made clear that the Carthusians had been given the right by Henry II and Henry III to 'franc-plege, wayf and strey, blodwyte' and that 'alle the kinges dere that come within our boundes we have hunted and kylled' (TNA SP1/86, f.57). The Carthusians at Hinton were also given free warren in their lands by Henry III in 1259, allowing them to kill any game which they hunted in the forest (TNA C53/49, m.1). This exemption really only applied to the lay brothers, who would be the ones doing the actual hunting. The lay brothers at Hinton were also granted permission to tan hides at the Friary and sell them after disputes had arisen between the Carthusians and local tradesmen over the price of the hides and the wages that the Carthusians were paying to secular workmen (TNA C66/254, m. 19).

The Carthusians used their complex knowledge of water management systems to divert rivers in order to flood fishponds near the charterhouses. Before 1232, dams were built over the River Frome to create fishponds at Witham and to serve a mill, and from 1525 Hinton owned a lease on a pond called Lachemere, which was stocked with bream, tench, perch and roach (Dunning 1991, 38; Coppack and Aston 2002, 30). Even the London Charterhouse had a fishpond nearby which apparently yielded 300 carp per year (TNA SP1/139, ff.148-152). As was discussed in Chapter 4, however, the ponds seem to have kept fish for emergencies, or special occasions, as the accounts for the London Charterhouse in 1492-3 indicate purchases of large amounts of sea and river fish (Barber and Thomas 2002, 61), and the lease for Hinton's fish pond states 'for the comfort and sustentacion off them and their successor in tyme commyng… [in case they] myght have noo Fysshe from the seey' (TNA STAC 2/32/42).

5.5 Carthusian Estates

The types of land that the Carthusians were given varied, including granges, tenements, churches and alien priories[4] as well as some urban properties in various cities. A cursory look at the estates of each house shows that Sheen (fig. 5.10) and London (fig. 5.11) were patronised far more than any of the other houses, and owned property across the country. At other houses, such as Beauvale, Hinton, Witham and Hull there are indications of a strong regional tie to their lands, likely given as part of the original endowment, or given by local benefactors. The three remaining English houses, Axholme, Coventry, and Mount Grace, owned property that was more dispersed and located further afield from their own precinct. Axholme's properties were mostly located around Coventry. This spread of properties does seem to have caused some problems for the English charterhouses, as notes from the General Chapter in 1425 indicate that the province was ordered to consolidate their estates, in keeping with the customs of the order (Hogg 1987, 65; LPL MS 413, f. 58r), although this never actually came to fruition, and many of the houses continued to hold land and parishes despite the rulings of the Consuetudines and the General Chapter. The earlier houses, Witham and Hinton, appear to have kept to the statutes more stringently than later monasteries.

The Carthusian Order was also granted a number of alien priories when the monks of these houses were expelled in 1378[5], and their lands were given to other religious institutions, which was completed during Henry V's reign in 1414. The Carthusian Statutes (41:1) gave specific instructions as to the ownership of property, which reads 'the inhabitants of this place [the charterhouse] can possess absolutely nothing outside the limits of our desert. Namely, neither fields, nor vineyards, nor gardens, nor churches, nor cemeteries, nor oblations, nor tithes, nor anything of that sort'. This was obviously ignored by the fourteenth century when charterhouses in England began to be endowed with large areas of land. Coppack and Aston (2002, 26) asserted, however, that the priories could own only as much land as was needed to support themselves, and any surplus crops or goods should be donated to local religious houses in need. For Hinton and Witham, the original endowment gave them only the original manors of their precincts, whereas the houses established from Beauvale (1343) onwards, are given much larger holdings. Dependent on the land they were given, they were able to increase their influence in the area. As has already been discussed, Beauvale owned a number of coal mines, which were given to them as part of the original endowment and allowed them to lease them to lay miners creating a new stream of revenue for the charterhouse. The house at Sheen is somewhat of an exception. As a royal foundation of Henry V, it was endowed with a great number of manors and churches from its establishment, with few later additions (Jurkowski and Ramsay 2007, 486-491).

Rosenwein (1989, 38) noted that secular benefactors often gave land, and particularly churches, to monastic houses because it ensured remembrance after their death. They would be buried in the monastic cemetery and would be memorialised in the masses for the dead, but the foundation (and therefore giving of land) of monasteries also functioned as a status symbol for many elite patrons (Milis 1992, 32). The fact that a charterhouse could be easily founded by more than one person (as exemplified at the London Charterhouse), lent itself to the popularity of the order by the laity in the later Middle Ages, as it allowed those lay persons unable to found a whole monastery to still reap the benefits of a founder. Duby (1962, 174) also postulated that the reason for gifting land to a monastic order was in to expiate one's sins; 'an act of piety deserving salvation'. This theory has already been referred to in Chapter 4, with the discussion of wills, but the gift of land represents a much larger commitment to a religious order, and therefore with the expectation of a larger return, such as burial in the monastic cemetery and perpetual remembrance.

Those who gave land to the charterhouses, such as Hugh de Cressy of Selston, and his wife Cecilia, did so with the expectation of a return, in this case, they gave the gift of the manors of Kimberly and Newthorpe to Beauvale, on the condition that Hugh would receive a pension of £7 10s. during his life from the priory, or should his wife Cecelia survive him, she would receive £4 11s. (BL Add. MS 6060, f. 32). Likewise, Henry de Lacy, 3rd Earl of Lincoln gave the hamlet of Midford to the charterhouse at Hinton in 1275, on the proviso that the monks would pray for his soul (Feet of Fines, 237). This case, however, indicates familial ties, as Henry was married to Margaret Longespée, the great-granddaughter of William and Ela Longespée, who founded Hinton Charterhouse. As has been indicated in Chapter 4, familial connections were often factors in the benefaction and patronage of a particular religious order or monastic house, and this was no different for the Carthusian Order.

5.6 Conclusions

The desert wilderness of the Carthusians was a clear barrier to the outside world, whether the house was situated in a city, on its fringes, or nestled in an uninhabited valley, and was bolstered by foundation stories which gave credence to their origins, tradition, and daily practice. For the rural houses, the availability of natural resources was of vital consideration, and water management could alter the layout and orientation of the monastic complex. The provision of water and removal of waste can be explored further in the archaeological record; fragments of lead pipe were recovered from the London Charterhouse, and the drainage channels behind the cells and Mount Grace Priory

---

[4] Alien priories were small religious institutions that were directly controlled by foreign religious houses.
[5] In April 1403, Beauvale Charterhouse was granted the alien priory of Bonby in Lincolnshire, which was a cell of St Fromond Priory in France. The grant included the possessions of the priory, including the rectory of the parish church, pensions of 13s. 4d. of two churches and the advowson of a further three churches (TNA C 66/369, m. 31).

Communal Solitude

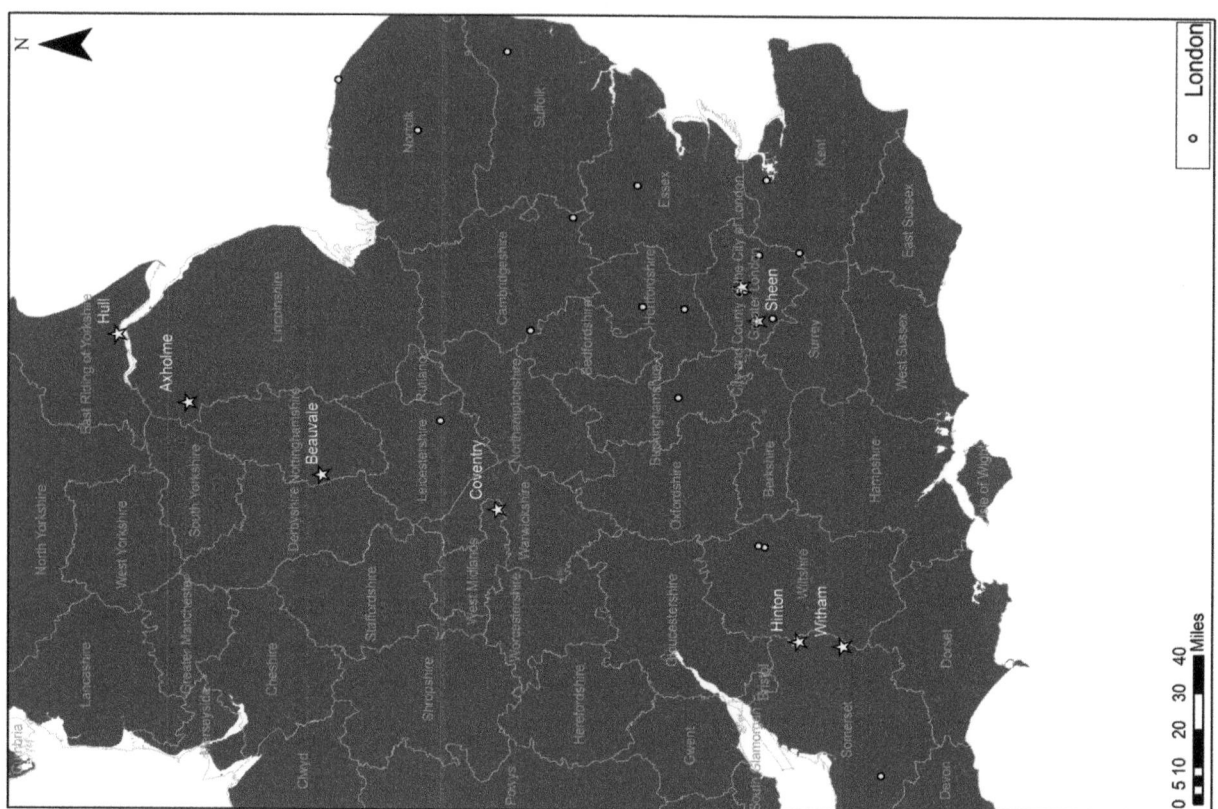

Figure 5.10. Map of estates owned by Sheen Charterhouse.

Figure 5.11. Map of estates owned by London Charterhouse.

are still visible. The topographic analysis examined in the course of this chapter has demonstrated that earthworks related to resource management and building remains can be identified through LiDAR data, and how this method is useful for viewing a large area of land quickly. In order to give a more accurate understanding of the landscape, the resolution of the LiDAR data would need to be greater than 1m, as currently, the results for the friary sites and Witham Friary, in particular, cannot be used to increase knowledge of these areas.

In addition to the bequests which were discussed in the previous chapter, the benefaction of land was another method utilised by the laity to ensure safe passage for their souls after death. Further, the exploitation of this land provides an interesting view of the relationship between the Carthusians and their secular patrons, as each impacted the other, in particular through wool fairs held by Hinton Priory and the income the monks gained from rents on mines and land. That the Carthusians were able to grow food and herbs, and cultivate livestock and fish meant that they did not need to rely solely on local produce[6], and therefore decreased the amount of secular interaction that was required. The sheep sleights and granges of Witham and Hinton on the Mendip Hills have never been archaeologically investigated as concerns the monastic occupation of these areas, although this would increase understanding of the agricultural business of the communities and may give insight into the lives of the lay brothers who maintained the granges.

---

[6] This self-reliance is not a uniquely Carthusian attribute, all monastic houses grew crops and tended livestock, but within the realm of Carthusian isolation, being able to avoid secular interaction made self-sufficiency an even more desirable objective.

6

Material Culture of the Charterhouse

The study of material culture recovered from excavations at charterhouses allows for insight into a peculiar environment. The nature of the monks' cells, encircled by high walls, made them particularly isolated, enclosed areas, providing excellent conditions to examine one particular individual's possessions at one point in time: the eve of the Dissolution. This opportunity is unparalleled elsewhere, as the walls allow for a minimal migration of materials from one distinct area to another (Coppack 2008, 174). At no other monastic site is it possible to investigate the personal preferences of one specific person, especially in comparison to other individuals in close proximity. This singular setting allows for a study of the occupation of the last inhabitant of each cell at the Dissolution and sheds light on some of the activities of the Carthusians in the 1530s.

This chapter aims to assess the material culture of five English charterhouses in order to understand their utility in investigating the monks and lay brothers themselves. To this end, three categories of finds have been analysed: pottery, items relating to book manufacture, and dress accessories. This is in no way an exhaustive list and does not include all the items recovered from the sites but allows for a detailed discussion of the main types of materials excavated from the charterhouses, and the occupations of the inhabitants.

The three categories of material culture were selected because their functions encompass a number of different areas of monastic life. The ceramic evidence addresses not only food and cooking, but also the furnishing of the cell, as well as the networks of consumption available to the charterhouse. Largely, the pottery has been examined as a whole, rather than on a cell-by-cell basis, as many of the cells featured very few ceramic finds, so it was more appropriate to discuss the entire assemblage. The items related to the creation of books are concerned with the manual labour of the monks, the inter-monastic channels of communication, and how the monks were able to influence secular life through their religious writings. Finally, the dress accessories can be used to infer social status, conspicuous consumption, and the material environment of not only the monks and lay brethren who inhabited the charterhouse, but also their secular visitors.

6.1 A Comparative Study of Monastic Material Culture recovered from English Charterhouses.

Mount Grace Priory is one of the most fully excavated charterhouses in England and therefore provides an excellent case study to examine the material culture. As the assemblage is so rich and can give so much information about the monastic occupation of the site, the Mount Grace finds will be used to drive the discussion throughout this study. Prior to Coppack and Keen's excavations, Sir William St John Hope conducted archaeological investigations at the site in the late nineteenth and early twentieth century (Hope 1905, 271). These investigations only partially excavated some of the cells, and so they cannot be taken as representative of the whole assemblage, finds excavated by Hope will not be considered in this current investigation.

In order to establish how typical Mount Grace was for an English charterhouse, the material culture has been compared with other excavated houses at London and Coventry, founded in 1371 and 1385 respectively. Looking again at the categories of ceramics, writing implements, and dress accessories, it will be possible to assess these cell assemblages for similarities between the houses. The two Somerset houses, Witham and Hinton have also been integrated into the discussion, providing a rounded view of the furnishing of the cell. However, for the site at Hinton Priory, unfortunately, no trace remains of any material culture. The excavation reports written by Major Philip Fletcher (1951, 1958) make no note of any finds other than worked stone, and his correspondence with the Ministry of Works equally offers no contributions to an understanding of the material culture (TNA, WORK 14/2006). This is disappointing, and no archive is mentioned where items may have been deposited. It must be surmised that any objects that had been found are now lost or remain in a private collection.

6.1.1 Ceramic Cooking and Dining Vessels

The ceramic evidence from Mount Grace has allowed for accurate dating of each cell or area of excavation. In total, 6053 sherds were excavated, representing a minimum of 2490 vessels (Hayfield 2019, 315). The great majority of the pottery sherds recovered are of domestic wares, with imported goods making up only 17% of the total (fig. 6.1). Within these broad categories are a wide range of fabrics, from plain utilitarian vessels to the more decorative items for display. For analysis of fabric types, the sherds excavated have been grouped into four categories, illustrated in table 6.1.

The distribution of the ceramics was well spread across all of the cells and the rest of the site. No one cell boasted a particularly high percentage of any one group of fabrics. It should be noted, however, that Cell 8 was more thoroughly excavated than any other and provides a better view of the construction of the cell and build-up of materials. The domestic wares cover a large range of

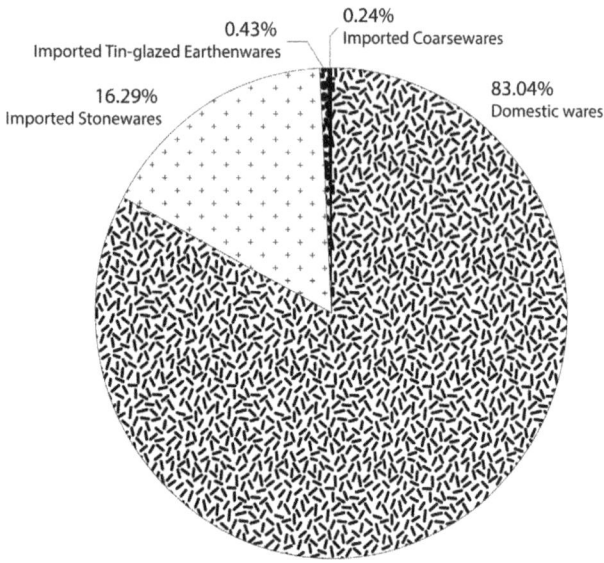

Figure 6.1. Chart showing the percentage of domestic and imported ceramics excavated at Mount Grace Priory.

fabrics, and represent the majority of the sherds excavated, from particularly local styles, such as Brandsby-type ware and Humber ware, to fabrics like Midlands Purple, which were manufactured at other English kiln sites. The fabric types excavated from Mount Grace Priory show that domestic wares by far represented the greater part of the total assemblage. This is to be expected since the vessels were cheaper and more readily available than those that required importation. Certainly, Ryedale wares made up the great majority of jugs excavated from the site. For other vessels, pancheons were mostly of early sixteenth-century Sandy ware, and mugs were of Cistercian ware or German stoneware. Cooking pots were largely made of local gritty wares and these vessels would have fulfilled more than one type of function. They were likely used for not only cooking but also for the storage of foodstuffs and other functions outside of the kitchen (Willmott 2018, 698). Accordingly, the majority of the ceramic fabrics represented at Mount Grace were not indicative of any particular high status, including the imported goods. German Stoneware such as Raeren, Langerwehe and Siegburg was mass-produced and traded across Europe in the sixteenth century, being a cheap, hardwearing material, and which was already flooding the market of north-west Continental Europe (Gaimster and Nenk, 1997, 173; Hurst, Neal, and van Beuningen 1986, 176). The fabric was one that could have been found in any status household during that period and does not represent a luxury item (Roebuck, Coppack, and Hurst 1987, 18). The mugs, in particular, were especially cost-effective compared to their wooden counterparts (Courtney 1997, 98). Despite this, imported stonewares made up 14.38% of the vessels or

Table 6.1. Types of pottery excavated at Mount Grace Priory according to categories.

Domestic Wares	Imported Coarsewares	Imported Stonewares	Imported Tin-Glazed Earthenwares
Gritty wares	Low Countries Red	Siegburg	South Netherlands Maiolica
Brandsby types	Pisa Slipware	Langerwehe	Pisa Maiolica
Scarborough wares		Raeren	Valencia Lustreware
Humber wares		Beauvais	Columbia Plain
Late Gritty wares		Westerwald	
Hambleton wares			
Rydale wares			
Developed Humber wares			
Post-medieval Sandy			
Midlands Purple			
Midlands Yellow			
Cistercian wares			
Cistercian copies			
Reversed Cistercian wares			
Tudor Green			
Staffordshire wares			
Staffordshire types			
Stamford type			

591 sherds. This is likely due to its renown as being cheap and hardwearing, as well as being impervious to liquids, unlike coarsewares. The imported coarsewares and tin-glazed earthenwares were not as popular. This may be due to expense, or simply that the fabrics were not as popular or as easily available in Northern England at the time.

Equally, the presence of South Netherlands Maiolica and other tin-glazed earthenwares, albeit in small portions, are of similarly modest standards, which would have been relatively easily available and cheap (Hurst 1999, 91; 95). The two-handled South Netherlands Maiolica flower vase was the most popular vessel of this fabric. Some featured monograms reading 'IHS', suggesting that they may have been used for private devotion, explaining their presence in the cells of the Carthusian monks (Hurst, Neal, and van Beuningen 1986, 117; Hurst 1999, 91; 95).

Only the Valencia lustreware, of which 2 sherds were found in cell 8, suggests a slightly higher level of status. This was an admired vessel fabric, manufactured in rich blues and copper tones, and made by Islamic craftsmen in Valencia and Andalusia between the thirteenth and sixteenth centuries (Henisch 1976, 171). Gaimster and Nenk (1997, 175) have suggested that this type of luxury ware was a status symbol, indicating perhaps that this was a gift from a lay patron. It has been noted, however, that it would be rather archaic to own a Valencia dish in the 1530s, as it was supplanted by Netherlands tin-glazed ware, suggesting this was a vessel that had been passed from monk to monk and well looked after (Roebuck, Coppack and Hurst 1987, 20).

Furthermore, the presence of Columbia plain earthenware was also rather unusual. This is a Spanish fabric, which was issued to Spanish sailors, and was quickly imported to the Caribbean and wider Spanish colonies. It is the second most common fabric found on Spanish shipwrecks and in North American colonial settlements, rarely occurring on English sites (Marken 1994, 139; Deagan and Cruxent 2002, 153). At Mount Grace, a bowl and two dishes of this fabric were recovered from the garden of cell 8 and are thought to have been deposited at the Suppression (Coppack and Keen 2019, 106). The presence of Columbia plainware and Valencia lustreware indicate that the monk who was in possession of these vessels had direct contact with Spain, either via a Spanish visitor, or because he was himself Spanish (Roebuck, Coppack, and Hurst 1987, 20). The deed of surrender holds the signatures of all the monks present at the dissolution of the monastery, and none appear to be of Spanish heritage, indicating other links to Spain (TNA E 315/234). Hayfield (2019, 323) has further postulated that the presence of these vessels indicates Mount Grace's high status within the monastic landscape. However, their presence may also be evidence of a network of both monastic and lay contacts for Mount Grace. Both Doyle (1989a, 130) and Cariboni (2013, 47) have noticed that by sending monks from current monasteries to found new ones or to help those in difficulty, close-knit networks were forged that allowed channels of trade to open up.

Certainly, monks from the Low Countries were sent to found Sheen Charterhouse, and following the Dissolution, the remaining Carthusian monks fled back to the Low Countries where they established the charterhouse of Sheen Anglorum (Doyle 1989a, 130). The circulation of texts discussed by Doyle (1989a) also includes individuals at the Universities of Oxford and Cambridge who were recipients of Carthusian-manufactured texts, as well as other lay people. As it has been established that there was already a flourishing book network, there seems no reason to exclude the trade or gifting of ceramic items from these social networks, and a number of charterhouses had been founded in Spain by the time of the Dissolution in the 1530s.

The suggestion that these ceramics were not being imported specifically to Mount Grace but were instead being brought with the monks themselves as they relocated to the North Yorkshire priory from elsewhere is not impossible. There are many records of English monks staying in Europe and vice versa. One Dan Henry was professed at Bruges but died at Hinton in the late fifteenth century (Thompson 1930, 284); Dan Richard Dixton of Axholme was also a monk of Hinton, stayed at Mont-Dieu and died at St Martin's in Naples in 1473 (Thompson 1930, 286) and in 1429 Dom John Joliis was sent from Beauvale to the Charterhouse of the Holy Spirit at Gosnay in France (Thompson 1930, 287). Despite the restrictions on the monks owning personal property, certain items for furnishing the cell would have likely been maintained and used by one person, and therefore transferred with the monk.

The example of Thomas Golwynne, a monk of the London Charterhouse, exemplifies this transferal of goods perfectly. Golwynne relocated to Mount Grace Priory in January 1520, and a document dated the 25th of that month lists all the items which he brought with him (TNA SP 1/19, f. 169). The following passage refers to vessels he carried with him:

> Be yt Remembyrd that I Dane Thomas Golwyne monke professyd of the howse of London hadde wt me by the lycens of the honorable Fader prior of the sayd howse of London Dan Wylliam Tynbegh: when I departyd from London un to Mownte Grace All these things under wrytten the xxv day of January in the year of owre lord ml cccccxix...

> ...Item a lytell brasyn morter wt a pestyll gven by the gyfte of a frende of myn

> Item ij pewtyr dysshes ij sawcers an a podynger & a lytell sqware dysshe for butter

> Item a new chafyng dysshe of laten gevyn to us and ij new tyne botylles gevyn by a kynsman of owrs

> Item a brasyn chafer that ys to hete in water

> Item a brasse panne of a galon gevyn to us lyke wyse...

...Item a dwbyll styll to make wt aqua vite that ys to say a lymbeke wt a serpentyn closyd both yn oon.

Although monks were prohibited from owning personal property, this does not seem to have been enforced quite as stringently as one might expect. Golwynne explicitly refers to items that have been given to him by lay patrons. 'by the gyfte of a frende of myn', 'gevyn by a kynsman of owrs'. The vessels he brings with him – a pestle and mortar, dishes, saucers, podinger (porringer), butter dish, chafing dish, bottles, chafer, pan and a double still – are largely for cooking purposes, items one may expect to find in the cell. Golwynne does not specifically mention ceramic items, but as Henisch (1976, 174) and Brears (2012, 222) have suggested, often ceramics would not be seen to be worth noting, as largely disposable, they could be easily replaced and represented no great value for the owner (Hammond 1993, 103). The items listed are of greater value, and it may have been that Golwynne would have been supplied with ceramic vessels when he reached Mount Grace, removing the need to carry them with him (Hayfield 2019, 323). Largely the items are made of brass, spelt 'brasse' or 'brasyn', with the exception of the pewter dishes. These are not expensive materials, but they would be long lasting, not as fragile as ceramics. There was a ready market for these vessels at the Suppression, as the metal could be melted down, and this is most likely the reason why no examples of metal vessels were excavated from Mount Grace (Roebuck, Coppack, and Hurst 1987, 23).

It has been suggested by Hayfield (2019, 323) that the Carthusian monks would have been issued a standard set of ceramic items for their cell from a central store, which seems to be represented in the archaeological record by the high number of local wares such as Ryedale ware. This ware constituted 31.8% of the total vessels excavated and is by far the largest group of ceramics (fig. 6.2). This centralised distribution questions how far personal preference may be accounted for if the monks were all provided with the same items. The theory of a central ceramic store is further exemplified by the chapter from the Carthusian statutes on the furnishing of the cell. This passage (C.C. 28.5) illustrates the items given to the monk for cooking and eating, to be kept for his own use:

...And since, like other necessary tasks which suit abjection and humility, we also make for ourselves our kitchen, the hermit is given two pots, two bowls, a third for bread or in its place a towel. A fourth bowl, quite large, is used for washing; two spoons, a knife for bread, a pot, a cup, a receptacle for water, a salt cellar, a small plate, two small bags for vegetables, a hand towel. For fire, two small logs, tinder, a flint, a stock of wood, and an axe. And for work, a curved axe...

Whether the vessels stated above would all be ceramic is debatable, as although it has been established that pottery made up a lot of tablewares, storage vessels, cooking pots and urinals, this evidence comes solely from the archaeological record, rather than from any contemporary documentation (Roebuck, Coppack and Hurst 1987, 20). It is likely that some items would be wooden, being easier to produce quickly within the precinct. Certainly, the dishes would be wooden or metal, as ceramic dishes were not produced in England until the seventeenth century (Willmott 2018, 702).

Another passage in the Statutes reads 'For all monks, but us especially, should certainly wear humble and used

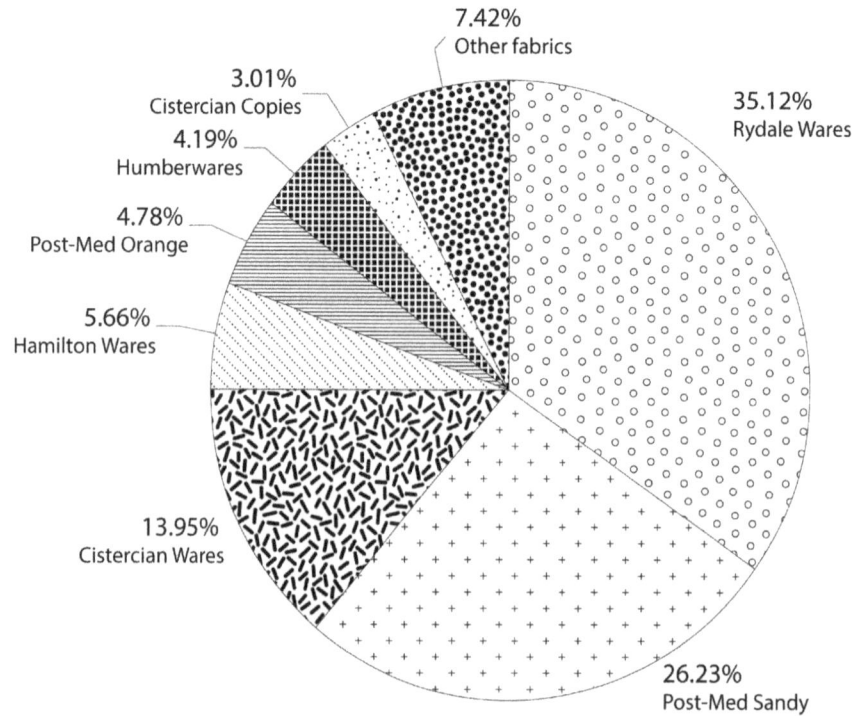

Figure 6.2. Proportions of domestic fabric types excavated at Mount Grace Priory.

clothing, and everything else we use should be worthless objects, poor and meagre.' (C.C. 28) It could be suggested, based on this statement, that the ceramic products the monks owned not from the central store, were donated to the priory, likely from wealthy benefactors or patrons, and therefore there was no choice on the part of the monks as to what quality or quantity they were given.

Overall, the ceramic assemblage from the site seems to fit with the norm for monastic sites in North Yorkshire. Comparison with the assemblage from Kirkstall Abbey, also in North Yorkshire, indicates that Mount Grace had a much wider range of wares. At Kirkstall, 98.67% of the excavated pottery was domestic (Moorhouse and Wrathmell 1987, 66-70), and of that, only 3.36% was non-local, coming from the Midlands, and the south-east (Moorhouse and Wrathmell 1987, 107). There were also very small amounts of imported wares excavated from Kirkstall: stoneware constituted 1.16% of the assemblage, while tin-glazed earthenware was only represented by 0.17% of the 595 vessels (Moorhouse and Wrathmell 1987, 66-70). There was no imported coarseware. It should be noted, however, that the Kirkstall assemblage was located largely in service areas, as well as some pieces from the cloister and refectory, compared to the majority of Mount Grace's pottery being situated in the cells.

Mount Grace's wider assemblage may stem from the international nature of the order, the acquisition of items by individual monks from different locations, and the collection of pottery in one specific individual place, rather than communally, as in a conventional monastery. However, the large presence of Ryedale ware, a fabric local to Mount Grace, is highly suggestive of a central store of ceramics to supply the monks. Every cell featured at least one sherd of Ryedale, and it is likely that this was a readily available, cheap fabric that the monks could easily get hold of. The ceramic evidence from Mount Grace indicates both its high status as a monastery and its desire for austerity, an interesting combination, which demonstrates the varied and international nature of the charterhouse.

The pottery assemblage from the London Charterhouse was not quite as extensive as that of Mount Grace, and the excavation was not able to recover the whole site. Nonetheless, a large range of fabric types was located, utilitarian Borderwares being the most numerous, with some imported ceramics also (Blackmore 2000, 3). The most noticeable thing about the London assemblage is the high number of local wares compared to Mount Grace (fig. 6.3). This is true for Coventry as well. At both sites, between 92% and 95% of the pottery consisted of local fabrics, compared to only 85% at Mount Grace. This may be explained by London and Coventry's close proximity to a number of pottery centres, and therefore there was no need to import other fabrics (Goddard 2004, 58; Orton 1979, 358; Blackmore and Pearce 2010, 19-20, 235-236; McCarthy and Brooks 1988, 73). Soden (1995, 91) noted that at Coventry, a large proportion of tablewares and storage vessels in local fabrics were found in the cells, where these fabrics were not found elsewhere on the site. This suggests that the house's central store of dining vessels was only of local fabrics, and an alternative, perhaps harder-wearing fabric was preferred for cooking vessels.

The site at Witham, on the other hand, produced few items which may be compared with the other assemblages. The pottery was very sparse, with only 39 fragments recovered (Burrow and Burrow 1990, 171). These were mostly jugs and cooking pots, and the majority of the sherds were recovered from trench XIII, which was the garden of the only cell excavated. The excavators decided that the small

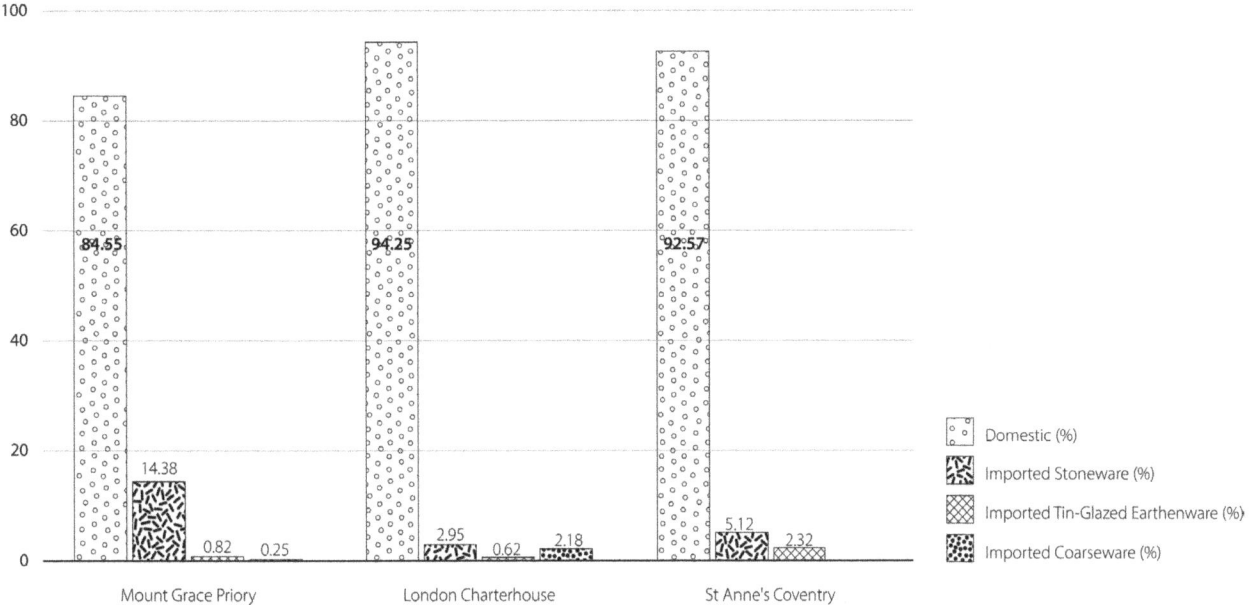

Figure 6.3. Chart comparing the proportions of domestic and imported ceramics recovered from excavations at Mount Grace Priory, London Charterhouse, and St Anne's, Coventry.

size of the assemblage did not justify further analysis, and so there is no information as to the fabric type of any of the sherds. The assemblage would merit reanalysis in comparison with other Carthusian sets of finds.

6.1.2 Writing and Book Manufacture Implements

Although a number of religious orders manufactured books both for their own and secular use, none surpassed the Carthusians in their circulation of texts, extending their network beyond Britain, and conspicuous in their leading role in the manufacture of books (Doyle 1989b, 114). Six of the cells surrounding the Great Cloister at Mount Grace provided evidence for book manufacture within the charterhouse, cell 8 and cells 10-14. Within these six cells, it is possible to identify five distinct occupations of the monks. In order to examine the material culture succinctly, this section will evaluate the finds within these occupations of scribe, corrector, illuminator, binder and printer.

Guigo I, the fifth prior of La Grande Chartreuse was a propagator of learning and book production. He ensured that in writing the Carthusian Statutes all those entering the house would be trained as scribes. The statutes outline the items a monk would be provided in his cell for book production: 'And for writing: a writing desk, pens, chalk, two pumice stones, two inkwells, a knife, two razors to level the surface of the parchment, a punch, an awl, a lead weight, a ruler, a board for ruling the page, tablets, a writing stylus' (C.C. 28:2). Guigo also discussed the spiritual benefits of the books, describing them as 'immortal food for our souls', (C.C. 28:3) and explained that as the monks are unable to leave the cell to conduct charitable works in secular society, this is their way of contributing to the spiritual well-being of the public: 'Because we cannot preach the word of God by mouth, we may with our hands'. However, the Carthusians' skill in book production cannot only be attributed to Guigo's enthusiasm. There are other factors in this, including the growing desire by lay persons to have access to devotional texts, and the understanding that the laity were able to access religion by listening to these texts, of which more will be discussed in the course of this chapter. The Carthusians were not the only order to produce books, but from the early thirteenth century, book production was not the main focus of other orders' manual activity, and members of secular society began to work as scribes (Thomson 2008, 166). However, as Doyle (1990, 13) has stated, 'the monastic order for which proportionately the most explicit evidence survives of book production by its members is the Carthusian'. Book production thus became an important element of Carthusian identity in Britain.

Although only 12 books have been linked by Ker (1964, 132) to Mount Grace, Doyle (1998, 122) notes that a further 106 books are known to be of Carthusian origin, but are yet to be assigned a house. This is due to a number of factors, including the movement of the monks across the country and continent, making it often difficult to establish a place of origin, especially without an *ex libris* or scribe's name. Furthermore, the Dissolution of the Monasteries meant that many books were lost, and as book lists for the English charterhouses have not survived, it is impossible to say how many may have been destroyed or taken to other charterhouses abroad following the suppression.

The production of books began with animal skins (sheep, goat, or calf) that had been stretched, scraped, and dried (Howsam 2016, 140). These skins were cut to the desired dimensions and collected into sets of 4 sheets (8 pages) or 5 sheets (10 pages), to make a quire (Howsam 2016, 142-3). These quires were not constructed into a book, however, until the writing and illuminating were finished. First, margins were pricked onto the page to guide the rulings using a parchment pricker or awl (fig. 6.4). Next, lines would be ruled on the page, using a ruler and a writing lead. This ensured the writing would be straight and each line would be equidistant from each other. Though quills may have been used for writing (Thomson *et al.* 2008, 81), copper alloy pens are more likely. They could be used on parchment or paper and were longer lasting than quills, and pens of this type dating to as early as the thirteenth century have been found in London excavations (Egan 1998, 271). In cells 10 and 11 a number of items definitely related to writing were recovered; pens, writing leads, graphite, and book mounts or clasps which may have been accidentally disposed of or which were scraps ready to be recycled and reused.

Ready-made inks were available to the charterhouses, but it is likely that the monks made their own ink, as a grinding stone was recovered from cell 12. If letters were to be illuminated, the scribe would leave space for these to be filled in, although there are many examples of where this did not happen such as the example of letters patent from July 1461 granting Hinton Charterhouse 50 marks annually (fig. 6.5) (TNA E 328/310). The scribe would then write out the text and may have highlighted capital letters in red, a process known as rubrication. Later readers often wrote notes in the margins also, as in this example from BL Harley MS 2373, f. 15v (fig. 6.6)

Although no specific cell for a corrector has been established, it is highly likely that one of the monks would have been responsible for correcting the manuscripts before they were bound together. A Carthusian miscellany attributed to one of the Northern charterhouses (BL Add. MS. 37049) shows a number of pages which have been corrected in red ink (fig. 6.7). In some cases, the scribe would leave space, perhaps where they were unsure of the correct translation, for the corrector to add the right sentence in (fig. 6.8). The scribe would have also been instructed to leave space for any decoration or illuminated letters (Morgan 2008, 93). Coppack (2008, 174) has already asserted that Cell 8 contained large amounts of scrap metal, likely ready to be melted down and recycled into new book fittings. Largely these scraps are of book mounts or clasps, but also present are the tongs or pliers used to manipulate the metals, and a paint or inkwell which contained a red pigment of some sort, along with part of what may have been a pen (Keen 2019, 344-345).

Figure 6.4. Example of margin pricking to guide ruled lines from BL Lansdowne MS 1201, f. 9r. This manuscript belonged to Sheen Charterhouse and contains rules for the Carthusian Order.

The presence of these last two objects suggests that the binder may have needed to do last-minute correction.

Cells 12 and 13 contained items perhaps more associated with illumination, such as the oyster shell palettes, and the grinding stone, as well as finds such as tweezers, which may not be immediately obvious, but were used for placing gold leaf onto the page (Keen 2019, 344-345). Similarly, the writing leads recovered from cells 10 and 13 were likely used to trace the outline of figures or letters to be illuminated onto the page before colouring, or for ruling lines before writing (Morgan 2008, 92). The outlines being drawn, the colour would have been added next, the inks held in oyster shell palettes, and white highlights were sometimes added to give depth to the image (Morgan 2008, 94). Finally, the outlines were redrawn in black ink, and detail was added (Morgan 2008, 94). As with the spaces left by scribes for lines of text, some manuscripts were never fully illuminated and were left with either a space or the empty lead-drawn outline on the page, such as in a document from December 1574, selling the granges previously owned by Hinton Charterhouse (fig. 6.9) (CRES 38/514/6/1).

The coloured inks found in the oyster shell palettes in cells 12 and 13 are indicative of some of the colours used to illuminate letters and images in the books they were producing. Both green and red pigments were found at Mount Grace (Coppack and Keen 2019, 140, 147, 344), although the examples of illumination from a book copied at the London Charterhouse indicate a much wider range of colours (CUL MS Ee.4.30, f. 4r, in Smith 2016).

Once the illumination was completed, the quire would be passed to the binder, who collected all the quires together to bind them into one volume. The quires were sewn with a thick thread to straps of leather along the width of the spine (Gullick and Hadgraft 2008, 103). These straps were then attached to stiffened boards to make the cover, and then the whole volume was covered in leather, which was sometimes dyed (Gullick and Hadgraft 2008, 104). Fastenings may also have been added, which tended to be leather straps attached to a catch or clasp or mounts added to the covers, which prevented the leather from getting too worn (Gullick and Hadgraft 2008, 105). Not all manuscripts were bound, however. Some were attached to a simple parchment cover or remained in loose quires. This may have allowed them to be more easily transported (Clemens and Graham 2007, 50).

A casting mould for gothic type was recovered from Cell 11 and suggests an attempt at printing (Coppack and Keen 2019, 134). Experiments with the mould have proved that it would have been possible to cast metal letters from it (Sessions 1983, 109), and the letter shapes are similar to that of handwritten documents of the period. The printing could not have been large scale, but it has been suggested by Coppack (2008, 176) that they may have been attempting to print letters of confraternity for secular visitors or benefactors. Handwritten letters are known to have been given out to members of the public (Coppack 2008, 176), but the evidence suggests that the monks of cells 11 and 14 were trialling printed letters of confraternity.

In addition to this, lead plaques were recovered from Cells 11 and 14, with the raised retrograde phrase 'iefus nazarenus' (Coppack and Keen 2019, 134, 152), and it

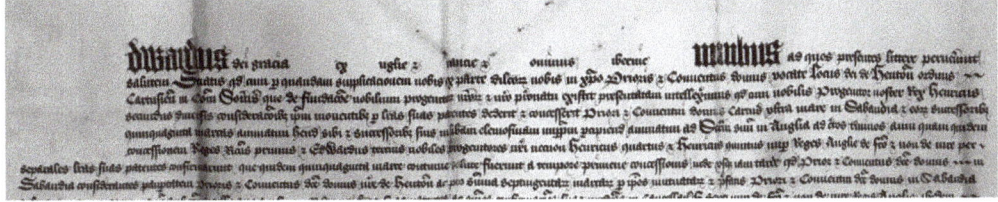

Figure 6.5. Example of missing illumination from TNA E 328/310, letters patent granting the Charterhouse at Hinton 50 marks annually. The top line is missing its capital letters, it should read 'Edwardus dei gratia Rex Anglie et Francie et Dominus Hibernie Omnibus ad quos presentes littere pervenerint'.

Communal Solitude

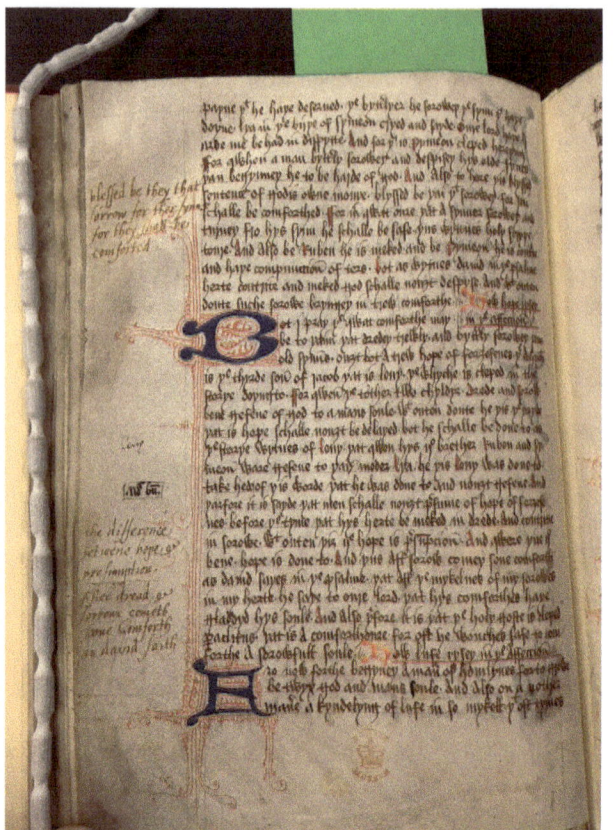

Figure 6.6. Folio 15v from BL Harley MS 2373, where a reader has added notes to the margins of the manuscript. The manuscript was made at Mount Grace Priory in around 1450.

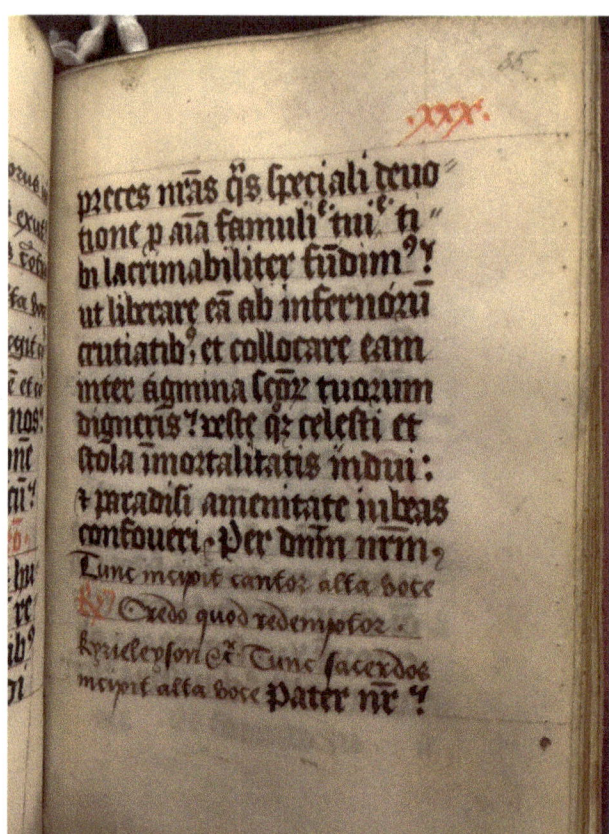

Figure 6.8. Another example from BL Lansdowne MS 1201, f. 35r, where space has been left for another scribe to add the correct sentence. The additions have been made in black ink, and in a distinctively different hand to the original scribe.

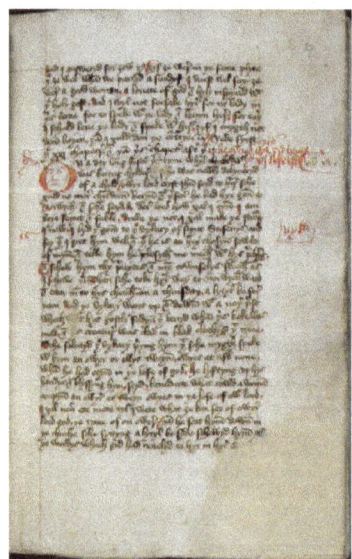

Figure 6.7. Example of correction of a manuscript in red ink from BL Add. MS 61823, f. 19r. This manuscript is the only known copy of Margery Kempe's autobiography and belonged to Mount Grace Priory.

Figure 6.9. Lead-drawn illustration of Queen Elizabeth I, filling the 'O' of 'omnibus', never fully illuminated, from a document detailing the sale of granges owned by Hinton Priory (TNA CRES 38/514/6/1).

has been suggested that these are evidence of a different type of industry amongst the monks and are related to the sale of indulgences. As Mount Grace lay on the pilgrim route between York and Durham, Coppack (2008, 176) has suggested that the monks may have been trying their hand at printing indulgences to sell to pilgrims staying in the guest house. The intercession of monks was highly valued, as evidenced in various royal foundations[1], and in the numerous bequests to the monks, so it is likely that this was a plausible and lucrative business (Hughes 1988, 76, 110). Sessions (1983) suggested that Mount Grace was the location of one of the first printing centres outside London and Westminster. However, as Coppack (2008, 176) clearly states, until one of these printed documents is discovered, this remains a theory.

The monks, as demonstrated by the material culture, were 'producing books on an industrial scale' (Coppack 2008, 175), likely to be distributed not only to other charterhouses but also to the secular world. Both Mount Grace and Beauvale copied religious literature for their secular patrons (Hughes 1988, 109), and at the foundation of the London Charterhouse in 1371, the bishop of London, Michael Northburgh, wrote to the houses at Witham and Hinton informing them that it was their duty 'to teach and edify others' (Hughes 1988, 108). In August 1532, John Houghton, the Prior of the London Charterhouse, wrote to the Cologne Charterhouse (who owned a printing press), ordering ten copies of the opera of Denys the Carthusian, and twenty copies of *De contemptu mundi* and *Scala religiosorum*, as the English Carthusians were unable to keep up with the public demands for these books (Jones and Walsham 2010, 121; Erler 2013, 127). Large (1975, 202) has suggested that Houghton had hoped that loaning copies of the works of Denys the Carthusian to members of the public would 'prove conducive to the conversion of many who had fallen into heresy'. This may also, however, refer to the impact of hearing the books being read, and preaching on those topics. Although it is not stated, it must be assumed that these heretical persons must have been able to read at least basic Latin in order for the texts to have any effect on their spiritual health. Whilst the Carthusians did translate texts into the vernacular, such as the *Orologium Sapiencia*, it is unlikely that those ordered from Germany by John Houghton were printed in English (Brantley 2007, 53).

The Carthusians' use of the vernacular in the great majority of their texts points to an ideal for greater accessibility of spiritual texts than using Latin, which isolated a large portion of the population. Vincent Gillespie (1989, 317) noted a growing desire of the laity to read texts previously limited to the cloistered religious. He demonstrates this through the second translation into English of Thomas Kempis' *De Imitacione Christi,* and Suso's *Orologium Sapientie*, which were both made at the request of lay people (Gillespie 1989, 319). Key to this is also the realisation of the potential of devotional texts for lay audiences, and even those members of the clergy who were less literate (Gillespie 1989, 318). Even if the public were unable to read the texts, they were still able to access the divine by listening to someone else read the texts out loud, and so English translations were vital.

---

[1] See Chapter 4 for discussion of the intercessory value of the Carthusians.

The assemblage of items relating to book manufacture is very interesting at Mount Grace Priory because they can be linked to several specific cells, allowing for an interpretation which places scribes, illuminators and binders in their own specific environments. The presence of printing materials adds a new facet of understanding, suggesting that the monks, perhaps inspired by the printing press recently installed at the Cologne Charterhouse, were pursuing a different type of industry, and manufacturing letters of confraternity. This illustrates their connection to the outside world despite their inability to leave the cell.

A comparison of writing implements between Mount Grace, Coventry, and London draws some interesting points. At London, only one find referred to as a 'possible' book clasp was located from the whole site (Barber and Thomas 2002, 69). This very low recovery rate may be due to excavation bias but is more likely to stem from the method in which the charterhouse was dissolved and subsequently re-used.

From 1535, the London Carthusians were under observation by the King's commissioners, following the execution of John Houghton, the previous prior. For two years, members of the King's court confiscated the possessions of the monks and attempted to convert them to Protestantism (BL Cotton Cleopatra E/IV, ff. 42-43). It is possible that during this time, the number of books being produced, and therefore the number of writing implements required had significantly diminished, leading to a smaller archaeological record. The monks leaving the priory in 1537 also took the items of their cell with them, leaving only those tools which were of no further use (TNA SP 1/139, f. 148) As previously discussed, the monastery was later used as a store, and the cells were rented to families. This immediate reoccupation of the site, unlike Mount Grace, which was left derelict for many years, may have contributed to the low recovery of writing implements and book fittings.

Similarly, the charterhouse at Coventry yielded few writing implements or items related to book manufacture (Soden 1995, 128, 130). Two stylus points or parchment prickers were found in the garden of Cell III and in the church (Soden 1995, 129). In the garden of Cell III was also a corner reinforcement piece for a book (Soden 1995, 129). Three other book reinforcement plates were found during the excavation, one within grave 37, which was located in the nave of the church (Soden 1995, 49, 73, 129). The only other item was a finely worked bone handle, thought to be part of a stylus or awl (Soden 1995, 126).

Although not as low a recovery rate as in London, the finds from Coventry are still few. The item found within grave 37 likely belonged to a secular benefactor, as Carthusian monks tended not to be buried in the church, but in the garth of the great cloister. Coventry also had close relations with local society, much more so than Mount Grace. Without an excavation of the whole site, it is difficult to draw conclusions comparative to Mount Grace, as only four of the cells were excavated at Coventry. With the significantly reduced size of excavation, it is not surprising that fewer items relating to book manufacture were recovered.

At Witham Charterhouse, two mounts and a plate were recovered relating to book manufacture, all in copper alloy (Burrow and Burrow 1990, 173-174). Although no writing implements were recovered, it is unlikely that the Witham monks were not involved in book manufacture. In fact the author of *Liber de quadripartito exercito cellae*, a treatise on the four-fold spiritual contemplation of the cell, was a Witham monk, Adam of Dryburgh (Herbert McAvoy 2011, 59-60; Thompson 1932, 483), and one of the most prolific Carthusian scribes, Stephen Dodesham began his profession at Witham (Doyle 1997, 96) so there must have been some provision for writing, copying and binding.

6.1.3 Dress Accessories

The category of dress accessories refers here to items which are used both functionally in dress, such as pins and buckles, as well as those decorative items such as strap ends and mounts, which serve as a highly visible indicator of social status. The items are often made of metal, usually copper alloy or iron, but can also be made from bone. This section will consider the dress accessories excavated at Mount Grace Priory by functional type, and relate them to available documentary sources, allowing for some reconstruction of monastic life at the priory.

Dress accessories can be interpreted as simply indicating the types of clothing worn by an individual, but on a more personal level, they indicate the status of that person or the persona they wished to project. For monks, these may have been characteristics such as humility, poverty, and modesty. Although items such as belt fittings could be highly decorative, dress accessories served a higher purpose in the 'construction, maintenance and subversion of identity' (Cassels 2013, 2). Despite being everyday items, the objects were symbolically significant, defining the socio-economic status of the wearer, at a time when these items were worn ubiquitously by all levels of society (Cassels 2013, 3-5).

At Mount Grace Priory dress accessories were recovered from the south west cloister range, the kitchen, and cells 8-12 and 14 (table 6.2). The location of these finds can be indicative of the status of the owner, as areas such as the kitchen would have been exclusively the environ of the lay brothers, and as such, one can expect to recover items in keeping with the activities conducted here.

Buckles were attached to leather straps and used to fasten articles of clothing. In some cases, buckles were also used on shoes (Egan and Pritchard 2002, 53). Egan and Pritchard (2002, 50) have articulated how difficult it can be to differentiate between buckles used for horse equipment, and those used for dress, as both categories use similar forms and materials. The buckle plate provided a more secure means of attaching the buckles to the leather strap (Egan and Pritchard 2002, 55). A single piece of metal would be folded around the frame of the buckle and attached to the strap with rivets. Where a plate was not used, the leather was folded back on itself around the frame, and secured with stitching (Egan and Pritchard 2002, 55). Aesthetically, the flat surface of the buckle plate could be decorated (Egan and Pritchard 2002, 56).

Similar to the buckle fittings, belt plates could be added to a leather strap for decoration. Mounts were further used in this manner, providing a means of decorative expression for the wearer. Mounts were often made from sheet metal, incised with designs, and attached using a rivet through the leather. As with the buckles, there is no way of differentiating between mounts that were used as dress accessories, and those used for furniture, book covers, horse harnesses or animal collars (Egan and Pritchard 2002, 162; Cassels 2013, 42).

Lace chapes, also known as points, or aiglets were tubes of metal attached to the ends of laces to prevent fraying and to facilitate threading through eyelets in clothing (Egan

Table 6.2. Dress accessories excavated from different areas at Mount Grace Priory.

	Buckle	Buckle Fitting	Belt Fitting	Lace Chape	Pin	Mount	Strap End
Cell 8	3	2	4	1		5	2
Cell 9	1	1	1				
Cell 10			1	1			
Cell 11	1						
Cell 12	1				1		
Cell 14				1	1	1	
SW Cloister	1		1	7	4	2	
Kitchen	1			5	1		
Total	8	3	7	15	7	9	2

and Pritchard 2002, 281). They were manufactured from sheet metal rolled into tubes, with a straight seam down one side. There were a number of methods of finishing the chape, either with an edge-to-edge or overlapping seam, and a finished end or folded tab. Chapes would be used on shoelaces, but also on lacing for hose and dresses.

Pins were used widely in dressing ladies' hair, but in a monastic setting, they would have been used to fasten pieces of clothing, for example, to hold the edges of a gown around the shoulders (Egan and Pritchard 2002, 297). Thicker pins were also used to fasten heavy outer garments (Egan and Pritchard 2002, 297).

Strap ends were attached to the end of a belt strap. Manufactured from sheet metal, some were folded from a single sheet and attached with rivets, and some were made from two separate sheets, joined together with rivets. They protected the end of the leather or fabric strap and prevented it from being worn away, whilst also facilitating it being passed through the buckle loop (Cassels 2013, 36). Furthermore, they provided another space for decoration on the clothing (Egan and Pritchard 2002, 129)

The number of items recovered from Mount Grace Priory relating to dress is not vast. There may be some confusion with mounts which could be used both on belts or on books, as they are similar in size and shape, so cannot always be distinguished. A number of buckle fittings were recovered, as well as a large number of lace chapes and pins. Belt fittings were similarly popular. A comparison with the religious sites assessed by Standley (2013, 12) shows that the assemblage is fairly average as concerns the frequency of items. The great majority of items were manufactured from copper alloy which as a relatively cheap metal, Standley (2013, 17) suggests would be more suitable and in keeping with the ideals of humility and poverty. This was also in keeping with the Sumptuary Law enacted in 1363, which restricted the types of metals that could be worn by the lower classes, leaving copper alloy as a suitably low-status material (*Statutes of the Realm* I, 380-382).

The inventory of clothes for Dan Andrew when he moved to Witham, is both useful on its own and in conjunction with the statutes (TNA E135/2/46). Dated to the reign of Henry VII, the inventory lists a habit, 5 kirtles, a cowl, and another of wool, a woollen shirt, 2 caps, a singlet, 2 lined coats, a pilcher, a pair of short hose, a pair of socks, and a shaving cloth. These are all common items to be owned by a monk of the charterhouse. The woollen shirt is likely the same as that in the statutes, a hair shirt.

Similarly, the statutes list cowls, socks, caps, pelisses and tunics (C.C. 28:1). The shaving cloth may be a sort of face towel but could refer to the sharpening strap for the razor. The statutes also list a belt and four pairs of shoes (C.C. 28:1), which have more lasting material elements in the archaeological record than the aforesaid items. Belt fittings such as strap ends and buckles were among the assemblage from Mount Grace, as were a large number of lace chapes from the ends of shoelaces or other lacing (Keen 2019, 344). The statutes specify that the Carthusian monk should wear 'humble and used clothing' and therefore no items of particular luxury (C.C. 28:1). Likewise, neither the assemblage nor Dan Andrew's list gives any indication of high-status items:

> Imprimis iij habytes as they come by cowrse
>
> Item ij newe stamyn shyrtes and j olde
>
> Item ij newe stamyn colys and j olde
>
> Item ij newe hodys and j olde
>
> Item a new coote lynyde & an olde mantell
>
> Item a wyde sloppe furryd to put over all my gere by the gyfte of my lady Conway
>
> Item a newe cappe and an olde
>
> Item a newe pylche of the gyft of Mr Saxby
>
> Item an olde pylche. And iij payer of hosen
>
> Item iij payer of new sokkes & ij payer of olde
>
> Item iij olde syleces and a lumbare
>
> Item a new payer of korkyd shone lynyd and j payer of doble solyd shone
>
> Item a payer of blankettes & ij goode pylows and ij lyttle pylows & a kosshyn to knele on
>
> Item a newe mantell by the gyfte of syr John Rawson Knyght of the Roodes
>
> (TNA E135/2/46)

The new items the monk brought with him, 'ij newe stamyn shyrtes...' do not denote any luxury. 'Stamyn' was a type of coarse worsted cloth, noted for being worn by ascetics (OED) and given as a suitable fabric in the Ancrene Riwle (BL Cotton MS Cleop. C/VI).

The combination of archaeological and documentary evidence allows for an excellent understanding of dress within the Carthusian world. The accessories' importance as social indicators has here been put to use highlighting the humility and austerity of the wearer, in contrast to secular decorative items. That the monks were provided with specific items of clothing points to a strong homogeneity among the monks, opting for plain, coarse styles of dress that emphasise their adherence to the Carthusian life.

The comparison of dress accessories draws some different conclusions to that of book manufacture. Those found at the London Charterhouse all originate in the western part of the precinct, the inner court and the service area. None of these items therefore can be said with any certainty to have belonged to the monks. It is unlikely that the monks would have visited this area of the precinct at all, and the finds are much more likely to have been the possessions of the lay brothers or secular guests, which will be discussed in due course. It was not unheard of for the London Carthusians to host a secular guest for a period of time. Indeed, Sir Thomas More lived at the charterhouse for four years (Barber and Thomas 2002, 71; Marius 1999, 34-35), and the Visitation of 1405 forbid preaching to the laity in the inner court (Hope 1925, 43), so the secular contribution to the archaeological record should not be dismissed as ephemeral.

As none of the London dress accessories can be connected with the monks, it is not particularly suitable for comparison with the Mount Grace assemblage. The finds from Coventry however, were recovered from across the site, and feature a wide range of accessories. These finds included a large number of pins, as well as belt eyelets, strap ends, studs, buttons, and lace chapes (Soden 1995, 129-138). Compared to Mount Grace the assemblage is small, yet the size of the excavation was equally small, so this is to be expected. As at Mount Grace, the Coventry assemblage is largely made from copper alloy, which could be regarded as a cheaper and more readily available alternative to gold and silver, thus reflective of Carthusian ideals of austerity. None of the dress accessories were decorative, which is in keeping with the plain items seen at Mount Grace, and the theory that plain dress accessories were a method of increasing congruity amongst the monks.

The dress accessories recovered from Witham were again plain, as at Coventry and Mount Grace. As only one cell was excavated, this may explain the relatively low level of finds from this site, which consisted of a lace chape, mount, strap end, and thimble (Burrow and Burrow 1990, 171-173).

6.1.4 Summary

Comparison of the five charterhouses has proved difficult in parts. Hinton Priory could offer no material culture evidence whatsoever, and Witham's finds were scant. Both London and Coventry provided good if small, assemblages to compare with Mount Grace which showed a number of similarities and differences between the urban and rural charterhouses.

For writing implements and book manufacture items, compared to the vast assemblage from Mount Grace, London and Coventry had very few items. This was due to a number of factors including re-use of the site, recovery bias and the size of the excavation, and meant that it was not possible to understand the occupations of the monks quite so vividly as at Mount Grace.

Overall, the excavation and finds at Mount Grace greatly surpass any other British Carthusian site, and owes this to the excellent preservation immediately following the Dissolution, as well as the whole site excavation. Although some comparisons could be drawn from the various assemblages, largely it was impossible to make refined conclusions due to the huge difference in the volume of the finds.

6.2 Material Culture of the Lay Brethren

So far, this discussion has focussed solely on the professed members of the monastery. However, the lay assemblages from excavated charterhouses therefore should be investigated similarly, and where possible, in comparison with the monastic assemblages. Identifying the laity within the monastic precinct presents a new challenge, as there are no set rules as to what material items denote a lay brother as opposed to a monk. It may prove that there is no material difference between the two communities that lived in such close quarters, and that it is only through finds locations that one may make tentative assumptions about the ownership of these items.

Pursuing this theory, three excavated sites have made specific reference to the material culture of the lay brothers, Mount Grace and the charterhouses at London and Coventry, and it is these three sites that will form the basis of this investigation.

6.2.1 Mount Grace Priory

The excavation at Mount Grace examined the six cells surrounding the lesser cloister, which are known to have housed lay brothers in the sixteenth century, as well as the kitchen and area of the south west cloister (Coppack and Keen 2019, 244). Of the six cells excavated at Mount Grace, only one provided any material culture from its occupation, cell 20. This comprised 104 sherds of pottery from a variety of domestic wares, and 25 sherds of Siegburg stoneware (Coppack and Keen 2019, 248-250). It is worth drawing some comparisons between the collections from cell 20 and that of the cells of the great cloister.

First, the range of pottery is immediately apparent as being much poorer than that of the monks. Although a number of imported stoneware mugs were present, they were of one basic type, unlike the different varieties present within the monks' assemblages. The Siegburg mugs represent the only items of imported pottery within the cell; the rest of the vessels are domestic wares and produced locally. Although cell 20 produced vessels of the same fabrics as that of the monks' cells, the number and variety of fabrics are much less than that of the monastic areas.

Comparison with some of the assemblages of other monks' cells surrounding the great cloister shows that the materials excavated are of a similar quality to that of cell 20. The finds from cell 5, for example, comprised only 4 sherds of domestic wares, and 1 sherd of a Raeren mug (Coppack and Keen 2019, 79). Although this is not representative of the cell as a whole, it is a vital point to make as there are a variety of factors that affect the interpretation of an assemblage, and that recovery bias within each cell means that the interpretation of the material culture is subject to the contextual information provided by the accompanying report. It would appear that the lay brother's cell does feature lesser quality materials than the majority of the monks' cells.

6.2.2 The London Charterhouse

As members of the public were allowed entry to the outer court at the London Charterhouse, this means that the assemblage recovered from that area cannot be assured to be representative of only the lay brother. Barber and Thomas (2002, 30) noted that the refuse deposits excavated from buildings 1 and 2 and Open Area 2 may have contained items dumped by local citizens as well as the material produced by the activity of the lay brothers. This makes it more difficult to define the difference between the secular items and those of the lay brothers, especially as the items owned by both parties were very similar.

Barber and Thomas (2002, 28) suggested that Buildings 1 and 2 and Open Area 2 would have served as the inner court of the charterhouse, where food preparation and storage were conducted, and where service functions were carried out. This would have included making habits for the monks, and other manual tasks vital for the upkeep of the monastery. As the lay brothers were in charge of receiving visitors, the inner court would have witnessed a greater level of lay influence and interaction, resulting in the mixed material culture already stated.

The material culture from these lay areas was characterised by a restricted range of pottery, mostly utilitarian vessels, charred grains, fruit seeds, and some interesting accessioned finds (Barber and Thomas 2002, 29). These items, in particular, illustrate the merging of religious and secular. Finds included a copper alloy scabbard chape, decorative copper alloy pins, a double strap end, and a 30g lead weight (Barber and Thomas 2002, 29). Although it is impossible to say for certain, the decorative pins were unlikely to have been owned by members of the Carthusian community. The scabbard chape, depending on whether it was intended to hold a sword or dagger, could be construed as of either religious or secular origin, as the lay brothers may have carried daggers, depending on their occupation.

Therefore, once again, it is difficult to interpret the lay brothers' influence on the material culture of the London Charterhouse, as it is entwined with that of the secular visitors, and of the local citizens. The similarities in pottery types makes it impossible to distinguish between the two, and the few accessioned finds do little to help this confusion.

6.2.3 Coventry Charterhouse

At Coventry, no area specifically belonging to the lay brethren was excavated, but note was made that areas such as the kitchens would have predominantly been used by the laity, rather than the monks, and as such, personal items located in these areas may be supposed to be of lay origin (Soden 1995, 91). The charterhouse was not wholly excavated, but of the areas that were, the excavators noted a marked difference between the monks and lay brothers in their material culture (Soden 1995, 91). Particular fabric types and pottery forms were only found in certain areas. Tablewares were of local origin, and distribution was focused on the cells, the fabrics being unique to those areas (Soden 1995, 91). The domestic, or lay area, however, was characterised by a focus on storage and food preparation vessels, such as cisterns, jugs, and cooking pots (Soden 1995, 92). Largely these vessels were of Midlands Purpleware (Soden 1995, 92). This area did also feature a large amount of fine tableware, double that of the cells, suggesting more secular interaction, not unlike the situation at London (Soden 1995, 92). It is to be expected that service areas will feature large numbers of preparation vessels, and likewise, that the cells would feature vessels of consumption. However, as no lay cell was excavated at Coventry, it is impossible to make a more meaningful comparison.

As for the small finds, a number of iron items are strikingly obvious as belonging to the lay community of the monastery. A buckle from horse furniture, an animal shoe, and shears all point to some sort of animal husbandry, whereas the stonemason's wedge and chisel point to masonry work, both types of manual work the lay brothers were involved in, contrasting with the items related to the monks' work – largely related to book manufacture (Soden 1995, 139-140).

6.2.4 Documentary Evidence

As was possible with the material culture of the monks, there is some documentary evidence for material items relating to the lay brothers. The British Library manuscript Add. MS. 11303 contains a series of statutes for the lay brothers, specifically those who resided at Sheen. For the most part, the manuscript instructs the laity on how they should comport themselves during mass, their role within the Carthusian community, and the rules for everyday life in the monastery. The passage on items for the cell reads:

Other usuall or necessarie thynges belongynge eyther to table or other uses, let be geven eache one as ye Pryour shall iudge reasonable or nedfull, Let them fynallie kepe nothinge at all what so ever by them: But what they have with lycense (Pask-Matthews 1931, 120).

Given that the lay brothers were provided with clothes from the monks' hand-me-downs (Kerr 2009, 60), it may be assumed that any tablewares would also be second-hand, and therefore there was no specific list of items that the lay brother should have in his cell. This is, of course, assuming that the statutes applicable at Sheen were similar to those across the country. Should this be true, however, it may explain some of the similar ceramic fabrics found in both the monks' and lay brothers' cells.

Those items they were allowed to keep 'with lycense' refers to the items specific to their occupation. These occupation-specific objects would very definitively distinguish monk from lay brother, as the monks would have had no part in these types of labour-intensive activities. The ironwork finds from Coventry above illustrates this distinction well. But equally, these items were located in areas of the monastery known to be frequented by the lay brothers, rather than the monks, such as the stables and other buildings of the inner court, so the distinction is also defined by its find location.

6.2.5 Summary

As has been demonstrated, the lay brothers can be much harder to identify as distinct in their material culture from the monks, or indeed from local citizens. The assemblages they produce are largely similar to that of the monks, and it is often only with the interpretation of find location that it is possible to make any distinction between ordained and lay.

Where the small finds can be very useful in this regard is in understanding the occupations of the lay brethren. From the statutes, it is known that possible manual work for the lay brothers was varied, and therefore finds such as horseshoes, shears or kitchen equipment strongly indicate lay activity. These items are consistent with find locations, usually recovered from kitchen areas, stables and workshops, which would have been the typical daily environment of the lay brother.

As far as the pottery evidence is concerned, it varies between sites as to whether there is a marked difference between a monk and lay brother or whether they are largely similar. This is unique to each house, and is likely to be a result of their location in the country, having a bearing on how readily available different pottery fabrics and types were.

6.3 Conclusions

The singular nature of the Carthusian living conditions, where each cell was separated from the next by a high wall, has meant that a discussion of material culture from these sites can address each cell as a distinct assemblage, particular to one specific individual. This has led to a discussion of the occupations of the inhabitants, and the cross-European networks that may have been maintained by the monks.

From these discussions, it has been possible to establish a higher proportion of domestic ceramics in the city charterhouses, likely due to the local pottery industry. Of the imported wares at Mount Grace, a few more exotic or high-status vessels may have indicated personal contacts in Europe, that the monk who owned these items was from that country themselves or could be representative of gifts from benefactors. The high levels of similar, local wares indicated a central store of surplus ceramics which were provided to each new monk, or which could replace broken items. Those wares tended to be plain coarsewares.

For the lay brothers at Mount Grace, the pottery assemblage demonstrates that although they had a more restricted range of fabric types, the vessels themselves were not necessarily of poorer quality than that of the monks. Finds of other materials were not recovered from the lay brothers' cells, although items in service areas such as the kitchen would have been utilised by them. In some cases, as at London Charterhouse, the material of the lay brothers was mostly indistinguishable from that of the secular guests. With the exception of items such as a scabbard chape, there were no defining qualities that ensured an item could be established as belonging to a lay brother. At Coventry however, much of the iron finds could be positively attributed to the lay brothers, as they related to tasks, such as animal husbandry, that the lay brothers would have been involved in.

Uniquely, at Mount Grace, it was possible in a number of cells to identify the occupation of each individual. The material culture indicated activities related to book manufacture such as copying, binding and printing. The prominence of the Carthusians in writing is well known from documentary sources and these finds solidify that understanding. A large range of dress accessories was uncovered at Mount Grace, mostly plain, copper alloy objects. This collection was in keeping with assemblages found at other sites and was indicative of the avoidance of particularly luxurious or expensive metals, which would have been contrary to the practices of the Carthusians.

7

The Lower House: An Archaeological Investigation at the sites of Hinton and Witham Friary

Whereas the upper house protected the spiritual wellbeing of the monastery, the friary, or lower house, kept the community running. The friary maintained a more outward-looking approach to society than the upper house, through necessities of trade, labour and hospitality. As will be discussed, not all charterhouses were split in such a fashion. In the mid-fourteenth century, the complex layout tended towards a combined house for both the monks and lay brothers, whilst still maintaining certain layers of isolation for the monks. As discussed in previous chapters (see Chapters 3 and 6), the lay brothers were carefully integrated into the charterhouse, ensuring separation in the church, but were provided with individual cells like the monks.

7.1 A Divided House

The necessity of splitting the monastery into two parts, one for the monks and one for the lay brothers, came about from the style in which the first charterhouse, La Grande Chartreuse, was constructed. Set in the middle of the Chartreuse mountains near Grenoble, the upper house, for the monks, was built higher up the mountain than the lower house, for the lay brothers. Although after an avalanche the upper house was relocated to be closer to the lower house, the names remained and persisted into the new foundations that were built across Europe. Apart from the locational value of this monastic layout, the spiritual ideals of the Carthusian Order were further served in that the lower house acted almost as a gatehouse for the upper house. Any visitors to the charterhouse would be directed first to the lower house, where they could meet with the procurator, who would refer them to the prior if necessary.

The division of the upper and lower houses meant that only certain buildings were situated in each. The buildings in the lower house were where the majority of the work took place: the kitchen, bakehouse, brewery, cheese house, granary, storehouses and laundry, but also the location for the more secular side of Carthusian living – the guest house and stables (Coppack and Aston 2002, 27). The lay brothers also had their cells here, and a chapel was provided for worship. When the houses became joined, those buildings previously located in the lower house moved to the inner court, and so the monastery still maintained its zoned layout. This conjunction of upper and lower houses was definitely in effect in Britain by the foundation of the London Charterhouse in 1371 (Barber and Thomas 2002, 16). Coppack (forthcoming, 37-38) has posited that Beauvale also founded a separate lower house but there is some uncertainty as to whether or not this was the case at Kilnalahanin.

In addition to the service buildings of the lower house, charterhouses also relied on external granges as a source of income. Hinton Priory owned granges in the Mendip Hills, at Green Ore and Whitnell, whilst Witham owned one at Charterhouse-on-Mendip[1] (Jurkowski and Ramsay 2007, 431-432; 439-440). Largely, these granges were used for sheep grazing, even though Charterhouse-on-Mendip had been used for mining lead since the Roman period and further charters were received in the twelfth-thirteenth century to mine lead (Fradley 2009, 10). The rights to mine coal were also rented out by the Carthusians at Beauvale in 1397 to William Monash of Costall for one of their granges at Kirkstall, in Yorkshire (TNA E 326/1782). The granges were maintained by a number of the lay brothers, as well as some *mercenarii* (hired labourers) working under their leadership. The granges likely served to supply their own houses with wool for bed coverings and clothing, and any surplus was sold. The charterhouses also made their own cheese from sheep's milk, but there are no records to indicate whether surplus supplies were sold at markets.

As already stated, the lower house acted as a buffer between monastic and secular life. The Carthusians discouraged any guests from staying, although guest houses were part of the monastic complex. At Witham Friary, records from the bishop of Bekynton show that the monastic community requested permission to build a guest house at the lower house and to place a baptismal font in the chapel of the lay brothers (*Reg. Bekynton*, 315-6). The charterhouse at Mount Grace seems to have been built with a guesthouse already included, and it was this structure that was converted into a mansion house following the Dissolution and the sale of land to secular patrons (Coppack and Aston 2002, 143). While the Carthusians were staunchly vegetarian, they did not limit their guests to the same dietary restrictions. The contemporary water supply plan from London Charterhouse indicates a building called the 'Flessche Kitchen,' where meat was prepared (CM MP/1/14a). The London Charterhouse was in a singular position, as the city location gave the community the opportunity for many more secular interactions than any of the other British Carthusian houses, likely due to how close the house was to other monasteries and residential areas, and its location in the middle of the West Smithfield Black Death cemetery. The presence of a separate meat kitchen may indicate that they were entertaining sufficient numbers of guests for this to become a necessity, and indeed, records from the General Chapter show that the London Charterhouse was reprimanded on more than one occasion for its lax appreciation for the Carthusian

---

[1] See Chapter 5 for further discussion of granges.

statutes, with monks eating and drinking with company in their cells (Bodl. Rawlinson MS D.318, f. 106 bis v).

The singular situation of a separate or distinct area for the lay brothers makes the investigation of the two Somerset correries particularly interesting. Although much has been written about the layout of La Grande Chartreuse, there is no certain evidence to indicate how the British lower houses were organised, and therefore the following research is of the utmost importance in understanding these sites.

7.2 Case Study 1 – Witham Friary

Witham Charterhouse is situated in Northeast Somerset, around 18 miles south of Bath (fig. 7.1). The sites of the *domus superior* and the *domus inferior* lie roughly a kilometre away from each other, the *domus superior* at Witham Hall Farm, and the *domus inferior* at Witham Friary. The charterhouse remains have been cut by the Great Western Railway, running through the northern conventual buildings (Wilson-North and Porter 1997, 82). The medieval fishponds of the charterhouse still remain to the west and are fed by the River Frome.

For the lower house, only the church and the dovecote remain, in the village of Witham Friary. A kitchen built of wattles was located to the west of the church, and nearby was the timber-built guest house (*Magna Vita*, 219). This was in the earlier phases of construction, as the *Magna Vita S. Hugonis*, from which the reference is taken, was written by Adam of Eynsham in the early thirteenth century. Wooden structures were normally connected with the oldest phases and replaced within the first few years of habitation (Coppack and Aston 2002, 28).

Prior to the foundation of the Carthusian community in Witham, the community of Augustinian canons at Bruton Abbey owned a chapel in the village of Witham Friary. The Bruton monks built the first church in around 1142, and the Carthusians were granted it as part of the original endowment when they first arrived in 1178. They were, therefore, able to make use of the church while their own buildings were in construction (McGarvie 1989, 10; Hunt and White 1878, 24).

As part of the building effort, the Carthusians renovated the church under the leadership of the third prior, Hugh of Avalon, who arrived in 1180. The vaulted ceiling was added (fig. 7.2), the walls were thickened, and it became the chapel for the lay brethren of the priory (Hunt and White 1878, 26; Mayr-Harting 2011, 193).

Details of the everyday life of the monastery are scant, there are few extant documents that illustrate the situation of the priory. Consequently, it is not known exactly how the Black Death in the mid-fourteenth century affected the charterhouse. From the Patent Rolls, it can be inferred that a good many of the lay brethren had died, but there are no details concerning the monks. The community petitioned Edward III on 16 January 1354 and on 20 October 1362, to allow them to bring in labourers from other parts of the country as the land was unworked and the harvest had not been gathered (TNA C66/239, m. 20; TNA C66/266, m. 7). The petition states that 'their servants and household in the last pestilence died totally' (TNA C66/239, m. 20) and 'their servants and household almost wholly perished in the last pestilence' (TNA C66/266, m. 7). They also petitioned to pay their labourers an elevated wage above that sanctioned by the Crown (TNA C66/246, m. 4).

The house was surrendered on 31 March 1539 to the Royal Commissioners John Tregonwell and William Petre, who valued the house at £227 1*s*. 8*d*. (Thompson 1896, 116; RCHME 1994, 2). After the Dissolution, the lay brothers' chapel was maintained for parochial use by the local community, and with the exception of the flying buttresses, which were added in 1875, it retains the same characteristic simplicity of the Carthusian Order (fig. 7.3; Wilson-North and Porter 1997, 82; McGarvie 1989, 12).

7.3 Case Study 2 – Hinton Friary

The second case study focuses on Hinton Friary, the lower house of the second Carthusian priory constructed in England. As seen in the previous section, there are few remaining features of the friary at Witham. The friary at Hinton has not been wholly built over and offers a singular opportunity to understand the layout of the lay quarters of a Carthusian house. With only a small amount of geophysical survey conducted on the site, and the land being largely undisturbed, there is potential for interesting results, which will shed new light on the life of a Carthusian lay brother. Hinton Friary (Monument No. 1030135) has only recently (December 2015) been recognised as the house of the lay brothers, highlighting the importance of this current research.

The precinct of Hinton is situated approximately 17.5 kilometres to the north of Witham Priory, near the village of Freshford, in Northeast Somerset (fig. 7.4). The sites of the Priory (NGR ST 77799 59160) and the Friary (NGR ST 78885 59189) are just over a kilometre away from each other, the Friary sitting on the west bank of the River Frome.

As at Witham, the Prior of Hinton petitioned Edward III in 1355, as their lay brethren and servants had perished in the Black Death (TNA C66/246, m. 4). They needed permission to hire new labourers from outside the area of their jurisdiction and to pay them higher than normal wages. There are no documents recording the effect of the pestilence upon the monks.

It is likely that the friary had been abandoned by the end of the fourteenth century, and the lay brothers moved to the main house, reflecting the move to a combined upper and lower house at the London Charterhouse and subsequent Carthusian monasteries (Aston 1990, 14). By 1535, the monks were definitely leasing out the Friary site, as is recorded in the *Valor Ecclesiasticus* (vol. 1, 156), 'Le Frary' brought in rents of 63*s*.

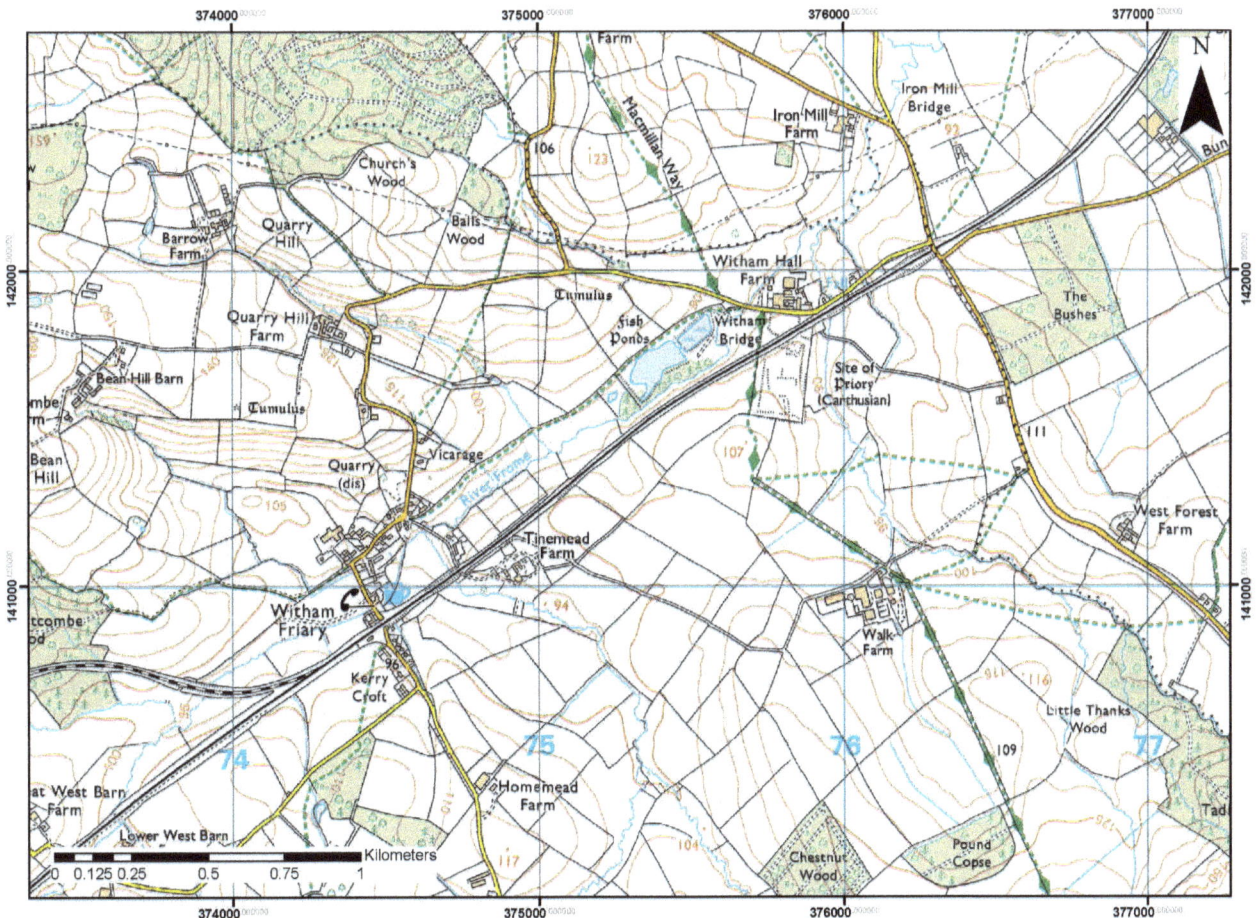

Figure 7.1. Location of Witham Friary and Witham Hall Farm in relation to each other. © Crown copyright and database rights 2022 Ordnance Survey (100025252).

Figure 7.2. Interior or the lay brothers' church at Witham Friary, showing the vaulted ceiling added by the Carthusians during renovations. © *Francesca Breeden 2022*.

7.4 Geophysical Survey

The geophysical surveys were conducted only on the lay brothers' quarters, so only these areas will be discussed. The first method to be considered will be the resistance survey. The results of each site are presented separately, including an interpretation of the recorded features. After this, the results of the magnetometer survey at Friary are discussed, with an accompanying interpretation. This will finally lead to a summary interpretation of the sites overall, and how they can be compared to each other, including inferences which can be made on the layouts of the site from their respective results.

7.4.1 Witham Friary Earth Resistance Survey

The resistance survey undertaken on the site was not able to reveal a great amount about the layout of the friary (fig. 7.5). As with the results of the LiDAR visualisations, previously discussed in chapter 4, the small open areas hindered the resistivity survey. Few anomalous features were recorded, and there were no real trends that indicated a wider context or layout for the upstanding buildings.

The only larger high-resistance anomaly revealed at Witham Friary was a rectangular feature, which likely resembles the remains of a building of some type, especially given its proximity to the medieval dovecote. The other areas

Figure 7.3. Exterior of the lay brothers' church at Witham Friary, showing the buttresses added in 1875. © *Francesca Breeden 2022*.

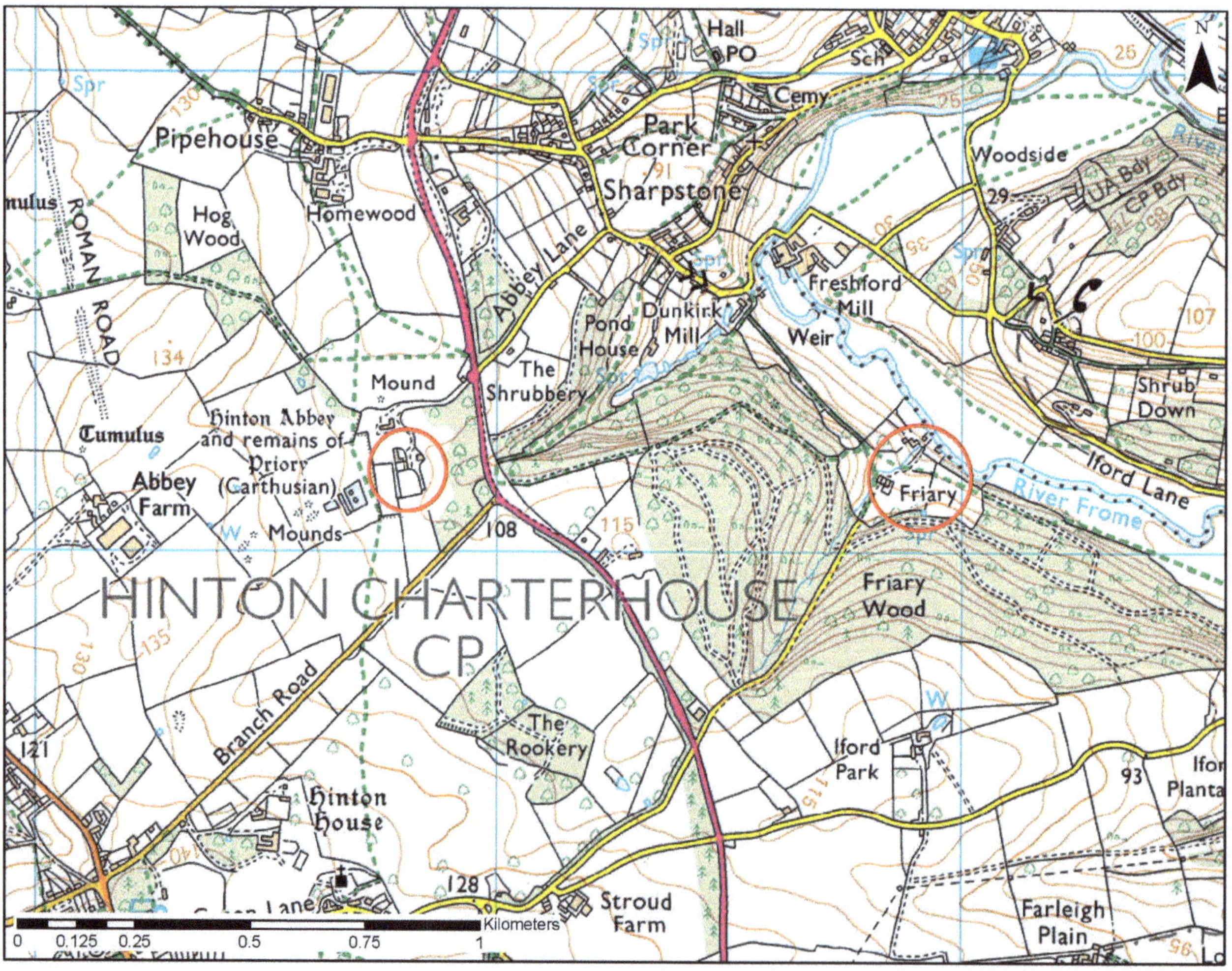

Figure 7.4. The site of Hinton Priory and the village of Friary in relation to one another. © Crown copyright and database rights 2022 Ordnance Survey (100025252).

of possible archaeological remains are not substantial enough to make any interpretation as to their original use, or their role in the layout of the wider complex. Since there is no apparent pattern or link between the areas of high-resistance features, it is impossible to even say if they are contemporary with the monastic occupation of the area. If a Friary layout could be constructed from other surveys or excavations, there would be potential to correlate the results of the resistivity survey with a floor plan, but as it stands, there is little remaining to make any accurate statements about the site.

7.4.2 Hinton Friary Earth Resistance Survey

As already noted, in chapter 3, a resistivity survey was previously conducted at Friary but covered only the area immediately around Woodman's Cottage (Hawke 2015). This survey has informed the author's research, and consequent resurvey of the site. The new survey has covered a larger area of ground in order to attempt to place into context the features already located. Re-surveying the area has also dealt with some of the issues of the previous survey, such as gaps in the survey plot, and the original method of processing the data.

The most important results of the survey are presented here, with detailed interpretation to follow (fig. 7.6). There is very definitive evidence for the presence of the Friary in this area, although the survey was somewhat hampered by new fencing and property boundaries which prevented the collection of data for the south-east of the complex. Despite this, the resistivity survey has revealed the majority of the Friary complex, as well as confirming the location of a post-medieval building to the north of the monastic buildings (fig. 7.7).

The central area appears to be the main location for the Friary. There are a large number of linear features that all lie on an east-west alignment. The few modern features have been identified through comparison with aerial photographs from 1945 to 1968 held by the Historic England Archive at Swindon. The photographs show a curved wall running from Woodman's Cottage and leading towards the river, correlating with feature 1. The wall had been removed by the time of the 1968 aerial photograph, but its footprint of it is still visible. A line of trees is also visible in the 1945 and 1946 photographs in the same position as the modern feature labelled 2. Perpendicular to this tree line, another linear feature (3) represents a modern pipeline, which was installed by the current owners of Woodman's Cottage. To the west of these features, two rectangular anomalies labelled 4 may be representative of a structure standing on a terraced area of the hillside. It seems unlikely that they are related to the monastic occupation, and more probably consist of the remains of a later agricultural building. At 5, there is a building which can be tied in with a map from 1785 of the Hinton Abbey Estate (SRO DD\FL/8). No name is given to the building on the map, so who the tenant was there cannot be traced. It may have been an agricultural building belonging to the estate. Like the features at 4, this structure may be of monastic date, but more likely represents the post-medieval phase of occupation.

The first feature which is relevant to the monastic occupation of the site is represented by a group of anomalous features labelled A, which are strongly indicative of a row of cells. The structure of the cell, with a small building and L-shaped garden, is identical to the cell layout of the Carthusian monks, as demonstrated by the geophysical survey conducted at Hinton Priory. At least three of these cells can be identified in the resistivity survey, but other adjoining cells may have been destroyed through subsequent land use. Opposite this range of cells, the group of features labelled B are perhaps indicative of another row of cells or other buildings facing the first.

Comparison with the layout of the correrie at La Grande Chartreuse is useful here. At the correrie a row of cells faces the cloister and a number of other buildings, with the church situated at one end, and an entrance way leading into the complex. This is very much in keeping with the evidence from the geophysical survey that a similar architectural style was being utilised at Friary. The feature marked C could be regarded as the entranceway leading towards the church. There is little evidence to suggest the location of the church, although it may be represented by the series of small linear features labelled D. Although some of the building styles of Friary are matched at La Correrie, some, such as the cell with the L-shaped garden, seem to have maintained the monastic style, as was used at Hinton Priory.

To the southwest of this group of features, there is evidence of another group of buildings. Labelled E, these could represent workshops for the lay brothers, including the kitchen, bakehouse, and stables, or perhaps a guest house for visitors. Since the lay brothers were the first point of contact for anyone wishing to communicate with the monks, the guest house was maintained at the lower house.

The results of the resistivity survey suggest a good level of preservation for the walls of the Friary, as they produced high-resistance anomalies which were easily visible in the results plot. The complexity of some areas of the Friary makes interpretation difficult, although comparison with the layout of the correrie at La Grande Chartreuse is of help in this case. Unfortunately, where modern building works have been situated restricts the completeness of the survey, as some parts of the complex seem to run into private gardens.

7.4.3 Hinton Friary Magnetometer Survey

The results of the magnetometer survey are well correlated with the resistivity survey, and confirm some postulations made about the nature of a number of the features revealed by the resistivity survey (figs. 7.8, 7.9).

At 1, the curved wall already located in the LiDAR data and resistivity survey is also visible through the magnetometer

Communal Solitude

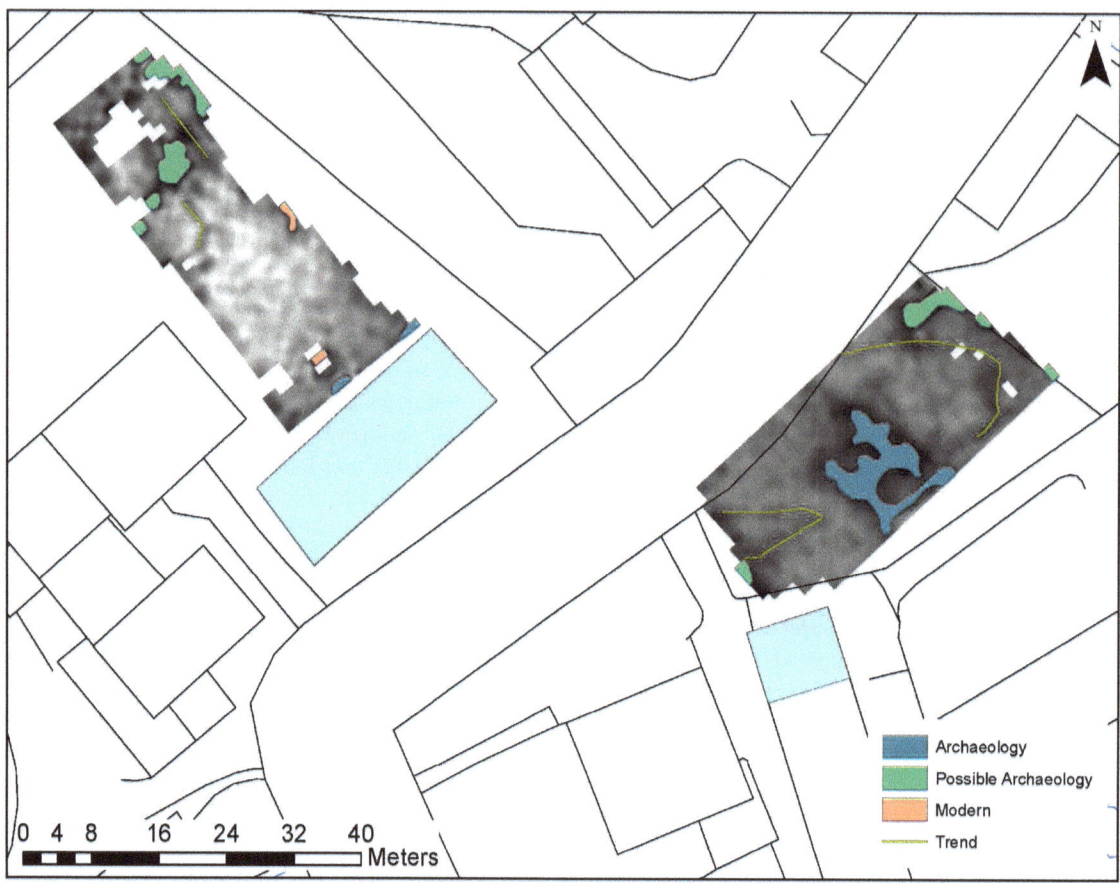

Figure 7.5. Interpretation of resistivity survey conducted at Witham Friary. © Crown copyright and database rights 2022 Ordnance Survey (100025252).

Figure 7.6. Resistivity survey results for Friary. © Crown copyright and database rights 2022 Ordnance Survey (100025252).

The Lower House: An Archaeological Investigation at the sites of Hinton and Witham Friary

Figure 7.7. Interpretation of resistivity survey data at Friary. © Crown copyright and database rights 2022 Ordnance Survey (100025252).

Figure 7.8. Magnetometry survey results for Friary. © Crown copyright and database rights 2022 Ordnance Survey (100025252).

results. This is the same for the pipeline at 2, which was visible in the resistivity survey. The tree line has not been picked up by this survey.

For the monastic buildings, there are a number of features of interest. Firstly, at A, several short linear features are in a similar placement to the location of the workshop buildings as revealed by the resistivity survey. At B, the grouping of linear anomalies again correlates with the features located by the resistivity survey. The magnetometer has picked up on the location of walls where they have perhaps been robbed out, which is why they would not appear as strong anomalies on the resistivity survey. By utilising both techniques of prospection, it is possible to build up a more accurate view of the layout of the Friary. In the next section, the results of both these methods will be combined with the LiDAR data to yield the most pertinent information and begin to create a ground plan for the Friary.

7.5 Synthesis of Data

Combining the results of the techniques discussed in the course of this chapter provides an overview of a potential layout for the Friary at Hinton. Figure 7.10 illustrates the combination of LiDAR, Resistivity Survey and Magnetometer Survey interpretations. Ignoring the features that have been shown to be modern leaves a ground plan of the Friary during the monastic occupation. Three cells are well defined here, and whether there ever were more could only be established through an excavation of the site. The correrie at La Grande Chartreuse featured six cells in this area, but the monastic community there was considerably larger than that of Hinton, so this can perhaps be explained in this way. Excavations at the correrie of Liget in France (constructed at the same time as Witham) have shown that the lay brothers there slept in a dormitory, but there is no archaeological evidence to suggest this was the case at Friary (Dufaÿ 2014, 28).

A complex group of walls south of the cells becomes visible through this visualisation; likely service areas, such as the kitchens, buttery, and storehouses. The structure of the workshop area has also been extended through the combined interpretation of techniques, indicating a likely layout for the buildings, although not as clearly defined as that of the cells. Similarly undefined is the area to the east of the cells, which may represent the aforementioned dormitory. The western wall of this structure appears to create a boundary for the cloister, and given its location, could just as likely be interpreted as the refectory.

A photo from 1909 (fig. 7.11) which recently came to light provides some additional information in creating a potential plan of the site at Friary. The image shows Woodman's Cottage, with the field that Friary sits in behind the house. To the right of Woodman's Cottage are what appears to be upstanding medieval remains, with a central, bricked-up window. The site of these remains has now been buried by a garage building. This photo extends the Friary complex to the west and may represent the western end of a church.

A potential layout (fig. 7.12) can be constructed from the survey interpretations and comparative plans, but this would have to be ground-truthed through excavation. The layout suggests a similar architectural style to the correrie at La Grande Chartreuse, although the location of some buildings cannot yet be attributed to ground features. A combined interpretation of the data at Friary, in particular, has allowed all anomalous readings from the three data collation techniques to be collected together and demonstrates how the techniques both complement and enhance each other.

7.6 Conclusions

Investigation of Witham Friary and the Friary at Hinton through geophysical techniques has allowed for a better understanding of the layout of the Carthusian correrie. Where the charterhouse complex was split into two precincts, the lower house served as a gatehouse and the majority of the work took place there. Subsequently, buildings such as the stables, guest house, kitchens and brewery were all located within this complex. Though this has not been an exhaustive investigation, preliminary studies have been able to provide a potential layout for the site at Hinton. The resistivity survey results illustrated an east-west aligned complex, with three cells clearly visible on the northern side of the precinct. A series of buildings to the south are likely indicative of the service buildings and the location of the stables and guesthouse.

The resistivity survey at Witham Friary was unable to provide any useful results, and it is unfortunate that the location of the complex has been largely built over as the village has grown. However, it may be worth conducting a larger-scale magnetometer survey around the village to prospect potential outlying buildings. Now that a layout for the correrie at Hinton has been established, it may be possible to work off that to estimate locations for buildings at Witham, based on the location of the church and dovecote, which are still standing.

This study has shown the particular utility of combining a number of techniques in order to gain as full an understanding of the site as possible. There is much scope for further investigation of the Friary at Hinton to continue prospection on the site with a view to excavation. This would be the first excavation of a correrie in the United Kingdom and would be instrumental in providing an understanding of the Carthusian lay brother.

The Lower House: An Archaeological Investigation at the sites of Hinton and Witham Friary

Figure 7.9. Interpretation of magnetometry survey results at Friary. © Crown copyright and database rights 2022 Ordnance Survey (100025252).

Figure 7.10. Combined interpretation of Friary resistivity and magnetometry interpretations with LiDAR interpretation. © Crown copyright and database rights 2022 Ordnance Survey (100025252).

Communal Solitude

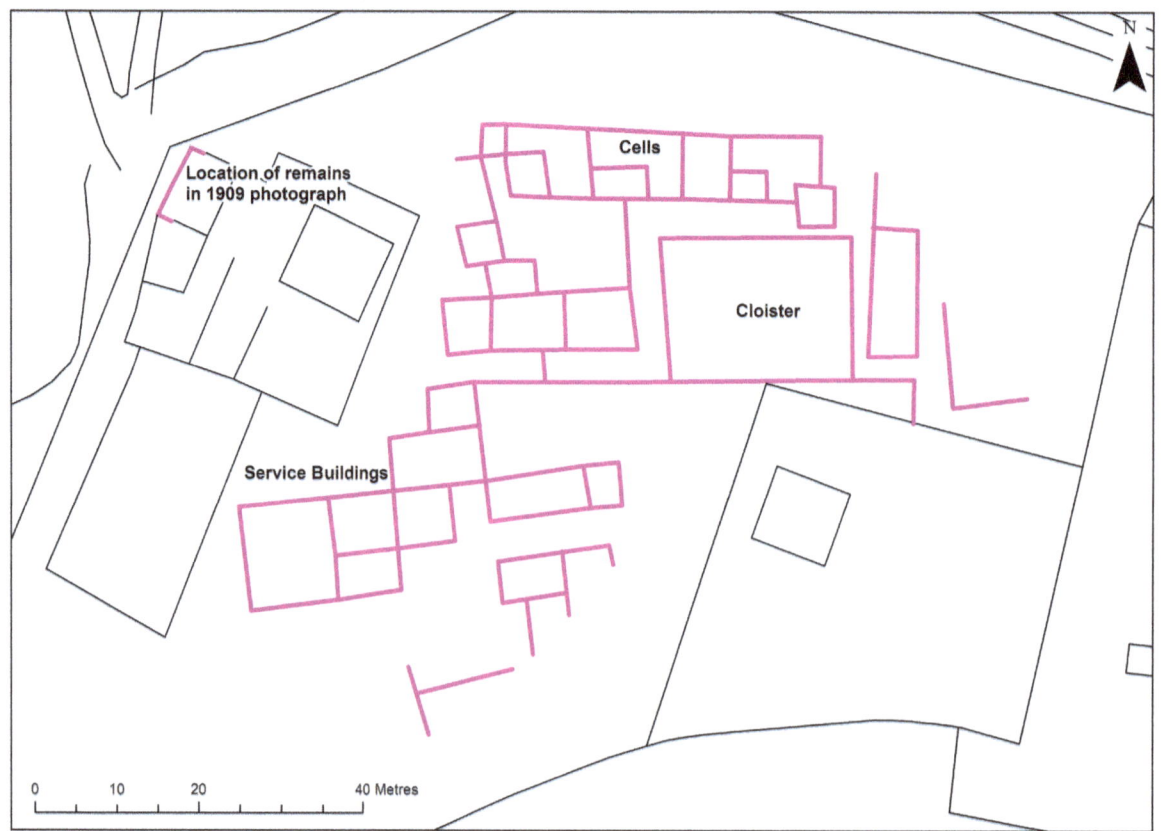

Figure 7.11. Photograph of Woodman's Cottage in Friary from 1909 facing south east, with upstanding remains in foreground, possibly site of lay brothers' church. © *Akeman Press 2017*.

Figure 7.12. Potential layout of the lay brothers' complex at Friary based on survey data and 1909 photo.

8

Conclusions

This study aimed to examine the role of the lay brother in Carthusian communities and did so by compiling the available archaeological data with documentary evidence to provide a historically contextualised study of the English, Scottish and Irish charterhouses. In particular, this research posed two principal questions: whether it was possible to identify the lay brethren as an archaeologically distinct element of the community, and how the lay brothers' precinct was arranged and organised. The first question was addressed by analysing material culture assemblages from three English charterhouses, where specific lay areas could be identified, and the second question was answered through topographic analysis and geophysical survey.

8.1 Can the Lay Brother be identified as archaeologically distinct?

The material culture evidence discussed in this study has demonstrated that contrary to an assumption that the lay brothers' cooking and eating vessels would be poorer in nature than that of the monks, there was no discernible difference in the quality of the vessels found. Though there was an apparent restriction in the range of ceramic fabric types used by the lay brothers at Mount Grace Priory, there was variation in the quality of the monks' assemblages also, some containing a similarly small range of fabrics. The advantage of analysing Carthusian pottery assemblages is that the cells ensure that each recovered collection refers to only one individual. Unfortunately, there are no records to provide the names of the inhabitants of each, which would enable greater exploration in detail of the lives of the monks and lay brothers on the eve of the Dissolution. This discussion was somewhat limited in that only one of the six lay cells excavated at Mount Grace provided any material culture, and at neither London nor Coventry Charterhouses were lay cells excavated.

Where areas of lay activity were excavated at the London and Coventry Charterhouses, it was evident that some of the items recovered belonged to secular guests. A scabbard chape, for example, found in one of the lay areas at London Charterhouse, indicates lay interaction within the walls of the monastic precinct. This prevented any accurate discussion of the assemblage relating to the lay brothers, as it was impossible to differentiate. The finds from Coventry were more distinctive, where iron horse material and shears obviously relate to animal husbandry, just as the stonemason's wedge and iron chisel provide evidence of masonry work, but still, it cannot be definitively shown that this does not indicate lay interaction, and one may just infer this conclusion.

In burial too, the lay brothers are indistinguishable. The Carthusian statutes state that monks and lay brothers were treated exactly the same in death, the only difference being the clothes they were dressed in. Where burial records survive, such as at Nieuwlicht Charterhouse, it is possible to identify specific individuals and their vocation, but none exist for the British and Irish charterhouses. The only burial segregation that seems to have been made at Nieuwlicht is between the monks and conversi, who were buried to the south of the Great Cloister, and the donati, who were buried to the north. Should the opportunity for archaeological exploration of an English Carthusian cemetery arise, it would be enlightening to investigate burial zoning in that context and compare it with the evidence from Nieuwlicht.

This study demonstrated that in making distinctions between monastic and lay populations in Carthusian houses, the find location of the material culture is crucial. Without the context of the recovery location, the distinction between the two groups of men in the charterhouses is impossible, as there is little difference in the quality of material, especially ceramics. With no documentary sources to indicate what items each lay brother should be provided within their cell, unlike the monks, this creates a further difficulty in understanding how the lay brothers can be distinguished in the archaeological record. This conclusion is, however, based on a small assemblage from only a few charterhouses, so further research should be conducted to compile a larger database of artefacts from more sites, which would produce more accurate results, and give a better understanding of the situation across Europe, rather than restricting the study to only England.

8.2 Layouts and Landscapes: Arrangement and Organisation

The discussion of the topography of the monastic precinct and wider landscapes has been an integral part of this study. The singular nature of the early charterhouses, where the monks and lay brothers were segregated into separate complexes has provided an opportunity to explore the arrangement of the lay brothers' accommodation and construct the first ground plan for an English Carthusian friary. This has a number of interesting implications for historical and archaeological scholarship of the Carthusians. First, the new Hinton Friary ground plan will begin further research and discussion into the archaeology of the site. The results of the resistivity survey were sufficient to create a conjectural plan of the site, and the magnetometer results added to this, revealing the location of at least three cells, as well as service buildings and other conventual structures. Further research here, especially with excavation, can ground-truth this plan, and provide material culture that gives a better understanding of the function of these buildings.

Second, as the only full layouts currently established in Great Britain and Ireland are of joined houses, where the monks and lay brothers lived together, the potential of Space Syntax Analysis has been restricted to this style of complex. The new Friary ground plan lends itself to a better understanding of how space was accessed by its inhabitants, and whether the levels of isolation and boundaries highlighted by the analysis carried out on the London Charterhouse and Mount Grace Priory are similar to that at Friary.

Should the lower houses at Beauvale or Kilnalahanin be located (if they existed in the first place), the research conducted at Hinton Friary will provide guidance for archaeological investigation at those sites. Though any ground plans arising from that research would be unlikely to match that of Hinton, it would be possible to identify similar features, and each site could inform research at the others.

As it was not possible to gain good results from either the LiDAR data or the geophysical surveys at Witham Friary, this creates another avenue for future research. The recent increase in the use of Unmanned Aerial Vehicles (UAVs) as a tool for archaeological prospection has shown that it is possible to create three-dimensional models of a site, and the level of resolution for these is much higher than that of the LiDAR available for Witham Friary. A 3D model created in this manner, as it is a non-invasive method of prospection, may be able to give a better understanding of the landscape of the current village, and identify earthworks that may be pertinent to the monastic occupation of the area.

8.3 Interactions with the Secular World

Though the aim of this study was to examine the role of the lay brother, this is inextricably linked with secular interaction, and therefore a discussion of the most salient findings relating to this theme must be considered. The most obvious way in which the secular world interacted with the Carthusians is in their benefaction of the houses. As the prayers of the Order came to be seen as the most effective method of spiritual intercession, donations of land and money constituted a spiritual trade, whereby the benefactor would receive divine rewards after their death. The expansion of the monastic churches at London and Coventry was in large part (if not the only reason) due to the need to append additional chapels where tombs could be placed. The will of Katherine de la Pole (1306-1382) (Test. Ebor. I, 119) indicated that she wished to be buried in the church at the Hull Charterhouse, next to the tomb of her husband, William (1302-1366), who was one of the co-founders of the monastery. Their children and grandchildren were subsequently buried at the charterhouse and were continued benefactors of the Carthusian community there.

As this study has discussed, however, it was not only the founders of charterhouses and their families who requested burial in the monasteries. A number of Lord Mayors of London, Mayors of Coventry and Hull, merchants and other noblemen also stipulated in their wills that they were to be buried in a charterhouse. Furthermore, the example of Nieuwlicht Charterhouse, where the necrology survives, has been used to illustrate how the Carthusians accommodated the laity. The necrology shows that the great cloister alley was reserved for male burials, where women could be buried in the little cloister, it being the most secular area of the monastic complex. The material culture gathered from London Charterhouse also showed that the laity were allowed access to the outer court, where a scabbard chape was recovered, and documentary evidence suggests that the Carthusians allowed entrance to the precinct as it lay in the midst of a Black Death cemetery.

8.4 The Role of the Lay Brother

The main topic for discussion throughout this study has been the role of the lay brother. The Carthusian Order recognised four classes of lay brother, the *conversi*, the *redditi*, the *donati*, and the *mercenarii*. Throughout this study, reference has been made to 'the lay brothers,' and in general, this has referred to the *conversi*, often seen as the true lay brother. The vocations available to the lay brother indicate the types of workshops that would have been necessary at the lower house or in the lay area of the charterhouse. Occupations such as baker, smith, and carpenter required specific tools and materials, and additionally, guest houses and stables were under the remit of the lay brethren. This knowledge, therefore, informs the types of material culture one would expect to find, should excavation uncover the area of service buildings within a Carthusian site.

An investigation into the food waste, where possible, would also make for an interesting study; the meals of the lay brethren were in some ways different to that of the monks. Records from the London Charterhouse in 1535 show that the lay brothers were provided with different foods on Sundays and Wednesdays, although they still did not consume meat, and maintained a pescatarian diet like the monks. If this, and other documentary sources could be accorded with archaeological data, it would be possible to augment our understanding of the Carthusian diet in the English Province, and how it differed from other monastic orders, if at all. The charterhouses also owned meadows, orchards, kitchen gardens, and fishponds, all of which supplemented their diet, and reduced the number of goods that needed to be bought from secular vendors. The granges on the Mendip Hills held sheep sleights and were worked only by lay brethren, and therefore the archaeological record for these sites can be assumed to hold only lay material culture. However, it would be impossible to differentiate between a Carthusian lay brother and a member of secular society through only the material culture.

Records for Hinton and Witham show that both houses were badly affected by the Black Death. At each, all of their lay brothers died, and they were required to request special dispensation to hire secular workers and to pay them at a higher rate than normal. Where the lay brothers had greater secular interaction than the monks, they were at higher risk of contracting disease. There is further research to be conducted on the lay-monastic interactions among Carthusian communities, notably, the effect of country-wide epidemics such as the Black Death, later plagues, and famines, on the monastic population.

8.5 Scope and Recommendations for Further Research

As with any fixed-term research project, this study has had a number of time-constrained limitations. Within the three years, it was not possible to comprehensively compare the British and Irish sites with their European counterparts, especially as concerns material culture. Likewise, the timescale did not allow for an excavation of the site at Friary, so no ground-truthing of the potential layout could be attained. The layout constructed in this study, therefore, is based on the results of the geophysical survey, and the ascribed room uses are conjectural based on a comparison with the layout at Hinton Priory. Permission has been given for excavation and the owners of the site are keen for investigation to continue. As concerns future research, this should be the first avenue of investigation as it is of primary importance for a fuller understanding of the site.

The geophysical survey at Witham Friary was constrained by the expansion of the village. The only open areas which could be surveyed were the churchyard, and the playground adjacent to the monastic dovecote. This limited the amount of information that could be gained from the survey, as the location of most of the lay brothers' complex has subsequently been built over, or roads lay over it. Subsequently, the results of the survey that could be conducted showed very few features, and none that could be positively ascribed to the monastic occupation.

The analysis of material culture was also restricted as only three sites could be sufficiently discussed. Some sites remain unexcavated, and, therefore, have no assemblage of material culture (Sheen, Axholme, Hull, Kilnalahanin and Perth), and some of the excavated sites were only partially excavated, which included no lay areas, or the material culture recovered from the site is now missing or uncatalogued (Witham, Hinton and Beauvale). Furthermore, the excavation at Coventry Charterhouse was not as extensive as that of the London Charterhouse or Mount Grace Priory, and, therefore, the assemblage is smaller, which implicated the level of analysis that could be carried out. Continued research at Friary would allow for effective analysis and comparison of the material culture of the lay community with the monastic community and would be the first (and likely only) excavation of a Carthusian correrie in Great Britain and Ireland. Further to this study, an archaeological study of the Carthusian granges in the Mendip Hills would be of great benefit in better understanding the material culture or archaeological footprint of lay activity in Carthusian communities, and in establishing whether different classes of lay brother can be distinguished in the archaeological record.

The results of this investigation may lead to comparison with similar European sites, which again, was not possible within this study. The European sites and their material culture may reveal much about the architectural style of the lay brothers' buildings, and a comparative study of material culture from excavated correries would provide analysis of definitively lay assemblages, where it is not always possible to differentiate between the monks and the lay brothers. Witham Friary would also benefit from more in-depth archaeological investigation, although excavation may not be possible given the nature of the subsequent growth of the village, prospection techniques such as ground-penetrating radar may have application in a site such as this.

Bibliography

Primary Manuscript Sources

Bodleian Library, Oxford

MS. Laud Misc. 517. 'The Manere of Good Lyvyng'

MS. Rawlinson D. 318, ff. 73-167. 'Chartae of the Carthusian General Chapter'. 1411-1499.

British Library

Additional MS 6060. 'Beauvale Chartulary'. 1486.

Additional MS. 11303. 'Statutes to be observed by the lay Brethren of the monastery of Shene, in Surrey'. c. 16th Century.

Additional MS. 28588. 'Correspondence with Charles V and his ministers'. August 1535 – June 1536.

Additional MS. 37049. 'A Carthusian miscellany of poems, chronicles, and treatises in Northern English, including an epitome or summary of Mandeville's travels'. 1460-1500.

Additional MS. 61823. 'The Book of Margery Kempe'. c. 1440.

Cotton MS. Cleopatra C/VI. 'Ancrene Riwle ; songs and prayers; a leaf from a Book of Hours'. 1200-1420.

Cotton MS. Cleopatra E/IV. 'Papers relating to the Dissolution of the Monasteries'. 1536-1540s.

Cotton MS. Cleopatra E/VI. 'Papers relating to the Reformation'. 2nd quarter of the 16th century.

Lansdowne MS. 1201. 'Formulare vel Consutudinarium Carthusianorum de Sheen in comitatu Surr". 13th-17th Century.

Harley MS. 237. 'Theological treatises'. 1450.

Harley MS. 2373. 'Theological miscellany, including 'The Cloud of Unknowing''. 1450.

Cambridge University Library

MS. Ee.4.30. Walter Hilton, 'Scale of Perfection'. c.1450-1500.

Charterhouse Muniments, Sutton's Hospital

MP/1/14a. 'Plan of Water Supply at London Charterhouse'. Mid-15th Century.

Glasgow University Library

MS Hunter 136. 'Musica Ecclesiastica'. 1502.

Lambeth Palace Library

MS 413. 'Records of the General Chapters of the Carthusian Order' 1417-1481.

The National Archives, Kew.

C 53. Charter Rolls. 1199-1517.

C66. Patent Rolls. 1201-2012.

CRES 38/514/6/1. 'Somerset Estates – Green Ore and Whitnell'. 24 December 1574.

E 117/12/22. 'Declaration of the goods of the London Charterhouse, 30 Hen VIII'. 1539.

E 135/2/24 'Fragment of a cartulary of the Carthusian prior of Epworth in the Isle of Axholme'. 15th Century.

E 135/2/46. 'Inventory of clothes sent from the Charterhouse, London to the Carthusian house of Witham (Somerset) for dan Andrew, and of those cloths he took with him when he left London'. 1485-1509.

E 135/9/15 'Copy of extract from the Valor Ecclesiasticus I. 361'. 1558-1603.

E 315/234. 'Augmentation Office Miscellaneous Books, vol. 234'. 1540-1541.

E 315/235. 'Augmentation Office Miscellaneous Books, vol. 235'. 1539-1543.

E 322/63. 'Deeds of Surrender: Coventry Charterhouse'. 16 January 1539

E 326/ 8775. 'Parties: Prior and convent of the Charterhouse by London & John Popham, knight. Place or subject: Spiritual benefits. The manor of Rolleston: Leic [Midd]' 1460.

E 326/1782. 'Mining lease by the Prior and Convent of Beauvale'. 20 January 1396/7.

E 328/310. 'Letters patent, giving 50 marks annually to Prior and Convent of Locus Dei, Henton, co. Somerset'. 20 July 1461.

LR2/61. 'Cartulary of Charterhouse, London'. 1509-1547.

SP 1/19, f. 169. 'Inventory of items taken by Thomas Golwynne from London to Mount Grace'. 25 January 1520.

SP 1/86, f. 57. 'The Charterhouse, Witham'. 17 October 1534.

SP 1/92, ff. 26-35. 'Carthusians and the Supremacy'. 20 April 1535.

Communal Solitude

SP 1/97, f. 132. 'Fare of the monks and brothers at The Charterhouse' 13 October 1535.

SP 1/101, f. 85. 'Thomas Barnyngham, proctor and monk, to Cromwell'. 15 January 1536.

SP 1/102. 'The Compendium Compertorum'. 4 February – 23 March 1536

SP 1/139, f. 148-152. 'The Charterhouse'. 24 November 1538.

SP 1/142, f. 155. 'Tregonwell and Petre to Cromwell'. 26 January 1539.

SP 3/4, f. 141. 'John Husee to Lord Lisle'. 5 May 1534.

SP 3/7, f. 17. 'John Rokewood to Lord Lisle'. 15 May 1534.

STAC 2/32/42. 'Destruction of a fish pond at Emborrow'. 1509-1547.

WORK 14/2006. 'Hinton Prior excavations by owner'. 1940-1962.

Somerset Record Office, Taunton.

DD/FL/8. 'Map of Hinton Charterhouse'. 1785.

Universitatsbibliothek Basel

AK VI 21. 'Statuta Ordinis Cartusiensis, a domno Guigone prior cartusie edita'. 1510.

Primary Printed Sources

Adam of Eynsham. *Magna Vita S. Hugonis Episcopi Lincolniensis.* ed. J. F. Dimock. 1864. London: Longman, Green, Longman, Roberts and Green.

Calendar of Papal Registers Relating to Great Britain and Ireland. Volume 7: 1417-1431. ed. J. A. Twemlow. 1906. London: HMSO

Calendar of the Manuscripts of the Dean and Chapter of Wells. Volume 1. Historical Manuscripts Commission. 1907. London: HMSO.

Chauncy, M. 1550. *Historia aliquot nostri saeculi martyrum cum pia, tum lectu iucunda, nunquam antehac typis excusa.* Mainz.

English Episcopal Acta 37: Salisbury 1267-1297. ed. B. R. Kemp. 2010. Oxford: Oxford University Press.

Fisher, J. 1534. *Here Begynneth a Lytell Boke, That Speketh of Purgatorye.* London: Robert Wyer.

Fisher, J. 1532. *Hereafter Ensueth Two Fruytfull Sermons.* London: W. Rastell.

Guigo I. *Coutumes de Chartreuse.* Trans by 'Un Chartreux'. 2001. Paris: Les Éditions du Cerf.

Guigo I. *Les Méditationes.* Trans by 'Un Chartreux'. 1983. Paris: Les Éditions du Cerf.

The Hamilton Papers. Letters and Papers Illustrating the Political Relations of England and Scotland in the XVIth Century. Volume 1: 1532-1543. Ed. J. Bain. 1890. Edinburgh: H.M. General Register House.

Letters, S. *Online Gazetteer of Markets and Fairs in England and Wales to 1516.* Somerset. http://www.history.ac.uk/cmh/gaz/gazweb2.html [Last accessed 16 February 2018].

Letters and Papers, Foreign and Domestic of the Reign of Henry VIII. 21 volumes. 1862-1932. ed. J. S. Brewer, J. Gairdner, and R. H. Brewer. London: HMSO.

Lettres des premiers chartreux. Tome I. S. Bruno – Guigues – S. Anthelme. Ed. by 'Un Chartreux'. 1962. Paris: Cerf.

Lydgate, J. n.d. *The Lay Folks Mass Book or The Manner of Hearing Mass with Rubrics and Devotions for the People.* Ed. T. F. Simmons 1879. Early English Text Society Original Series 71. London: N. Trübner & Co.

Magna Vita S. Hugonis Episcopi Lincolniensis. Ed. J. F. Dimock. 1864. London: Longman, Green, Longman, Roberts and Green.

Migne, J.-P. (ed). 1880. *Patrologia Latina. Volume 153: S. Bruno Carthusiensium Institutor. Guigo I, Guigo II, Priores Carthusiae Majoris. S. Hugo Lincolniensis Episcopus.* Paris: Garnier

North Country Wills, 1383-1558. ed. J. W. Clay. 1908. Surtees Society 116.

Pask Matthews, C. 1930. 'The Laye Brethrens Statutes (Shene).' *Surrey Archaeological Collections* 38, 210-226.

Pask Matthews, C. 1931. 'The Laye Brethrens Statutes (Shene).' *Surrey Archaeological Collections* 39, 112-143.

Pedes Finium, commonly called Feet of Fines for the County of Somerset. Richard I to Edward I. AD 1196 to AD 1307. ed. E. Green. 1892. London: Harrison & Sons.

The Great Roll of the Pipe. 98 volumes. 1884-2016. London: Pipe Roll Society

The Register of Thomas Bekynton, Bishop of Bath and Wells, 1443-1465. Part I. Ed. H. C. Maxwell-Lyte and M. C. B. Dawes. 1934. Somerset Record Society, vol. 49.

Somerset Medieval Wills, 1383-1500. ed. Rev. F. W. Weaver. 1983. Gloucester: Alan Sutton.

Somerset Medieval Wills, 1501-1530. ed. Rev. F. W. Weaver. 1903. London: Somerset Record Society.

Somerset Medieval Wills, 1531-1558. ed. Rev. F. W. Weaver. 1905. London: Somerset Record Society.

Statutes of the Realm. Vol. 1. 1810. London: Dawsons.

'Testamenta Eboracensia, or, Wills Registered at York'. 6 volumes. 1836-1902. ed. J. Raine, L. Baker, J. Raine and J. W. Clay. *Surtees Society* 4; 30; 45; 53; 79; 106.

Testamenta Vetusta. 2 volumes. 1826. ed. N. H. Nicolas. London: Nichols & Son.

Valor Ecclesiasticus temp. Henry VIII auctoritate regia institutus. 6 vols. 1810-1834. London: Record Commission.

William of St Thierry. 'From the Vita *prima*'. Trans. and ed. by P. Matarasso. 1993. *The Cistercian World. Monastic Writings of the Twelfth Century.* Harmondsworth: Penguin.

Printed Secondary Sources

Allen, J. 2012. 'Carthusian Choir Stalls and the Misericord in Italy'. *The Antiquaries Journal* 92, 307-330.

Appleby, J. T. 1962. 'The ecclesiastical foundations of Henry II'. *Catholic Historical Review* 48, 205-215.

Archer, R. E. 2008. 'Mowbray, John (V), second duke of Norfolk (1392–1432)'. *Oxford Dictionary of National Biography*. Oxford: Oxford University Press. https://doi.org/10.1093/ref:odnb/19450 [Last accessed 16 February 2018]

Armitage Robinson, S. 1918. 'The foundation charter of Witham Charterhouse'. *Proceedings of the Somersetshire Archaeological and Natural History Society* 4, 1-29.

Arnold, E. F. 2013. *Negotiating the Landscape. Environment and Monastic Identity in the Medieval Ardennes*. Philadelphia, PA: University of Pennsylvania Press.

Aston, M. 2000. *Monasteries in the Landscape*. Stroud: Tempus

Aston, Mick. 1997. 'The Carthusian Project in the British Isles'. In G. De Boe and F. Verhaeghe (eds). *Religion and Belief in Medieval Europe – Papers of the 'Medieval Europe Brugge 1997' Conference – Volume 4*. Zellik: Institut voor het Archaeologisch Patrimonium, Wetenschappelijke instelling van de Vlaamse Gemeenschap, 33-41.

Aston, Mick. 1993. 'The Development of the Carthusian order in Europe and Britain'. In M. Carver (ed). *In search of cult: Archaeological Investigations in honour of Philip Rahtz*. Woodbridge: Boydell, 139-151.

Aravecchia, N. 2001. 'Hermitages and Spatial Analysis: Use of Space at the Kellia'. In S. McNally (ed). *Shaping Community: The Art and Archaeology of Monasticism*. International Series 941. Oxford: BAR Publishing, 29-38

Armitage Robinson, S. 1918. 'The foundation Charter of Witham Charterhouse' *Proceedings of the Somersetshire Archaeological and Natural History Society* 4, 1-29.

Baldwin, A. 2016. *An Introduction to Medieval English Literature, 1300-1484*. London: Palgrave Macmillan.

Bales, A. F. 2001. 'Mapping Rituals in a Carthusian Monastery: La Certosa di Calci'. *Journal of Architectural Education* 54:4, 264-267.

Barber, B. and Thomas, C. 2002. *The London Charterhouse*. London: MoLAS.

Barley, M. W. 1957. 'Cistercian Land Clearances in Nottinghamshire: Three Deserted Villages and their Moated Successor'. *Nottingham Medieval Studies* 1, 75-89.

Barlow, P. 1968. 'Witham Priory'. *79th and 80th Annual Reports of the Wells Natural History and Archaeological Society*, 7-11.

Barrell, A. D. M. 2000. *Medieval Scotland*. Cambridge: Cambridge University Press.

Bäuml, F. H. 1980. 'Varieties and Consequences of Medieval Literacy and Illiteracy'. *Speculum* 55:2, 237-265.

Beckett, W. N. M. 1988. 'The Perth Charterhouse before 1500'. *Analecta Cartusiana* 128, i-74.

Belisle, P-D. 2003. *The Language of Silence: The Changing Face of Monastic Solitude*. London: Darton, Longman and Todd.

Bellitto, C. M. 2001. *Renewing Christianity: A History of Church Reform from Day One to Vatican II*. Mahwah, NJ: Paulist Press

Bernáldez Sánchez, E. and Bazo Carretero, E. 2013. 'Los estudios paleobiológicos como herramienta para la gestión y conservación de la biodiversidad. Galápagos del siglo XVI en la Cartuja de Sevilla' In J. Jiménez Ávila, M. Bustamante and M. García Cabezas (eds). *VI Encuentro de Arqueología del Suroeste Peninsular*. Badajoz: Ecmo. Ayuntamiento de Villafranca de los Barros, 2573-2596.

Bernard, G. W. 2012. *The Late Medieval English Church. Vitality and Vulnerability before the break with Rome*. New Haven, CT: Yale University Press.

Bernard, G. W. 2011. 'The Dissolution of the Monasteries'. *History* 96: 324, 390-409.

Bernard, G. W. 2005. *The King's Reformation. Henry VIII and the Remaking of the English Church*. London and New Haven, CT: Yale University Press.

Bettey, J. H. 1989. *The Suppression of the Monasteries in the West Country*. Gloucester: Alan Sutton.

Bijsterveld, A-J. A. 2007. *Do ut des: Gift giving, Memoria, and Conflict Management in the Medieval Low Countries*. Hilversum: Uitgeverij Verloren

Blackmore, L. and Pearce, J. 2010. *A Dated Type Series of London Medieval Pottery: Part 5. Shelly-sandy ware and the greyware industries*. MoLA monograph 49. London: Museum of London Archaeology.

Blackmore, L. 2000. *The Pottery from Excavations at Charterhouse*. MoLSS unpublished specialist report.

Bligny, B. 1986. 'Saint Bruno et la Naissance des Chartreuses'. In B. Bligny. and G. Chaix. *La naissance des Chartreuses: colloque organisé par l'Association pour la Celelbration du IXe Centenaire de la Fondation de la Grande Chartreuses (12-15 septembre 1984)*. Grenoble: Editions des Cahiers de l'Alpe de la Société des Ecrivains Dauphinois, 7-14.

Bond, J. 2004. *Monastic Landscapes*. Stroud: Tempus

Bond, J. 1988. 'Monastic Fish'. In M. Aston (ed). *Medieval Fish, Fisheries and Fishponds in England*. BAR British Series 182, 69-112.

Bonde, S. and Maines, C. 2012. 'The Technology of Medieval Water Management at the Charterhouse of Bourgfontaine'. *Technology and Culture* 53:3, 625-670.

Boutrais, C. M. 1934. *The History of the Great Chartreuse*. London: Burns, Oates & Washbourne.

Bowlt, C. 2003. 'The Great Conduit at the London Charterhouse'. *London Archaeologist* 10:5, 121-123.

Brantley, J. 2007. *Reading in the Wilderness. Private Devotion and Public Performance in Late Medieval England*. Chicago: University of Chicago Press.

Braunfels, W. 1972. *Monasteries of Western Europe*. London: Thames & Hudson

Brears, P. 2012. *Cooking & Dining in Medieval England*. Totnes: Prospect Books.

Brett, C. J. 2012. 'Green Ore and Whitnell: Medieval and Post-Medieval Landholdings and Topography on Mendip'. *Proceedings of the Somerset Archaeological and Natural History Society* 155, 145-161.

Brett, C. J. 2002. 'The Fairs and Markets of Norton St Philip'. *Proceedings of the Somerset Archaeological and Natural History Society* 144, 165-196.

Brogden, T. 1941. 'The Carthusian Liturgy. Part 2'. *Magnificat: A Liturgical Quarterly* 3, 5-10.

Brown, A. 2003. *Church and Society in England, 1100-1500*. Basingstoke: Palgrave Macmillan.

Brown, D. 2011. *God and Grace of Body: Sacrament in Ordinary*. Oxford: Oxford University Press.

Brown, F. E. 1985. 'Medieval London – The Growth of a City'. *Journal of Architectural and Planning Research* 2:2, 77- 97

Bruce, S. G. 2007. *Silence and Sign Language in Medieval Monasticism. The Cluniac Tradition c. 900-1200*. Cambridge: Cambridge University Press.

Burton, J. 2006. *The Foundation History of the Abbeys of Byland and Jervaulx* York: University of York

Burton, J. 1994. *Monastic and Religious Orders in Britain, 1000-1300*. Cambridge: Cambridge University Press.

Burrow, I. and Burrow, C. B. 1990. 'Witham Priory: the first English Carthusian monastery'. *Proceedings of the Somerset Archaeological and Natural History Society* 134, 141-182.

Caie, G. D. 2004. 'Lay Literacy and the Medieval Bible'. *Nordic Journal of English Studies* 3:1, 125-144.

Caner, D. 2002. *Wandering, Begging Monks. Spiritual Authority and the Promotion of Monasticism in Late Antiquity*. Berkeley, CA: University of California Press.

Cariboni, G. 2013. "No one can serve two masters': Abbots and Archabbots in the monastic networks at the end of the eleventh century'. *Journal of Medieval Monastic Studies* 2, 39-74.

Clemens, R. and Graham, T. 2007. *Introduction to Manuscript Studies*. Ithaca, NY: Cornell University Press.

Cloake, J. 1977. 'The Charterhouse of Sheen'. *Surrey Archaeological Collections* 71, 145-198.

Cook, E. B. 1904. 'The Carthusian Order and its remains in Somerset'. *Wells Natural History and Archaeological Society Annual Reports*.

Coppack, G. Forthcoming. *A Synthesis of Archaeological and Historical Research and Building Recording at Beauvale Priory, Moorgreen, Greasley, Nottinghamshire (NGR SK 49234904)*.

Coppack, G. and Keen, L. 2019. *Mount Grace Priory: Excavations of 1957-1992*. Oxford: Oxbow

Coppack, G. and Aston, M. 2002. *Christ's Poor Men. The Carthusians in England*. Stroud: Tempus.

Coppack, G. 2008. "Make straight in the desert a highway for our God': The Carthusians and Community in Late Medieval England'. In J. Burton and K. Stöber (eds). *Monasteries and Society in the British Isles in the Later Middle Ages*. Woodbridge: Boydell, 168-179.

Courtney, P. 1997. 'Ceramics and the history of consumption: pitfalls and prospects'. *Medieval Ceramics* 21, 95-108.

Cowan, I. B. 1982. *The Scottish Reformation, Church and Society in sixteenth century Scotland*. London: Weidenfeld and Nicolson.

Cross, C. 2008. 'Monasteries and Society in Sixteenth-Century Yorkshire: The Last Years of Roche Abbey'. In J. Burton and K. Stöber (eds). *Monasteries and Society in the British Isles in the Later Middle Ages*. Woodbridge: Boydell, 229-240.

Crutchley, S. and Crow, P. 2009. *The Light Fantastic: Using airborne laser scanning in archaeological survey*. Swindon: English Heritage

Cunningham, A. and Kusukawa, S. (eds). 2010. *Natural Philosophy Epitomised: Books 8011 of Gregor Reisch's Philosophical Pearl (1503)*. Abingdon: Routledge.

Dalton, J. P. 1909a. 'The Abbey of Kilnalahan'. *Journal of Galway Archaeological and Historical Society* 6:1, 10-26.

Dauphin, C. 2001-2002. 'The Diet of the Desert Fathers in Late Antique Egypt'. *Bulletin of the Anglo-Israel Archaeological Society* 19-20, 39-63.

Deagan, K. A. and Cruxent, J. M. 2002. *Archaeology at La Isabela: America's First European Town*. New Haven, CT: Yale University Press.

Del Espino Hidalgo, B. and García Fernández, F. J. 2014. 'Broken Silence. An international approach to the integration processes of charterhouses in urban contexts'. *12th International Conference on Urban History: Cities in Europe, Cities in the World,* 1-14.

den Hartog, C. 2018. 'The Charterhouse of the New Light of the Holy Saviour at Bloemendaal outside the City of Utrecht, or Nieuwlicht Rediscovered'. *Journal of Medieval Monastic Studies* 7, 273-313.

Devereux, B. J., Amable, G. S., Crow, P., and Cliff, A. D. 2005. 'The potential of airborne lidar for the detection of archaeological features under woodland canopies'. *Antiquity* 79, 648-660.

De Weijert, R. 2011. 'Gift-giving practices in the Utrecht charterhouse. Donating to be Remembered?'. In R. De Weijert, K. Ragetli, A-J. Bijsterveld and J. van Arenthals (eds). *Living memoria. Studies in medieval and early modern memorial culture in honour of Truus van Bueren.* Hilversuum: Verloren, 147-164.

Dey, H. 2004. 'Building Worlds Apart. Walls and the Construction of Communal Monasticism from Augustine through Benedict'. *Antiquité Tardive* 12, 357-371.

Dimier, A. 1999. *Stones Laid Before the Lord. A History of Monastic Architecture.* Collegeville, MN: Liturgical Press.

Dixon, M. H. 2009. 'The Architecture of Solitude'. *Environment, Space, Place* 1, 53-72.

Doggett, N. 2001. 'The Demolition and Conversion of former monastic buildings in post-dissolution Hertfordshire'. In G. Keevil, M. Aston and T. Hall (eds). *Monastic Archaeology. Papers on the Study of Medieval Monasteries.* Oxford: Oxbow, 165-174.

Donaldson, G. 1960. *The Scottish Reformation.* Cambridge: Cambridge University Press.

Doneus, M., Briese, C., Fera, M., and Janner, M. 2008. 'Archaeological prospection of forested areas using full-waveform airborne laser scanning'. *Journal of Archaeological Science* 35, 882-893.

Doyle, A. I. 1998. 'English Carthusian Books not yet linked with a charterhouse'. In T. Barnard and D. Ó Cróinín (eds). *A Miracle of Learning: studies in manuscripts and Irish learning: essays in honour of William O'Sullivan.* Aldershot: Ashgate, 122-136.

Doyle, A. I. 1997. 'Stephen Dodesham of Witham and Sheen'. In P. R. Robinson and R. Zim (eds). *On the Making of Books. Medieval Manuscripts, their Scribes and Readers. Essays presented to M. B. Parkes.* Aldershot: Ashgate, 94-115.

Doyle, A. I. 1990. 'Book production by the monastic orders in England (c.1375–1530): assessing the evidence'. In L. Brownrigg (ed.). *Medieval book production: assessing the evidence. Proceedings of the second conference of the seminar in the history of the book to 1500, Oxford, July, 1988.* Los Altos Hills, CA: Anderson-Lovelace, 1-19

Doyle, A. I. 1989a. 'The European Circulation of Three Latin Spiritual Texts'. In A. J. Minnis (ed). *Latin and Vernacular. Studies in Late-Medieval Texts and Manuscripts.* Cambridge: D. S. Brewer, 129-146.

Doyle, A. I. 1989b. 'Publication by Members of the Religious Orders'. In J. Griffiths and D. Pearsall (eds). *Book Production and Publishing in Britain 1375-1475.* Cambridge: Cambridge University Press, 109-123.

Dubois, J. 1965. 'Les Limites des Chartreuses'. *Bulletin de la Société nationale des antiquaires de France* 108, 186-197.

Du Boulay Hill, Rev. A. and Gill, H. 1908. 'Beauvale Charterhouse, Notts.' *Transactions of the Thoroton Society* 12, 68-94.

Duby, G. 1962. *Rural Economy and Country Life in the Medieval West.* Columbia, SC: University of South Carolina Press.

Dufaÿ, B. 2014. 'La Corroirie de la Chartreuse du Liget à Chemillé-sur-Indrois (Indre et Loire). Étude historique et architecturale.' *Revue archéologique du Centre de la France* 53.

Duffy, E. 2005. *The Stripping of the Altars. Traditional Religion in England 1400-1580.* Second Edition. New Haven, CT: Yale University Press.

Dunn, M. 2003. *The Emergence of Monasticism. From the Desert Fathers to the Early Middle Ages.* Oxford: Blackwell

Dunning, R. W. 1991. 'The West Country Carthusians'. In C. Harper-Bill (ed). *Religious Belief and Ecclesiastical Careers in Late Medieval England. Proceedings of the conference held at Strawberry Hill, Easter 1989.* Woodbridge: Boydell, 33-42.

Dunning, R. W. 1983. A History of the Somerset. Bognor Regis: Phillimore & Co.

Dyas, D. 2005. ''Wildernesse Is Anlich Lif of Ancre Wununge': The Wilderness and Medieval Anchoritic Spirituality.' In D. Dyas, V. Edden and R. Ellis (eds). *Approaching Medieval English Anchoritic and Mystical Texts.* Cambridge: D. S. Brewer, 19-33.

Dyer, C. 1988. 'The Consumption of Fresh-Water Fish in Medieval England.' In M. Aston (ed). *Medieval Fish, Fisheries and Fishponds in England.* BAR British Series 182, 27-38.

Edwards, T. 1946. 'The Carthusians of Coventry'. *Pax* 36, 64-69; 115-119.

Egan, G. 1998. *The Medieval Household. Daily Living c. 1150-c. 1450. Medieval Finds from Excavations in London: 6.* London: The Stationery Office.

Egan, G. and Pritchard, F. 2002. *Dress Accessories c. 1150-c. 1450. Medieval Finds from Excavations in London: 3.* 2nd Edition. Woodbridge: Boydell.

Erler, M. C. 2013. *Reading and Writing during the Dissolution: Monks, Friars and Nuns 1530-1558*. Cambridge: Cambridge University Press.

Evans, D. H. 2018. 'The Fortifications of Hull between 1321 and 1864'. *Archaeological Journal* 175:1, 87-156.

Fairclough, G. 1992. 'Meaningful constructions – spatial and functional analysis of medieval buildings'. *Antiquity* 66:251, 348-366.

Farmer, D. H. 1989. 'Hugh of Lincoln, Carthusian Saint'. In M. G. Sargent (ed). *De cella in seculum: Religious and Secular life and devotion in Late Medieval England. An interdisciplinary conference in celebration of the eighth centenary of the consecration of St Hugh of Avalon, bishop of Lincoln 20-22 July 1986*. Cambridge: D.S. Brewer, 9-15.

Fawcett, R. and Hall, D. 2005. 'The Perth Charterhouse'. *Tayside and Fife Archaeological Journal* 11, 46-53.

Ferguson, J. 1910-11. 'The Carthusian Order in Scotland'. *Transactions of the Scottish Ecclesiological Society* 3, 179-192.

Finucane, R. C. 1981. 'Sacred Corpse, Profane Carrion: Social Ideals and Death Rituals in the Later Middle Ages'. In J. Whaley (ed). *Mirrors of Mortality. Studies in the Social History of Death*. London: Europa Publications, 40-60.

Fisher, C. T., Cohen, A. S., Fernández-Diaz, J. C., and Leisz, S. J. 2017. 'The application of airborne mapping LiDAR for the documentation ancient cities and regions in tropical regions'. *Quaternary International* (in press), 1-10.

Fletcher, P. C. 1958. 'Further Excavations at Hinton Priory, Somerset'. *Proceedings of the Somerset Archaeological and Natural History Society* 103, 76-80.

Fletcher, P. C. 1951. 'Recent Excavations at Hinton Priory, Somerset'. *Somerset Archaeological and Natural History Society Proceedings* 96, 160-165.

Foreville, R. 1973. 'La Place de la Chartreuse du Liget parmi les fondations pieuses de Henri II Plantagenet.' *Actes du colloque médiéval de Loches. Mémoires de la Société Archéologique de Tourain* 9, 13-22.

Fradley, M. 2009. *Charterhouse, Somerset. The Development of a Romano-British Mining Settlement and Associated Landscape*. Research Department Report Series 9. Swindon: English Heritage.

France, P. 1996. *Hermits: The Insights of Solitude*. London: Pimlico.

Gaffney, C. 1997. *Report on Geophysical Survey 'Sheen Charterhouse'*. Geophysical Surveys of Bradford Report No. 97/92

Gaffney, C. 1995a. *Report on Geophysical Survey 'Axholme Priory Humberside'*. Geophysical Surveys of Bradford Report No. 95/12.

Gaffney, C. 1995b. *Report on Geophysical Survey 'Hinton Charterhouse'*. Geophysical Surveys of Bradford Report Number 95/49

Gaffney, C. 1994. *Report on Geophysical Survey 'Witham Carthusian Monastery'*. Geophysical Surveys of Bradford Report No. 94/21.

Gaimster, D. and Nenk, B. 1997. 'English Households in Transition c. 1450-1550: the ceramic evidence'. In D. Gaimster and P. Stamper (eds). *The Age of Transition. The Archaeology of English Culture 1400-1600*. Oxford: Oxbow, 171-195.

Gee, H. 1890. 'The So-Called 'Friary' of our Somersetshire Charterhouses'. *Somerset and Dorset Notes and Queries* 1, 129-133.

Gilbert, B. 2014. 'Early Carthusian Script and Silence'. *Cistercian Studies Quarterly* 49:3, 367-397.

Gilchrist, R. 1995. *Contemplation and Action: The Other Monasticism*. London: Leicester University Press.

Gillespie, V. 1989. 'Vernacular Books of Religion'. In J. Griffiths and D. Pearsall (eds). *Book Production and Publishing in Britain 1375-1475*. Cambridge: Cambridge University Press, 317-344.

Goddard, R. 2004. *Lordship and Medieval Urbanisation: Coventry, 1043-1355*. Woodbridge: Boydell.

Goodman, A. 1971. *The Loyal Conspiracy: the Lords Appellant under Richard II*. London: Routledge

Gough, J. W. 1967. *The Mines of Mendip*. Newton Abbot: David & Charles.

Grattan Flood, W. H. 1907. 'The Carthusians in Ireland. Kilnalehin Priory (1280-1321)'. *Irish Ecclesiastical Record*, 4th Series 22: 477, 304-309.

Gray, A. 1959. 'Kinaleghin: A Forgotten Irish Charterhouse of the Thirteenth Century'. *Journal of the Royal Society of Antiquaries of Ireland* 89:1, 35-58.

Gray, J. M. 2013. *Oaths and the English Reformation*. Cambridge: Cambridge University Press

Greene, J. P. 1992. *Medieval Monasteries*. Leicester: Leicester University Press.

Gribbin, J. A. 2001. 'Health and Disease in the English Charterhouses: a Preliminary Study'. *Analecta Cartusiana* 157.1, 197-209.

Guinn-Chipman, S. 2013. *Religious Space in Reformation England: Contesting the Past*. London: Pickering & Chatto.

Gullick, M. and Hadgraft, N. 2008. 'Bookbindings'. In N. J. Morgan and R. M. Thomson (eds). *The Cambridge History of the Book Volume II: 1100-1400*. Cambridge: Cambridge University Press, 95-109.

Haigh, C. 1993. *English Reformations: Religion, Politics and Society under the Tudors*. Oxford: Clarendon Press

Hallam, E. M. 1977. 'Henry II as a Founder of Monasteries'. *Journal of Ecclesiastical History* 28:2, 113-132.

Hamilton, S. and Spicer, A. 2005. 'Defining the Holy: the Delineation of Sacred Space'. In A. Spicer and S. Hamilton (eds). *Defining the Holy: Sacred Space in Medieval and Early Modern Europe.* Aldershot: Ashgate, 1-26.

Hammond, P. W. 1993. *Food and Feast in Medieval England.* Stroud: Sutton

Hanna, R. 1994. "Meddling with Makings' and Will's Work'. In A.J. Minnis (ed). *Late-Medieval Religious Texts and their Transmissions. Essays in Honour of A. I. Doyle.* Cambridge: D. S. Brewer.

Harben, H.A. 1918. *A Dictionary of London.* London: H Jenkins.

Harrison, E. E. 1991. 'The History of the Charterhouse and its Buildings'. *Transactions of the Ancient Monuments Society* 35, 1-28.

Harvey, B. F. 2006. 'Monastic Pittances in the Middle Ages'. In C.M. Woolgar, D. Serjeantson and T. Waldron (eds). *Food in Medieval England. Diet and Nutrition.* Oxford: Oxford University Press, 215-227.

Harvey, B. 1993. *Living and Dying in England 1100-1540. The Monastic Experience.* Oxford: Clarendon Press.

Hawke, S. 2015. *Friary, Freshford: A Geophysical Survey of Church Field.* Unpublished report for Bath and Camerton Archaeological Society.

Hayfield, C. 2019. 'Pottery'. In G. Coppack and L. Keen. *Mount Grace Priory: Excavations of 1957-1992.* Oxford: Oxbow, 311-323.

Heal, F. 2003. *Reformation in Britain and Ireland.* Oxford: Oxford University Press.

Henisch, B. A. 1976. *Fast and Feast. Food in Medieval Society.* University Park, PA: Pennsylvania State University Press.

Herbert McAvoy, L. 2011. *Medieval Anchoritisms: Gender, Space and the Solitary Life.* Woodbridge: D.S. Brewer.

Herbert McAvoy, L. 2004. *Authority and the Female Body in the Writings of Julian of Norwich and Margery Kempe.* Cambridge: D. S. Brewer.

Hillier, B. 2014 'Spatial analysis and cultural information: the need for theory as well as method in space syntax analysis', In E. Paliou, U. Lieberwirth and S. Polla (eds.) *Spatial analysis and social spaces. Interdisciplinary approaches to the interpretation of prehistoric and historic built environments.* Berlin: De Gruyter, 19–48

Hogg, J. 2016. 'The Foundation of the Charterhouse of Sheen'. *Analecta Cartusiana* 302, 48-104.

Hogg, J. 2014. 'The Carthusians: History and Heritage'. In K. Pansters (ed). *The Carthusians in the Low Countries: Studies in Monastic History and Heritage.* Leuven: Peeters, 31-56.

Hogg, J. 1991. 'Carthusian Abstinence' In J. Hogg (ed). *Spiritualität Heute und Gestern.* Analecta Cartusiana 35:14, 5-15.

Hogg, J. 1987. 'Everyday Life in a Contemplative Order in the Fifteenth Century'. In M. Glasscoe (ed). *The Medieval Mystical Tradition in England. Exeter Symposium IV.* Woodbridge: D. S. Brewer, 62-76.

Hogg, J. 1980. 'Everyday Life in the Charterhouse in the Fourteenth and Fifteenth Centuries'. In *Klösterliche Sachkultur des Spätmittelalters. Internationaler Kongress Krems An Der Donau 18. Bis 21. September 1978. Veröffentlichungen des Instituts für mittelalterliche Realienkunde Österreiches 3.* Vienna: Verlagder Österreichischen Akademie der Wissenschaften, 113-146.

Hogg, J. 1977. 'Excavations at Witham Charterhouse'. *Analecta Cartusiana* 37, 118-133.

Hope, W. H. 1925. *A History of the London Charterhouse.* London: SPCK.

Hope, W. H. 1905. 'The Architectural History of Mount Grace Charterhouse'. *Yorkshire Archaeological Journal* 18, 270-309.

Horn, W. 1873, 'On the Origins of the Medieval Cloister'. *Gesta* 12: 1/2, 13-52.

Hoyle, R. W. 1995. 'The Origins of the Dissolution of the Monasteries'. *The Historical Journal* 38: 2, 275-305.

Hughes, J. 1988. *Pastors and visionaries: religion and secular life in late medieval Yorkshire.* Woodbridge: Boydell.

Hull City Council. 2010. *Charterhouse Conservation Area Character Appraisal.* Unpublished Report.

Hunt, E. and White, W. 1878. 'On the stone vaulting of the Carthusian Church at Witham'. *Proceedings of the Somersetshire Archaeological and Natural History Society* 24, 25-32.

Hurst, J. G. 1999. 'Sixteenth-century South Netherlands Maiolica imported into Britain and Ireland'. In D. Gaimster (ed). *Maiolica in the North: The Archaeology of Tin-Glazed Earthenware in North-West Europe, c. 1500-1600.* British Museum Occasional Paper, no. 122. London: British Museum 91-106.

Hurst, J. G., Neal, D. S., and van Beuningen, H. J. E. 1986. *Pottery produced and traded in north-west Europe 1350-1600.* Rotterdam Papers VI. Rotterdam: Stichting 'Het Nederlandse Gebruiksvoorwerp'.

Irvine, R. D. G. 2011. 'The Architecture of Stability: Monasteries and the Importance of Place in a World of Non-Places'. *Etnofoor* 23:1, 29-49.

Irving, B. and Jones, A. 2019. 'Fish Remains from the Kitchen and South-West Cloister Range'. In G. Coppack and L. Keen. *Mount Grace Priory: Excavations of 1957-1992.* Oxford: Oxbow, 333-340.

Jasper, D. 2004. *The Sacred Desert. Religion, Literature, Art and Culture.* Oxford: Blackwell.

Jenny, B. and Hurni, L. 2006. 'Swiss-Style Colour Relief Shading Modulated by Elevation and by Exposure to Illumination'. *The Cartographic Journal* 43:3, 198-207.

Johnson, S. F. 2014. *Monastic Women and Religious Orders in Late Medieval Bologna.* Cambridge: Cambridge University Press.

Jones, E. A. and Walsham, A. 2010. *Syon Abbey and its Books: Reading, Writing and Religion, c. 1400-1700.* Woodbridge: Boydell.

Jotischky, A. 2011. *A Hermit's Cookbook. Monks, Food and Fasting in the Middle Ages.* London: Continuum.

Jotischky, A. 1995. *The Perfection of Solitude. Hermits and Monks in the Crusader States.* University Park, PA: University of Pennsylvania State Press.

Jurkowski, M., and Ramsay, N., with Renton, S. 2007. *English Monastic Estates, 1066-1540: A list of manors, churches and chapels. Part Two. Lancashire to Surrey.* List and Index Society Special Series, Volume 41. Kew: The List and Index Society.

Keen, L. 2019. 'Small Finds'. In G. Coppack and L. Keen *Mount Grace Priory: Excavations of 1957-1992.* Oxford: Oxbow, 341-348.

Kennelly, P. 2008. 'Terrain maps displaying hill-shading with curvature'. *Geomorphology* 102, 567-577.

Ker, N. R. 1964. *Medieval Libraries of Great Britain. A List of Surviving Books.* 2nd Edition. London: Royal Historical Society

Kerr, J. 2009. *Life in the Medieval Cloister.* London: Continuum.

Kinder, T. 2002. *Cistercian Europe: Architecture of Contemplation.* Kalamazoo, MI: Cistercian Publications.

King, A. A. 1955. *Liturgies of the Religious Orders.* London: Longmans, Green and Co.

Knowles, D. 1959. *The Religious Orders in England. Volume 3: The Tudor Age.* Cambridge: Cambridge University Press.

Knowles, D. 1955. *The Religious Orders in England. Volume 2: The End of the Middle Ages.* Cambridge: Cambridge University Press.

Knowles, D. and Grimes, W. F. 1954. *Charterhouse: the medieval foundation in the light of recent discoveries.* London: Longmans, Green & Co.

Kreider, A. 1979. *English Chantries. The Road to Dissolution.* Cambridge, MA: Harvard University Press.

Lambres, B.-M. 1970. 'Le chant des chartreux'. *Revue belge de Musicologie* 24, 17-41.

Large, J. A. 1975. 'The libraries of the Carthusian Order in medieval England'. *Library History* 3:6, 191-203.

Lasocki, D. 1985. 'The Anglo-Venetian Bassano Family as Instrument Makers and Repairers'. *The Galpin Society Journal* 38, 112-132.

Leyser, H. 1987. 'Hugh the Carthusian'. In H. Mayr-Harting (ed). *St Hugh of Lincoln: lectures delivered at Oxford and Lincoln to celebrate the eighth centenary of St Hugh's consecration as bishop of Lincoln.* Oxford: Oxford University Press, 1-18.

Leyser, H. 1984. *Hermits and the new monasticism: a study of religious communities in Western Europe 1000-1150.* London: Macmillan.

Lindquist, S. C. M. 2003. 'Women in the Charterhouse: the Liminality of Cloistered Space at the Chartreuse de Champmol in Dijon'. In H. Hills (ed). *Architecture and the politics of gender in early modern Europe.* Aldershot: Ashgate, 177-192.

Lister, J. 1924. *The Early Yorkshire Woollen Trade. Extracts from the Hull Customs' Rolls, and Complete Transcripts of the Ulnagers' Rolls.* Cambridge: Cambridge University Press

Liturgy Office of England and Wales. n.d. *Universal Norms on the Liturgical Year and the General Roman Calendar.* Available at: http://www.liturgyoffice.org.uk/Calendar/Info/GNLY.pdf [Last accessed 17th March 2018]

Lockhart, R. B. 1985. *Halfway to Heaven: The Hidden Life of the Sublime Carthusians.* London: Thames Methuen.

Luxford, J. M. 2011. 'The Space of the Tomb in Carthusian Consciousness'. In F. Andrews (ed). *Ritual and Space in the Middle Ages. Proceedings of the 2009 Harlaxton Symposium.* Donington: Shaun Tyas, 259-281.

MacCulloch, D. 2014. *Silence: A Christian History.* London: Penguin.

MacCulloch, D. 2009. *A History of Christianity.* London: Penguin

Madigan, K. 2015. *Medieval Christianity. A New History.* New Haven & London: Yale University Press.

Magnusson, R. J. 2001. *Water Technology in the Middle Ages. Cities, Monasteries and Waterworks after the Roman Empire.* Baltimore, MD: The Johns Hopkins University Press.

Maisons de l'ordre des Chartreux: vues et notices. 4 vols. 1913-1919. Parkminster: St Hugh's Charterhouse.

Maitland, F. W. 1941. *The Constitutional History of England.* Cambridge: Cambridge University Press.

Malden, H. E. (ed). 1967. *A History of the County of Surrey: Volume 2.* London: Victoria County History.

Marius, R. 1999. *Thomas More: a Biography.* Cambridge, MA: Harvard University Press.

Marken, M. W. 1994. *Pottery from Spanish Shipwrecks 1500-1800*. Gainsville, FL: University Press of Florida.

Marshall, P. 2002. *Beliefs and the Dead in Reformation England*. Oxford: Oxford University Press.

Mayr-Harting, H. 2011. *Religion, Politics and Society in Britain 1066-1272*. Harlow: Pearson

McCarthy, M. R. and Brooks, C. M. 1988. *Medieval Pottery in Britain, AD 900-1600*. Leicester: Leicester University Press.

McGarvie, M. 1989. *Witham Friary. Church and Parish*. Church Histories 1. Frome: Frome Historical Research Group.

McLean, T. 1981. *Medieval English Gardens*. New York: Viking Press.

Merton, T. 1999. *Thoughts in Solitude*. New York: Farrar, Straus & Giroux.

Milis, L. J. R. 1992. *Angelic Monks and Earthly Men. Monasticism and its Meaning to Medieval Society*. Woodbridge: Boydell.

Monti, D. V. 2003. 'The Friars Minor: An Order in the Church?' *Franciscan Studies* 61, 235-252.

Moorhouse, S. 1991. 'Ceramics in the medieval garden'. In A. E. Brown (ed). *Garden archaeology. Papers presented to a conference at Knuston Hall, Northamptonshire, April 1988*. Council for British Archaeology Research Report 78. London: Council for British Archaeology, 100-117.

Moorhouse, S. and Wrathmell, S. 1987. *Kirkstall Abbey Volume 1. The 1950-1964 Excavations: A Reassessment*. Wakefield: West Yorkshire Archaeology Service.

Morgan, N. 2008. 'Illumination – pigments, drawing and gilding'. In N. J. Morgan and R. M. Thomson (eds). *The Cambridge History of the Book*. Cambridge: Cambridge University Press, 84-95.

Nagel, E. 2015. 'Five Steps Downhill. The Typological Sequence of Carthusian Architectural Adaptation to New Surroundings'. *Mittelalter: Interdisziplinäre Forschung und Rezeptionsgeschicte*. Available at: http://mittelalter.hypotheses.org/7336 (last accessed 30/08/2017).

Nissen, P. 2008. 'Topography of Solitude. Places of Silence in Early Carthusian Spirituality'. In H. Blommestijn, C. Caspers, R. Hofman, F. Mertens, P. Nissen, and H. Welzen (eds). *Seeing the Seeker: Explorations in the Discipline of Spirituality*. Leuven: Peeters, 201-213.

Orton, C. 1979. 'Medieval Pottery from a Kiln Site at Cheam'. *London Archaeologist* 3, 300-304, 355-359.

Page, W. (ed). 1974. *A History of the County of York: Volume 3*. London: Victoria County History

Palmer, T. 1921. 'The Site of Witham Priory or Charterhouse'. *Somerset and Dorset Notes and Queries* 17, 90-92.

Paravy, P. 2010. *Les Cartes de Chartreuse. Désert et Architecture*. Grenoble: Éditions Glénat.

Patterson, P. J. 2011. 'Preaching with the Hands: Carthusian Book Production and the Speculum devotorum'. In C. Cannon and M. Nolan (eds). *Medieval Latin and Middle English Literature*. Woodbridge: DS Brewer, 134-151.

Pingel, T. J. and Clarke, K. 2014. 'Perceptually Shaded Slope Maps for the Visualisation of Digital Surface Models'. *Cartographica* 49:4, 225-240.

Popović, S. 2007. 'Dividing the Indivisible: The Monastery Space – Secular and Sacred'. *Zbornik radova Vizantoloskog instituta* 44, 47-65.

RCHME. 1994. *Witham, Somerset. The Carthusian Monastery and the Post-Dissolution Landscape*. Unpublished survey report held in the National Monuments Record, Swindon.

Reid, R. and Barlow, P. 1966. 'Witham Priory'. *77th and 78th Annual Reports of the Wells Natural History and Archaeological Society*, 6-7.

Reid, W. S. 1973. 'The Coming of the Reformation to Edinburgh'. *Church History* 42:1, 27-44.

Remensnyder, A. G. 1995. *Remembering Kings Past. Monastic Foundation Legends in Medieval Southern France*. Ithaca, NY: Cornell University Press.

Richardson, A. 2003. 'Corridors of power: a case study in access analysis from medieval England'. *Antiquity* 77: 296, 373-384.

Ritchey, S. 2014. *Holy Matter: Changing Perceptions of the Material World in Late Medieval Christianity*. Ithaca, NY: Cornell University Press.

Rodwell, W. 2012. *The Archaeology of Churches*. Stroud: Amberley.

Roebuck, J., Coppack, G. and Hurst, J. G. 1987.'A Closely Dated Group of Late Medieval Pottery from Mount Grace Priory'. *Medieval Ceramics* 11, 15-24.

Rosenwein, B. H. 1989. *To be the Neighbour of Saint Peter. The Social Meaning of Cluny's Property, 909-1049*. Ithaca, NY: Cornell University Press.

Rousseau, M.-H. 2011. *Saving the Souls of Medieval London. Perpetual Chantries at St Paul's Cathedral, c. 1200-1548*. Farnham: Ashgate.

Sargent, M. G. and Hennessy, M. V. 2008. 'The Latin Verses over the Cell Doors of London Charterhouse'. In J. M. Luxford (ed). *Studies in Carthusian Monasticism in the Late Middle Ages*. Turnhout: Brepols, 179-197.

Sargent, M. 2004. 'Chauncy, Maurice (c. 1509-1581). *Oxford Dictionary of National Biography*. Oxford: Oxford University Press. https://doi.org/10.1093/ref:odnb/5199 [Last accessed 16 February 2018].

Schama, S. 1996. *Landscape and Memory*. London: Fontana.

Schirmer, E. 2005. 'Reading Lessons at Syon Abbey: The Myoure of Oure Ladye and the Mandates of Vernacular Theology'. In L. Olson and K. Kerby-Fulton (eds). *Voices in Dialogue: Reading Women in the Middle Ages*. Notre Dame, IN: University of Notre Dame Press, 345-376.

Serjeantson, D. and Woolgar, C.M. 2006. 'Fish Consumption in Medieval England'. In C.M. Woolgar, D. Serjeantson and T. Waldron (eds). *Food in Medieval England. Diet and Nutrition*. Oxford: Oxford University Press, 102-130

Sessions, W. K. 1983. *A Printer's Dozen. The First British Printing Centres to 1557 after Westminster and London*. York: The Ebor Press.

Signori, G. 2014. 'Cell or Dormitory? Monastic Visions of Space Amidst the Conflict of Ideals'. *Journal of Medieval Monastic Studies* 3, 21-49.

Smith, A. C. 2016. 'An ex libris puzzle in Cambridge, University Library, MS Ee.4.30'. *The Manuscripts Lab*. 23 September 2016. Available at: https://www.english.cam.ac.uk/manuscriptslab/an-ex-libris-puzzle-in-cambridge-university-library-ms-ee-4-30/#more-432 [Last accessed 4-11-16]

Soden, I. 2001. 'The Planning and Development of a Carthusian Church – the example of St Anne's Charterhouse, Coventry'. In G. Keevil, M. Aston and T. Hall (eds). *Monastic Archaeology. Papers on the Study of Medieval Monasteries*. Oxford: Oxbow, 161-164.

Soden, I. 1995. *Excavations at St Anne's Charterhouse, Coventry, 1968-87*. Coventry: Coventry City Council.

Solt, L. F. 1990. *Church and State in Early Modern England, 1509-1640*. Oxford: Oxford University Press.

Standley, E. R. 2013. *Trinkets & Charms. The use, meaning and significance of dress accessories, 1300-1700*. Oxford University School of Archaeology Monograph 78. Oxford: School of Archaeology.

Stöber, K. 2007. *Late Medieval Monasteries and their Patrons: England and Wales, c. 1300-1540*. Woodbridge: Boydell.

Strickland, M. 2010. 'Longespée, William (I), third earl of Salisbury'. *Oxford Dictionary of National Biography*. Oxford: Oxford University Press. Available at: http://www.oxforddnb.com/view/article/16983 [Last accessed 11th April 2017]

Swanson, R. N. 2009. 'The Burdens of Purgatory'. In D. E. Bornstein (ed). *Medieval Christianity*. Minneapolis: MN: Fortress Press, 353-380.

Swanson, R. N. 1995. *Religion and Devotion in Europe, c.1215-c.1515*. Cambridge: Cambridge University Press.

Swanson, R. N. (ed). 1993. *Catholic England. Faith, Religion and Observance before the Reformation*. Manchester: Manchester University Press.

Tanner, N. and Watson, S. 2006. 'Least of the laity: the minimum requirements for a medieval Christian'. *Journal of Medieval History* 32:4, 395-423.

Thomson, R. M., Morgan, N., Gullick, M., and Hadgraft, N. 2008. 'Parchment and paper, ruling and ink'. In N. J. Morgan and R. M. Thomson (eds). *The Cambridge History of the Book*. Cambridge: Cambridge University Press, 75-84.

Thomson, R. M. 2008. 'Monastic and cathedral book production'. In N. J. Morgan and R. M. Thomson (eds). *The Cambridge History of the Book*. Cambridge: Cambridge University Press, 136-167.

Thompson, E. M. 1932. 'A Fragment of a Witham Charterhouse Chronicle and Adam of Dryburgh, Premonstratensian, and Carthusian of Witham'. *Bulletin of the John Rylands Library, Manchester* 16, 482-506.

Thompson, E. M. 1930. *The Carthusian Order in England*. London: SPCK.

Thompson, E. M. 1896. *A History of the Somerset Carthusians*. London: Hodge.

Tuck, A. 2011. 'Lords Appellant (act. 1387-1388). *Oxford Dictionary of National Biography*. Oxford: Oxford University Press. Available at: https://doi.org/10.1093/ref:odnb/53093 [Last accessed 19th March 2018]

'Un Chartreux'. 1984. *La Grande Chartreuse*.

van Hasselt, L. 1886. 'Het necrologium van het Karthuizer-klooster nieuwlicht of Bloemendaal buiten Utrecht'. *Bijdragen en Mededeelingen van het Historisch Genootschap* 9, 126-392.

Veronesi, F. and Hurni, L. 2015. 'A GIS tool to increase the visual quality of relief shading by automatically changing the light direction'. *Computers & Geosciences* 74, 121-127.

Villabos Hennessy, M. 2008. 'Three Marian Texts, Including a Prayer for a Lay-Brother, in London, British library, MS Additional 37049'. In A. S. G. Edwards (ed). *Regional Manuscripts 1200-1700. English Manuscript Studies 1100-1700*, Volume 14. London: British Library 163-179.

Vrána, J. 2006. 'The Construction of the Charterhouse 'Domus vallis Josaphat' near Olomouc'. In J. Hogg, A. Girard and D. Le Blévec (eds). *Kartäusische Kunst und Architektur mit besonderer Berücksichtigung de Kartausen Zentraleuropas*. Analecta Cartusiana 207:2. Salzburg: Institut für Anglistik und Amerikanistik, Universität Salzburg, 75-94.

Waddell, H. 1962. *The Desert Fathers*. London: Fontana.

Webb, D. 2007. *Privacy and Solitude in the Middle Ages*. London: Continuum

Whatmore, L. E. 1983. *The Carthusians under King Henry the Eighth*. Analecta Cartusiana 109. Salzburg: Institut für Anglistik und Amerikanistik, 45-70.

Williams, J. E. H. D., Penoyre, J. and Hale, B. C. H. 1987. 'The George Inn, Norton St Philip, Somerset'. *Archaeological Journal* 144, 317-327.

Willmott, H. 2018. 'Cooking, Dining, and Drinking'. In C. Gerrard and A. Gutiérrez (eds). *The Oxford Handbook of Later Medieval Archaeology in Britain.* Oxford: Oxford University Press, 697-712.

Wilson North, R. and Porter, S. 1997. 'Witham, Somerset: From Carthusian Monastery to Country House to Gothic Folly'. *Architectural History* 40, 81-98.

Wines, A. R. 2008. 'The founders of London Charterhouse'. In J. M. Luxford (ed). *Studies in Carthusian Monasticism in the late Middle Ages.* Turnhout: Brepols, 61-72.

Woolgar, C. M. 2006. *The Senses in Late Medieval England.* New Haven, CT: Yale University Press.

Unpublished Secondary Sources

Beckett, N. 1992. *Sheen Charterhouse from its Foundation to its Dissolution.* Ph.D. Thesis, University of Oxford.

Cassels, A. K. 2013. *The Social Significance of Late Medieval Dress Accessories.* Ph.D. Thesis, University of Sheffield.

De Weijert, R. 2015. *Schenken, begraven, gedenken Lekenmemoria in het Utrechtse kartuizerklooster Nieuwlicht (1391-1580).* Ph.D. Thesis, Universiteit Utrecht.

Gottschall, A. E. 2014. *The Pater Noster and the Laity in England, c. 700-1560.* Ph.D Thesis, University of Birmingham.

Howsam, C. L. 2016. *Book Fastenings and Furnishings. An Archaeology of Late Medieval Books.* Ph.D. Thesis, University of Sheffield.

Rowntree, C. B. 1981. *Studies in Carthusian History in Later Medieval England.* Ph.D. Thesis, University of York.

Shaw, A. N. 2003. *The Compendium Compertorum and the Making of the Suppression Act of 1536.* Ph.D. Thesis, University of Warwick.